The American Liberals and the Russian Revolution (1962)
The New Radicalism in America (1965)
The Agony of the American Left (1969)
The World of Nations (1973)
Haven in a Heartless World: The Family Besieged (1977)
The Culture of Narcissism (1979)

The
Minimal
Self

W·W·Norton & Company
New York · London

The Minimal Self

Psychic Survival in Troubled Times

Christopher Lasch

Copyright © 1984 by Christopher Lasch
All rights reserved.
Published simultaneously in Canada by Stoddart,
a subsidiary of General Publishing Co. Ltd, Don Mills, Ontario.
Printed in the United States of America.

The text of this book is composed in Janson Alternate, with
display type set in Modern #20. Composition and
manufacturing by the Haddon Craftsmen Inc
Book design by Bernard Klein

First Edition

Library of Congress Cataloging in Publication Data

Lasch, Christopher.
   The minimal self.

   Bibliography: p.
   Includes index.
   1. Self. 2. Human ecology. I. Title.
BF697.L26   1984   155.2   84–4103

ISBN 0-393-01922-5

W.W. Norton & Company, Inc., 500 Fifth Avenue, New York, N.Y. 10110
W.W. Norton & Company Ltd., 37 Great Russell Street, London WC1B 3NU
1 2 3 4 5 6 7 8 9 0

He is as full of valor as of kindness,
Princely in both.

Henry V, IV. iii

The entire modern deification of survival *per se*, survival returning to itself, survival naked and abstract, with the denial of any substantive excellence in *what* survives, except the capacity for more survival still, is surely the strangest intellectual stopping-place ever proposed by one man to another.

William James

Contents

IV
THE MINIMALIST AESTHETIC:
ART AND LITERATURE IN AN AGE OF EXTREMITY

V
THE INNER HISTORY OF SELFHOOD

VI
THE POLITICS OF THE PSYCHE

VII

THE IDEOLOGICAL ASSAULT ON THE EGO

Preface

IN a time of troubles, everyday life becomes an exercise in survival. People take one day at a time. They seldom look back, lest they succumb to a debilitating "nostalgia"; and if they look ahead, it is to see how they can insure themselves against the disasters almost everybody now expects. Under these conditions, selfhood becomes a kind of luxury, out of place in an age of impending austerity. Selfhood implies a personal history, friends, family, a sense of place. Under siege, the self contracts to a defensive core, armed against adversity. Emotional equilibrium demands a minimal self, not the imperial self of yesteryear.

Such is the thesis, in its simplest form, advanced in these pages, in which the reader will find, accordingly, no indignant outcry against contemporary "hedonism," self-seeking, egoism, indifference to the general good—the traits commonly associated with "narcissism." In this essay, I hope first of all to make clear what *The Culture of Narcissism* seems to have left obscure or ambiguous: that the concern with the self, which seems so characteristic of our time, takes the form of a concern with its psychic survival. People have lost confidence in the future. Faced with an escalating arms race, an increase in crime and terrorism, environmental deterioration, and the prospect of long-term economic decline, they have begun to prepare for the worst, sometimes by building fallout shelters and laying in provisions, more commonly by executing a kind of emotional retreat from the long-term commitments that presuppose a stable, secure, and orderly world. Ever since the Second World War, the end of the world has loomed as a hypothetical possibility, but the sense of danger has greatly increased in the last twenty years, not only because social and economic conditions have grown objectively more unstable but because the hope of a remedial politics, a self-reformation of the political system, has sharply declined. The hope that political action will gradually humanize industrial society has given way to a determination to survive the general wreckage or, more modestly, to hold one's own life together in the face of mounting pressures. The danger of personal disintegration encourages a sense of selfhood neither "imperial" nor "narcissistic" but simply beleaguered.

Even opposition movements—the peace movement, the environmental movement—take survival as their slogan. Of course they refer to the survival of humanity as a whole, not to the everyday psychic survival of individuals; but they still reflect and reinforce a survival mentality. They call for a "moral commitment to survival" (as Richard Falk puts it in his ecological manifesto, *This Endangered Planet*), oblivious to the danger that a commitment to survival, instead of leading to constructive political action, can just as easily lead to a mountain hideaway or to national policies designed to enable the country to survive a nuclear war. The peace movement and the environmental movement call attention to our society's criminal indifference to the needs of future generations, but they inadvertently reaffirm this attitude by dwelling, for example, on the dangers of overpopulation and the irresponsibility of bringing children into an already overcrowded world. Too often they substitute an abstract interest in the future for the kind of palpable, emotional interest that enables people to make sacrifices on its behalf. In the same way, emphasis on the global dimensions of the survival issue—on the need for global controls and for the development of a "global mind"—probably helps to undermine attachments to a particular place and thus to weaken still further the emotional basis on which any real interest in the future has to rest. Rootless men and women take no more interest in the future than they take in the past; but instead of reminding us of the need for roots, many advocates of disarmament and environmental conservation, understandably eager to associate their cause with the survival of the planet as a whole, deplore the local associations and attachments that impede the development of a "planetary consciousness" but also make it possible for people to think constructively about the future instead of lapsing into cosmic panic and futuristic desperation.

In the nuclear age, survival has become an issue of overriding importance; but the attempt to awaken the public to its collective implications often tends to strengthen the inertia it seeks to overcome. "The great danger of an apocalyptic argument," as Falk himself recognizes, "is that to the extent it persuades, it also immobilizes." Heedless of his own warning, he insists that unless the world's leaders create a new world order, "there is little hope that our children will avoid the apocalypse."

Do not mistake me: the growing opposition to the nuclear arms race, the growing awareness of ecology, the growing criticism of consumerism and high technology, criticism of the "masculine" psychology of conquest and competitive enterprise hold out the best hope for the future. By dramatizing the dangers ahead, opposition movements inadvertently strengthen the siege mentality, but they also provide the only effective antidote against it: a determination to mount a collaborative assault on the difficulties that threaten to overwhelm us. Political action remains the only effective defense against disaster—political action, that is, that incorporates our new understanding of the dangers of unlimited economic growth, unlimited technological development, and the unlimited exploitation of nature. Whether it tells us much about the psychological roots of the Promethean will-to-power to call it a purely masculine obsession, which can be countered by the "feminine" qualities of cooperation and loving care, is an important question on which I hope to shed some light; but it is a good idea to remind ourselves at the outset that militarism and runaway technology have social, economic, and political roots as well as psychological roots and that political opposition to these evils, even if it often rests on shaky psychological and philosophical premises, represents an indispensable beginning in the struggle to make our world fit for human habitation.

Recent controversies about the contemporary culture of "narcissism" have revealed two quite different sources of confusion. The first, alluded to already and examined in some detail in the first of the following chapters, is the confusion of narcissism with egoism and selfishness. An analysis of the siege mentality and the strategies of psychic survival it encourages (the subject of chapters II, III, and IV) will serve not only to identify characteristic features of our culture—our protective irony and emotional disengagement, our reluctance to make long-term emotional commitments, our sense of powerlessness and victimization, our fascination with extreme situations and with the possibility of applying their lessons to everyday life, our perception of large-scale organizations as systems of total control—but also to distinguish narcissism from ordinary self-seeking. It will show how the prevailing social conditions, especially the fantastic mass-produced images that shape our perceptions of the world, not only encourage a defensive contraction of the self but blur the boundaries between the self and its surroundings. As the Greek legend reminds us, it is this confusion of the self and the not-self—not "egoism"—that distinguishes the plight of Narcissus. The minimal or narcissistic self is, above all, a self uncertain of its own outlines, longing either to remake the world in its own image or to merge into its environment in blissful union. The current concern with "identity" registers some of this difficulty in defining the boundaries of selfhood. So does the minimalist style in contemporary art and literature, which derives much of its subject matter from popular culture, in particular from the invasion of experience by images, and thus helps us to see that minimal selfhood is not just a defensive response to danger but arises out of a more fundamental social transformation: the replacement of a reliable world of durable objects by a world of flickering images that make it harder and harder to distinguish reality from fantasy.

This brings us to the second source of confusion about narcissism: the equation of narcissism not, this time, with selfishness and egoism but precisely with the "feminine" desire for union with the world, which some see as a corrective to masculine egoism. The last three chapters in this essay attempt, among other things, to explain why the narcissistic desire for union cannot be assigned a gender and why, moreover, it cannot be counted on as a remedy for the Faustian will-to-power. I will argue that Faustian, Promethean technology itself originates—insofar as we can trace it to psychological roots—in the attempt to restore narcissistic illusions of omnipotence. But I have no intention of arguing against the growing influence of women in politics and in the workplace; nor should my analysis of the narcissistic elements in contemporary culture be mistaken for an attack on the "feminization of American society." Narcissism has nothing to do with femininity or masculinity. Indeed it denies any knowledge of sexual differences, just as it denies the difference between the self and the world around it. It seeks to restore the undifferentiated contentment of the womb. It seeks both self-sufficiency and self-annihilation: opposite aspects of the same archaic experience of oneness with the world.

The achievement of selfhood, which our culture makes so difficult, might be defined as the acknowledgment of our separation from the original source of life, combined with a continuing struggle to recapture a sense of primal union by means of activity that gives us a provisional understanding and mastery of the world without denying our limitations and dependency. Selfhood is the painful awareness of the tension between our unlimited aspirations and our limited understanding, between our original intimations of immortality and our fallen state, between oneness and separation. A new culture—a postindustrial culture, if you like—has to be based on a recognition of these contradictions in human experience, not on a technology that tries to restore the illusion of self-sufficiency or, on the other hand, on a radical denial of selfhood that tries to restore the illusion of absolute unity with nature. Neither Prometheus nor Narcissus will lead us out of our present predicament. Brothers under the skin, they will only lead us further down the road on which we have already traveled much too far.

The
Minimal
Self

I

Introduction: Consumption, Narcissism, and Mass Culture

Materialism and Mass Culture Denunciation of American "materialism" has a long history, but recent events have given it new urgency. The energy crisis, the American defeat in Vietnam, the hostage crisis, the loss of American markets to the West Germans and the Japanese have revived old misgivings about the links between cultural decadence and national failure. American know-how, it appears, no longer dominates the world. American technology is no longer the most advanced; the country's industrial plant is decrepit; its city streets and transport systems are falling to pieces. The question arises whether the faltering of the American economy and the failure of American foreign policy do not reflect a deeper failure of morale, a cultural crisis associated in some way with the collapse of "traditional values" and the emergence of a new morality of self-gratification.

In the right-wing version of this argument, governmental paternalism and "secular humanism" have sapped the moral foundations of American enterprise, while pacifism, "survivalism," and movements for unilateral disarmament have emasculated American foreign policy and made Americans unwilling to fight for freedom. Another version, more acceptable to liberals and neoconservatives, stresses the bad effects of consumerism. In July 1979, President Carter attributed the national "malaise" to the spirit of self-seeking and the pursuit of "things." The conventional critique of narcissism, as we might call it, equates narcissism with selfishness and treats consumerism as a kind of moral lapse that can be corrected by exhortations about the value of hard work and family life. It deplores the breakdown of the work discipline and the popularization of a "fun morality" that has allegedly crippled productivity, undermined American enterprise, and thus weakened the country's competitive position in the race for markets and national greatness.

A third position has recently emerged in reply to the critique of "narcissism." A number of journalists and social critics—Daniel Yankelovich, Peter Clecak, Paul Wachtel, Alvin Toffler, Theodore Roszak, Philip Slater, and Marilyn Ferguson, among others—have begun to argue that the apparent increase in self-absorption is only a by-product of more encouraging cultural changes. They dismiss the idea of a national malaise or crisis of confidence. Industrial society may be sick, in their view, but it is already giving way to a postindustrial society that will consolidate the achievements of industrialism on a new basis. Critics of consumerism, they argue, miss the movement away from competitive status-seeking toward self-sufficiency, self-exploration, personal growth, and nonmaterialistic forms of "self-fulfillment."

Those who take a hopeful view of recent cultural changes disagree among themselves about the difficulty of the "transition" ahead and about the nature of the society to which it is leading. The only thing that justifies treating them as a group is that all of them reject the diagnosis of our society as "narcissistic." As Yankelovich puts it, the "American quest for self-fulfillment" cannot be reduced to the "pathology of narcissistic personality disorders." Narcissism "is not the essence of the recent American search for self-fulfillment." "Far from being its defining characteristic, narcissism is a betrayal of it."

The controversy about narcissism, which revives in a new form earlier controversies about mass culture and the American national character, raises important questions and helps to call attention to the connections between social and economic changes and changes in cultural and personal life. Nevertheless, much of it is deeply confused. For one thing, the concept of narcissism remains elusive and obscure, even though it appears eminently accessible. Those who object to the description of advanced industrial culture as a culture of narcissism do not understand very clearly what the description implies, while those who accept it all too quickly accept it as a journalistic slogan that merely restates moralistic platitudes in the jargon of psychoanalysis. Narcissism is a difficult idea that looks easy—a good recipe for confusion.

Another source of confusion is the persistence of certain preconceptions derived from the controversy that divided critics of "mass culture" in the fifties and sixties from celebrants of cultural democracy and pluralism. Recent attempts to reformulate this debate—to salvage what was useful in the critique of mass culture by detaching it from an ill-conceived defense of cultural modernism—have been misunderstood as attempts to revive earlier positions in their original form. I have suggested elsewhere that the phenomenon of mass culture, too often treated from the point of view of its impact on aesthetic standards, raises questions about technology, not about the level of public taste. Advanced technologies of communication, which seem merely to facilitate the dissemination of informationon a wider scale than was possible before, prove on closer examination to impede the circulation of ideas and to concentrate control over information in a handful of giant organizations. Modern technology has the same effect on culture that it has on production, where it serves to assert managerial control over the labor force. The study of mass culture thus leads to the same conclusion prompted by a study of the mechanization of the workplace: that much advanced technology embodies by design (in both senses of the word) a one-way system of management and communication. It concentrates economic and political control—and, increasingly, cultural control as well—in a small elite of corporate planners, market analysts, and social engineers. It invites popular "input" or "feedback" only in the form of suggestion boxes, market surveys, and public opinion polls. Technology thus comes to serve as an effective instrument of social control—in the case of mass media, by short-circuiting the electoral process through opinion surveys that help to shape opinion instead of merely recording it, by reserving to the media themselves the right to select political leaders and "spokesmen," and by presenting the choice of leaders and parties as a choice among consumer goods.

This interpretation of mass culture and advanced technology may be wrong, but it is a different argument from the old accusation that mass culture lowers public taste or from the Marxist version of this accusation, according to which mass culture brainwashes the workers and keeps them in a state of "false consciousness." Yet the terms of the earlier debate remain so coercive that new arguments are immediately assimilated to old ones. Criticism of the narcissistic elements in our culture strikes many observers as a lament for the "morally tuned, well-crafted self," in the words of Peter Clecak. It is not my position, however, as Herbert

Gans tries to summarize it, that "if commercial popular culture were eliminated, workers could and would become intellectuals." Why should workers become intellectuals? I find it hard to imagine a less attractive prospect than a society made up of intellectuals. What is important is that working men and women have more control over their work. It is also important for intellectuals and workers alike to see that this question of control is not just a political or an economic question but a cultural question as well.

Mass Production and Mass Consumption Still another source of confusion, in recent controversies about contemporary culture, is the failure to distinguish a moralistic indictment of "consumerism"—typified by Carter's complaint about the obsession with "owning *things,* consuming *things*"—from an analysis that understands mass consumption as part of a larger pattern of dependence, disorientation, and loss of control. Instead of thinking of consumption as the antithesis of labor, as if the two activities called for completely different mental and emotional qualities, we need to see them as two sides of the same process. The social arrangements that support a system of mass production and mass consumption tend to discourage initiative and self-reliance and to promote dependence, passivity, and a spectatorial state of mind both at work and at play. Consumerism is only the other side of the degradation of work—the elimination of playfulness and craftsmanship from the process of production.*

*In *The Cultural Contradictions of Capitalism,* Daniel Bell argues that the culture of consumption encourages an ethic of hedonism and thus undermines industrial discipline. Advanced capitalism is at odds with itself, in his view: it needs consumers who demand immediate gratification and deny themselves nothing, but it also needs self-denying producers willing to throw themselves into their jobs, to work long hours, and to follow instructions to the letter.

The strength of Bell's argument lies in its understanding of the connection between advanced capitalism and consumerism, which so many observers attribute

In the United States, a consumer culture began to emerge in the twenties, but only after the corporate transformation of industry had institutionalized the division of labor that runs all through modern industrial society, the division between brain work and manual labor: between the design and the execution of production. Under the banner of scientific management, capitalists expropriated the technical knowledge formerly exercised by workers, reformulated it as science, and vested its control in a new managerial elite. The managers extended their power not at the expense of the owners of industry, as is so often said, but at the expense of the workers. Nor did the eventual triumph of industrial unionism break this pattern of managerial control. By the 1930s, even the most militant unions had acquiesced in the division of labor between the planning and execution of work. Indeed the very success of the union movement was predicated on a strategic retreat from issues of worker control. Unionization, moreover, helped to stabilize and rationalize the labor market and to discipline the work force. It did not alter the arrangement whereby management controls the technology of production, the rhythm of work, and the location of plants (even when these decisions affect whole communities), leaving the worker with the task merely of carrying out orders.

Having organized mass production on the basis of the new division of labor, most fully realized in the assembly

---

merely to permissive educators and parents, moral decay, and the abdication of authorities. Its weakness lies in equating consumerism so closely with hedonism. The state of mind promoted by consumerism is better described as a state of uneasiness and chronic anxiety. The promotion of commodities depends, like modern mass production, on discouraging the individual from reliance on his own resources and judgment: in this case, his judgment of what he needs in order to be healthy and happy. The individual finds himself always under observation, if not by foremen and superintendents, by market researchers and pollsters who tell him what others prefer and what he too must therefore prefer, or by doctors and psychiatrists who examine him for symptoms of disease that might escape an untrained eye.

line, the leaders of American industry turned to the organization of a mass market. The mobilization of consumer demand, together with the recruitment of a labor force, required a far-reaching series of cultural changes. People had to be discouraged from providing for their own wants and resocialized as consumers. Industrialism by its very nature tends to discourage home production and to make people dependent on the market, but a vast effort of reeducation, starting in the 1920s, had to be undertaken before Americans accepted consumption as a way of life. As Emma Rothschild has shown in her study of the automobile industry, Alfred Sloan's innovations in marketing—the annual model change, constant upgrading of the product, efforts to associate it with social status, the deliberate inculcation of a boundless appetite for change—constituted the necessary counterpart of Henry Ford's innovations in production. Modern industry came to rest on the twin pillars of Fordism and Sloanism. Both tended to discourage enterprise and independent thinking and to make the individual distrust his own judgment, even in matters of taste. His own untutored preferences, it appeared, might lag behind current fashion; they too needed to be periodically upgraded.

The Fantastic World of Commodities   The psychological effects of consumerism can be grasped only when consumption is understood as another phase of the industrial work routine. The repeated experience of uneasy self-scrutiny, of submission to expert judgment, of distrust of their own capacity to make intelligent decisions, either as producers or as consumers, colors people's perceptions both of themselves and of the world around them. It encourages a new kind of self-consciousness that has little in common with introspection or vanity. Both as a worker and as a consumer, the individual learns not merely to measure himself against others but to see himself through others' eyes.

He learns that the self-image he projects counts for more than accumulated skills and experience. Since he will be judged, both by his colleagues and superiors at work and by the strangers he encounters on the street, according to his possessions, his clothes, and his "personality"—not, as in the nineteenth century, by his "character"—he adopts a theatrical view of his own "performance" on and off the job. Outright incompetence, of course, still weighs heavily against him at work, just as his actions as a friend and neighbor often outweigh his skill in managing impressions. But the conditions of everyday social intercourse, in societies based on mass production and mass consumption, encourage an unprecedented attention to superficial impressions and images, to the point where the self becomes almost indistinguishable from its surface. Selfhood and personal identity become problematic in such societies, as we can easily see from the outpouring of psychiatric and sociological commentary on these subjects. When people complain of feeling inauthentic or rebel against "role-playing," they testify to the prevailing pressure to see themselves with the eyes of strangers and to shape the self as another commodity offered up for consumption on the open market.

Commodity production and consumerism alter perceptions not just of the self but of the world outside the self. They create a world of mirrors, insubstantial images, illusions increasingly indistinguishable from reality. The mirror effect makes the subject an object; at the same time, it makes the world of objects an extension or projection of the self. It is misleading to characterize the culture of consumption as a culture dominated by things. The consumer lives surrounded not so much by things as by fantasies. He lives in a world that has no objective or independent existence and seems to exist only to gratify or thwart his desires.

This insubstantiality of the external world arises out of the very nature of commodity production, not out of some character flaw in individuals, some excess of greed or "materialism." Commodities are produced for immediate consumption. Their value lies not in their usefulness or permanence but in their marketability. They wear out even if they are not used, since they are designed to be superseded by "new and improved" products, changing fashions, and technological innovations. Thus the current "state of the art" in tape recorders, record players, and stereophonic speakers makes earlier models worthless (except as antiques), even if they continue to perform the tasks for which they were designed, just as a change in women's fashions dictates a complete change of wardrobe. Articles produced for use, on the other hand, without regard to their marketability, wear out only when they are literally used up. "It is this durability," Hannah Arendt once observed, "that gives the things of the world their relative independence from men who produced and use them, their 'objectivity' which makes them withstand, 'stand against' and endure, at least for a time, the voracious needs and wants of their living makers and users. From this viewpoint, the things of the world have the function of stabilizing human life, and their objectivity lies in the fact that . . . men, their everchanging nature notwithstanding, can retrieve their sameness, that is, their identity, by being related to the same chair and the same table."

The changing meaning of "identity" illuminates the connection between changing perceptions of the self and changing perceptions of the outside world. As used in common speech, identity still retains its former connotation of sameness and continuity: "the sameness of a person or thing at all times or in all circumstances," in the language of the Oxford English Dictionary, "the condition or fact that a person or thing is itself and not something else; individuality, personality." In the 1950s, however, the term came to be used by psychiatrists and sociologists to refer to a fluid, protean, and problematical self, "socially bestowed and socially sustained," in the words of Peter L. Berger, and defined either by the social roles an individual performs, the "reference group" to which he belongs, or, on the other hand, by the deliberate management of impressions or "presentation of self," in Erving Goffman's phrase. The psychosocial meaning of identity, which has itself passed into common usage, weakens or eliminates altogether the association between identity and "continuity of the personality." It also excludes the possibility that identity is defined largely through a person's actions and the public record of those actions. In its new meaning, the term registers the waning of the old sense of a life as a life-history or narrative—a way of understanding identity that depended on the belief in a durable public world, reassuring in its solidity, which outlasts an individual life and passes some sort of judgment on it. Note that the older meaning of identity refers both to persons and to things. Both have lost their solidity in modern society, their definiteness and continuity. Identity has become uncertain and problematical not because people no longer occupy fixed social stations—a commonplace explanation that unthinkingly incorporates the modern equation of identity and social role—but because they no longer inhabit a world that exists independently of themselves.

Now that the public or common world has receded into the shadows, we can see more clearly than before the extent of our need for it. For a long time, this need was forgotten in the initial exhilaration that accompanied the discovery of the fully developed interior life, a life liberated at last from the prying eyes of neighbors, from village prejudices, from the inquisitorial presence of elders, from everything narrow, stifling, petty, and conventional. But now it is possible to see that the collapse of our common life has impoverished private life as well. It has freed the imagination from external constraints but exposed it more directly than before to the tyranny of inner compulsions and anxieties. Fantasy ceases to be liberating when it frees itself from the checks imposed by practical experience of the world. Instead it gives rise to hallucinations; and the progress of scientific knowledge, which might be expected to discourage the projection of our inner hopes and fears onto the world around us, leaves these hallucinations undisturbed. Science has not fulfilled the hope that it would replace discredited metaphysical traditions with a coherent explanation of the world and of man's place in it. Science cannot tell people, and at its best does not pretend to tell people, how to live or how to organize a good society. Nor does science offer the same check to the otherwise unrestrained imagination that is offered by practical experience of the world. It does not recreate a public world. Indeed it heightens the prevailing sense of unreality by giving men the power to achieve their wildest flights of fantasy. By holding out a vision of limitless technological possibilities—space travel, biological engineering, mass destruction—it removes the last obstacle to wishful thinking. It brings reality into conformity with our dreams, or rather with our nightmares.

A culture organized around mass consumption encourages narcissism—which we can define, for the moment, as a disposition to see the world as a mirror, more particularly as a projection of one's own fears and desires—not because it makes people grasping and self-assertive but because it makes them weak and dependent. It undermines their confidence in their capacity to understand and shape the world and to provide for their own needs. The consumer feels that he lives in a world that defies practical understanding and control, a world of giant bureaucracies, "information overload," and complex, interlocking technological systems vulnerable to sudden breakdown, like the giant power failure that blacked out the Northeast in 1965 or the radiation leak at Three Mile Island in 1979.

The consumer's complete dependence on these intricate, supremely sophisticated life-support systems, and more generally on externally provided goods and services, recreates some of the infantile feelings of helplessness. If nineteenth-century bourgeois culture reinforced anal patterns of behavior—hoarding of money and supplies, control of bodily functions, control of affect—the twentieth-century culture of mass consumption recreates oral patterns rooted in an even earlier stage of emotional development, when the infant was completely dependent on the breast. The consumer experiences his surroundings as a kind of extension of the breast, alternately gratifying and frustrating. He finds it hard to conceive of the world except in connection with his fantasies. Partly because the propaganda surrounding commodities advertises them so seductively as wish-fulfillments, but also because commodity production by its very nature replaces the world of durable objects with disposable products designed for immediate obsolescence, the consumer confronts the world as a reflection of his wishes and fears. He knows the world, moreover, largely through insubstantial images and symbols that seem to refer not so much to a palpable, solid, and durable reality as to his inner psychic life, itself experienced not as an abiding sense of self but as reflections glimpsed in the mirror of his surroundings.

Consumption and Mass Culture   The most plausible defense of consumerism and modern mass culture has always been that they make available to everybody an array of personal choices formerly restricted to the rich. "The new society is a mass society," Edward Shils has written, "precisely in the sense that the mass of the population have become incorporated *into* society." For the first time, the masses have emerged from their "immemorially old, clod-like existence" and achieved at least the "possibility of becoming full members of their society, of living a human life with some exercise of cultural taste." Herbert Gans makes the same point when he criticizes proposals "to do away with mass production and consumption only a generation or so since a large number of working- and middle-class Americans have had the chance to approach the comforts, conveniences, and pleasures heretofore limited to the rich and the *haute bourgeoisie.*" Gans's clinching argument against critics of mass culture is that they themselves, as intellectuals liberated from provincial constraints, have already made the arduous journey from tradition to modernity and now expect everyone else to share their own standards of "creativity and self-expression" and their own ethic of "individualism and individual problem-solving." With more than a little condescension, he maintains that "many working- and even middle-class Americans are still in the process of liberating themselves from traditional parental cultures and learning how to be individuals with their own needs and values." In other words, they are beginning to approach the lofty standards set by the enlightened elite; and the much-despised mass media, according to Gans, play a "progressive" role in breaking down the restrictive, patriarchal, "traditional" culture from which the common people are just beginning to free themselves. Thus the mass media liberate the working-class housewife from parental dictation, enabling her to make her own decisions and to act on her own judgment and taste. "For a housewife who has decided that she wants to decorate her home in her own way, rather than in the way her parents and neighbors have always done," the media "provide not only a legitimation of her own striving toward individual self-expression but an array of solutions from various taste cultures from which she can begin to develop her own." Furthermore, the "spate of women's liberation articles in popular women's magazines helps a woman still deeply immersed in a male-dominated society to find ideas and feelings that allow her to start to struggle for her own freedom."

According to this view of the "modernization" process, it is the very abundance of choices to which people are now exposed that underlies the malaise of modern man. "Where complex alternatives are available in a society," in the words of Fred Weinstein and Gerald Platt, "it becomes necessary for the individual to direct his own existence without traditional supports, i.e., without class, ethnic, or kinship ties." The need to make choices among a growing range of alternatives gives rise to "persistent feelings of discontent."

Here again we find an explanation of the modern "identity crisis" that confuses identity with social roles and concludes, rather complacently, that "persistent feelings of discontent" are the price people pay for freedom. Instead of assigning individuals to a preordained identity or social station, the argument runs, modern social arrangements leave them free to choose a way of life that suits them; and the choice can become disconcerting, even painful. Yet the same commentators who celebrate "modernization" as an ever-increasing abundance of personal choices rob choice of its meaning by denying that its exercise leads to any important consequences. They reduce choice to a matter of style and taste, as their preoccupation with "lifestyles" indicates. Their bland, innocuous conception of pluralism assumes that all preferences, all "lifestyles," all "taste cultures," as Gans calls them, are equally valid. Misapplying the dictum of cultural anthropology that every culture has to be judged on its own terms, they insist that no one has a right to "impose" his own preferences or moral judgments on anyone else. They appear to assume that moral values can no longer be taught or transmitted through example and persuasion but are always "imposed" on unwilling victims. Any attempt to win someone to your own point of view, or even to expose him to a point of view different from his own, becomes an intolerable interference with his freedom of choice.

These assumptions obviously preclude any public discussion of values at all. They make choice the test of moral and political freedom and then reduce it to nonsense. Thus Peter Clecak, whose recent study, *America's Quest for the Ideal Self*, follows in the footsteps of Shils and Gans, celebrates the diversity of American culture while discounting the possibility that it may intensify ethnic and religious conflicts. Most Americans, he claims, do not approach religion in a "sectarian" spirit—a remarkably misguided statement in view of the long history of American sectarianism, but one that fits snugly into a theory of pluralism, derived not merely from Shils and Gans but from Louis Hartz, Daniel Boorstin, and Richard Hofstadter, that emphasizes cultural consensus as opposed to conflict and exalts American practicality and the alleged American indifference to ideology. Adherence to these dogmas enables Clecak to avoid the conclusion that the current revival of evangelical, charismatic, and fundamentalist sects signals a growing split between the culture of Middle America and the enlightened, secular, therapeutic culture of educated elites, a split referred to by some analysts as a "cultural civil war." The hypothesis of cultural conflict has to be rejected, according to Clecak, because "these divisions do not threaten to destroy culture or to unravel the social fabric." (Not many conflicts in history would meet such a rigorous test.) "Traditional" values have persisted side by side with newer values. The mixture leads not to conflict but to "more cultural options than ever: clear old choices, clear new choices, and a fertile range of ambiguous syntheses of old and new." Like other pluralists, Clecak minimizes the persistence of ideological conflict by pretending that the exercise of cultural "options" has no consequences, since one choice never seems to preclude another. For most people, unfortunately, things seldom work out so smoothly. Those who choose, for example, to raise their children as Christians claim that the mass media and the schools subvert their efforts by propagating hedonism and "secular humanism," while modernists believe that demands for the restoration of the death penalty, strict laws against abortion, and the teaching of "creation science" threaten everything they believe in. In real life, as opposed to pluralist fantasy, every moral and cultural choice of any consequence rules out a whole series of other choices. In an age of images and ideology, however, the difference between reality and fantasy becomes increasingly elusive.

The pluralist conception of freedom rests on the same protean sense of the self that finds popular expression in such panaceas as "open marriage" and "nonbinding commitments." Both originate in the culture of consumption. A society of consumers defines choice not as the freedom to choose one course of action over another but as the freedom to choose everything at once. "Freedom of choice" means "keeping your options open." The idea that "you can be anything you want," though it preserves something of the older idea of the career open to talents, has come to mean that identities can be adopted and discarded like a change of costume. Ideally, choices of friends, lovers, and careers should all be subject to immediate cancellation: such is the open-ended, experimental conception of the good life upheld by the propaganda of commodities, which surrounds the consumer with images of unlimited possibility. But if choice no longer implies commitments and consequences— as making love formerly carried important "consequences," for instance, especially for women—the freedom to choose amounts in practice to an abstention from choice. Unless the idea of choice carries with it the possibility of making a difference, of changing the course of events, of setting in motion a chain of events that may prove irreversible, it negates the freedom it claims to uphold. Freedom comes down to the freedom to choose between Brand X and Brand Y, between interchangeable lovers, interchangeable jobs, interchangeable neighborhoods. Pluralist ideology provides an accurate reflection of the traffic in commodities, where ostensibly competing products become increasingly indistinguishable and have to be promoted, therefore, by means of advertising that seeks to create the illusion of variety and to present these products as revolutionary breakthroughs, breathtaking advances of modern science and engineering, or, in the case of the products of the mind, as intellectual discoveries the consumption of which will bring instantaneous insight, success, or peace of mind.

Industrial Technology, Mass Culture, and Democracy
Conservative critics of popular education and popular culture have always taken the position that "high culture" can be appreciated only by elites and that efforts to extend it to the masses inevitably lead to a debasement of standards. Even leftist critics of mass culture have adopted the view that the "great cultures of the past have all been elite affairs," as Dwight Macdonald wrote in 1960. Having given up the hope that elite cultures would ever find a popular audience, Macdonald and other opponents of mass culture came to argue for a cultural policy that would at least keep the "two cultures" separate (high culture and mass culture) and encourage the emergence of "a number of smaller, more specialized audiences." This is pretty much the position later taken by Herbert Gans, who advances it, however, not as an attack on "masscult" but as an attack on Macdonald's "elitism."

The debate about mass culture—revived in the eighties in the form of a debate about "narcissism," the decline of educational "excellence," and the cultural roots of America's declining position in the world market—remains mired in the old ruts because those who reject the critique of mass culture nevertheless accept its major premise. They too believe that "high culture [has lost] much of its social authority," as Clecak puts it; that "authoritative standards of judgment [are] increasingly difficult to discover"; that democracy brings a certain "cheapening of opinion, a lowering of taste, lapses of civility"; and that the "bourgeois ideal of leisurely, gracious living has neither survived well among the very privileged nor spread throughout society." At the same time, they agree with Herbert Gans that "poor people are as entitled to their own culture as anyone else" and that intellectuals' efforts to "impose" high culture on other people violate their right to a culture that "relates to their own experience."

Since both parties to this debate agree that "modernization" leads to the democratization of society and culture, the difference between them comes down to the issue of whether social and economic progress compensates for the dilution and vulgarization of high culture. Those who see themselves as cultural democrats believe that the past was a better time only "for certain elite groups," in Clecak's words. Most people in the past, they claim, led hard, unhappy lives. Industrialism has brought common people, for the first time, a "vast expansion of possibilities for personal fulfillment." If they exploit these possibilities in ways that offend intellectuals, the important thing is that they have the right to choose. They enjoy a "range of cultural options" formerly available only to aristocrats. They live "longer and healthier lives than people did in the past," according to Paul Wachtel, and they enjoy "greater opportunities for education and for entertainment." The excesses deplored both by conservative intellectuals and by "Tory radicals," as Clecak calls them, are the excesses of immaturity and will give way in time to something better. The "thickening textures of middlebrow culture," together with the "rising political sophistication of a better-educated citizenry," have persuaded Clecak that popular culture has already achieved the beginnings of a new maturity.

As for the new "narcissism" and the "culture of selfishness," they can be dismissed as "excesses," "unavoidable byproducts," "troubling side effects" of social and economic progress—"extreme instances of more salutary trends." Intellectuals who see only the negative side of progress see American society through a framework of nostalgia. According to Wachtel, critics of contemporary narcissism obscure the "valuable features of the search for personal fulfillment" by "tarring them with the same brush used to describe severe psychopathology." "To gauge American character by means of a rising index of selfishness," Clecak argues, "seems to me as unprofitable as assessing progress in cardiac surgery during the sixties and seventies by counting the number of patients who die in operating rooms."

In the form in which it has been conducted now for the last forty years, the debate about what used to be called mass culture and is now called narcissism can never be resolved. The debate has turned on the controlling conception of cultural change as a balance sheet, in which material gains offset cultural losses. It turns on the question of whether material progress exacts too heavy a price in the loss of cultural "excellence." But who is to say whether the gains of social and economic democracy outweigh its cultural "side effects"?

Suppose the question is misconceived. What if we reject the premise behind this whole discussion, that industrialism fosters political and economic progress? What if we reject the equation of industrialism with democracy and start instead from the premise that large-scale industrial production undermines local institutions of self-government, weakens the party system, and discourages popular initiative? In that case, cultural analysis can no longer content itself with balancing the social and political gains allegedly attendant on industrial progress against cultural losses. It will have to decide instead whether the invasion of culture and personal life by the modern industrial system produces the same effects that it produces in the social and political realm: a loss of autonomy and popular control, a tendency to confuse self-determination with the exercise of consumer choices, a growing ascendance of elites, the replacement of practical skills with organized expertise.

Clecak's passing reference to cardiac surgery indicates what is wrong not just with his own argument but with the entire controversy about mass culture and "narcissism." He equates technological progress with material and social progress, whereas in fact there is no connection between them. Once again, the point is not that material achievements—in this case, the prolongation of life mistakenly attributed to sophisticated surgical techniques—have an undesirable side-effect: a growing population of old people unable to support themselves and confused about the moral meaning of old age. The point is that modern surgery, taken as a whole, has done very little, if anything, to improve the general level of health and physical well-being or even to prolong life.* All medical technology has done is to increase patients' dependence on machines and the medical experts who operate these "life-support systems." The development of modern technology, not only in medicine but in other fields as well, has improved human control over the physical environment only in a very superficial way, by enabling scientists to make short-term modifications of nature, of which the long-term effects are incalculable. Meanwhile it

---

*Long-term increases in life expectancy, which began in the eighteenth century, derive from improvements in diet and in the general standard of living. As for the recent decline in deaths from cardiovascular diseases, no reliable authorities attribute it to improvements in cardiac surgery, the "progress" of which Clecak and other champions of modernization take for granted. Even those who emphasize medical reasons for the decline of deaths from heart disease, as opposed to healthier eating habits and exercise, attribute the decline to improvements in diagnosis, not to surgery. According to Eileen Crimmins, "There is general agreement that the number of people who have actually had [coronary bypass] surgery is so small that it could not have played a very significant role in the recent mortality decline." The effect of intensive care units for heart patients is also "being debated."

has concentrated this control in a small elite of technicians and administrators.

Modern technology and mass production have been defended, like mass culture, on the grounds that although they may have taken some of the charm out of life, they have added immeasurably to the comforts enjoyed by ordinary men and women. "I have no quarrel with tradition," Gans writes. "I am in favor of washing machines over washboards, and over river banks, however." But it is precisely the democratizing effects of industrial technology that can no longer be taken for granted. If this technology reduces some of the drudgery of housekeeping, it also renders the housekeeper dependent on machinery—not merely the automatic washer and dryer but the elaborate energy system required to run these and innumerable other appliances— the breakdown of which brings housekeeping to a halt. As we have seen, modern technology undermines the self-reliance and autonomy both of workers and consumers. It expands man's collective control over his environment at the expense of individual control; and even this collective control, as ecologists have pointed out again and again, is beginning to prove illusory as human intervention threatens to provoke unexpected responses from nature, including changes in climate, depletion of the ozone layer, and the exhaustion of natural resources. Nor can it be argued that advanced technology expands the range of options. Whatever its power to create new options in theory, in practice industrial technology has developed according to the principle of radical monopoly, as Ivan Illich calls it, whereby new technologies effectively eliminate older technologies even when the old ones remain demonstrably more efficient for many purposes. Thus the automobile did not simply add another form of transportation to existing forms; it achieved its preeminence at the expense of canals, railways, streetcars, and horse-drawn carriages, thereby forcing the population to depend almost exclusively on automotive transport even for those purposes for which it is obviously unsuited, such as commuting back and forth to work.

Our growing dependence on technologies no one seems to understand or control has given rise to a widespread feeling of powerlessness and victimization. The proliferation of protest groups, seen as an assertion of "personhood" in the arguments advanced by Clecak, Gans, and other pluralists, actually arises out of a feeling that other people are controlling our lives. The dominant imagery associated with political protest in the sixties, seventies, and eighties is not the imagery of "personhood," not even the therapeutic imagery of self-actualization, but the imagery of victimization and paranoia, of being manipulated, invaded, colonized, and inhabited by alien forces. Angry citizens who find themselves living near poisonous chemical dumps or nuclear power plants, neighbors who band together to keep out schools for retarded children or low-income housing or nursing homes, angry taxpayers, opponents of abortion, opponents of busing, and minority groups all see themselves, for different reasons, as victims of policies over which they have no control. They see themselves as victims not only of bureaucracy, big government, and unpredictable technologies but also, in many cases, of high-level plots and conspiracies involving organized crime, intelligence agencies, and politicians at the upper reaches of government. Side by side with the official myth of a beleaguered government threatened by riots, demonstrations, and unmotivated, irrational assassinations of public figures, a popular mythology has taken shape that sees government as a conspiracy against the people themselves.

The Decline of Authority   The myth of modernization, which dominates debates about consumerism, technology, mass culture, and mass politics, assumes that "move-

ments toward autonomy," in the words of Weinstein and
Platt, have "separat[ed] the individual from authority,"
brought about a "relaxation of external controls" and a new
"flexibility of social mandates," and thus made it possible for
a citizen to "choose his personal goals from a wide scope of
legitimate ends." The declining respect for authority, allegedly a concomitant of the rise of mass parties and universal suffrage, generates the same kind of controversies as the
controversies about the decline of craftsmanship and the
decline of educational "excellence." Conservatives lament
the collapse of authoritative leadership, whereas progressives claim, once again, that the democratization of politics
makes up for the raucous quality of modern political culture,
the lack of deference shown to opponents or to authorities,
and the unthinking contempt for tradition. According to
Clecak, it is an "embattled intellectual elite" that mourns the
collapse of standards and the "democratization of American
culture." Blind to the "vitality and variety" of American life,
full of status anxiety and status resentment, mistaking the
decline in their own genteel status for a general decline of
politics and culture, intellectuals assume a posture of moral
superiority and denounce their fellow citizens as self-
centered and narcissistic. Their "mood of defeat," their
"pessimism," the "haze of nostalgia" through which they see
the past bespeak an elitist disdain for democracy, even when
they pose as radicals. With a judicial and impartial air, Clecak notes that the "painful tensions between elitist cultural
values and the results of democratic participation admit no
easy resolution." He quotes Hofstadter, one of the founders
of pluralist theory, to support his contention that criticism
of modern politics and culture originates in the "unresolv-
able conflict," as Hofstadter put it, "between the elite character of [the intellectual's] own class and his democratic
aspirations." Like other pluralists, Clecak finds this trite
formula so appealing that he simply closes his mind to argu-

ments that fail to conform to it—arguments, for example, that criticize modern society on the grounds not that it is too democratic but that the democratization of culture and politics remains an illusion.

The decline of authority is a good example of the kind of change that promotes the appearance of democracy without its substance. It is part of a shift to a manipulative, therapeutic, "pluralistic," and "nonjudgmental" style of social discipline that originated, like so many other developments, with the rise of a professional and managerial class in the early years of the twentieth century and then spread from the industrial corporation, where it was first perfected, into the political realm as a whole. As we have seen, managerial control of the work force created a passive work force, excluded from decisions about the design and execution of production. Passivity, however, created new problems of labor discipline and social control—problems of "morale," of "motivation," of the "human factor," as they were known to the industrial sociologists and industrial psychologists who began to appear in the twenties. According to these professional students of "human relations," modern industry had created a feeling of drift, uncertainty, anomie: the worker lacked a sense of "belonging." Problems of labor discipline and "manpower recruitment" demanded an extension of the cultural reforms already inaugurated by the rise of mass marketing. Indeed the promotion of consumption as a way of life came to be seen as itself a means of easing industrial unrest. But the conversion of the worker into a consumer of commodities was soon followed by his conversion into a consumer of therapies designed to ease his "adjustment" to the realities of industrial life. Experiments carried out at Western Electric by Elton Mayo and his colleagues at the Harvard Business School—the famous Hawthorne studies—showed how complaints about low wages and excessive supervision could be neutralized by psychiatric counseling and observation. Mayo and his colleagues found, or claimed to find, that changes in the physical conditions of work, wage incentives, and other material considerations had little influence on industrial productivity. The workers under observation increased their output simply because they had become the object of professional attention and for the first time felt as if someone cared about their work. Interviews instituted with the intention of eliciting complaints about the quality of supervision, which might in turn have enabled management to improve supervisory techniques, turned up instead subjective and intensely emotional grievances having little relation to the objective conditions of work. The workers' complaints, according to Mayo, had no "external reference," and the new sense of freedom expressed by the workers under study had to be taken, therefore, not as an objective description of an actual change in the conditions of work but as "prejudiced judgments," as symptoms, as, in short, "simply a type of statement almost inevitably made when a not very articulate group of workers tries to express an indefinable feeling of relief from constraint." As Mayo took pains to point out, "Their opinion is, of course, mistaken: in a sense they are getting closer supervision than ever before, the change is in the quality of the supervision."

It would be hard to find a statement that captures so clearly the shift from an authoritative to a therapeutic mode of social control—a shift that has transformed not only industry but politics, the school, and the family. On the strength of such studies, sophisticated administrators came to regard moral exhortation, or even appeals to enlightened self-interest in the form of wage incentives, as outmoded techniques of industrial management. They envisioned a change in the "quality of supervision," described by Douglas MacGregor of MIT in *The Human Side of Enterprise* (1957)—another study that has had enormous impact on

managerial thought and practice—as a change from an authoritarian style of control, relying on rewards and punishments, to a more "humanistic" style that treated the worker
not as a child but as a partner in the enterprise and sought
to give him a sense of belonging. Note the irony of this talk
of "partnership," as misleading as the talk of "expanding
options" that also figures so prominently in the rhetoric of
pluralism. The new style of management defines the worker
(just as he is defined by the advertising industry) as a creature of impulse: shortsighted, irrational, incapable of understanding the conditions of his work or even of formulating
an intelligent defense of his own interests. Drawing not only
on their own experiments but also on a vast body of sociological and psychological theory, members of the new administrative elite have replaced the direct supervision of the
labor force with a far more subtle system of psychiatric
observation. Observation, initially conceived as a means to
more effective forms of supervision and control, has become
a means of control in its own right.

Politics as Consumption The systematic observation of symptomatic data, even before it became a technique
of labor discipline and social control, had already come to
serve as the basis of a new system of industrial recruitment,
centered on the school. The modern system of public education, remodeled in accordance with the same principles of
scientific management first perfected in industry, has replaced apprenticeship as the principal agency of training
people for work. The transmission of skills is increasingly
incidental to this training. The school habituates children to
bureaucratic discipline and to the demands of group living,
grades and sorts them by means of standardized tests, and
selects some for professional and managerial careers while
consigning the rest to manual labor. The subordination of
academic instruction to testing and counseling suggests that

agencies of "manpower selection" have become part of a larger apparatus of counseling or resocialization that includes not only the school but also the juvenile court, the psychiatric clinic, and the social-work agency—in short, the whole range of institutions operated by the "helping professions." This tutelary complex, as it has aptly been called, discourages the autonomous transfer of power and authority from one generation to the next, mediates family relationships, and socializes the population to the demands of bureaucracy and industrial life.

All these institutions operate according to the underlying principle that a willingness to cooperate with the proper authorities offers the best evidence of "adjustment" and the best hope of personal success, while a refusal to cooperate signifies the presence of "emotional problems" requiring more sustained therapeutic attention. As an agency of manpower selection, the school system, supplemented by other tutelary agencies, serves as an effective device for rationing class privilege in a society that feels uneasy about privilege and wants to believe that people get ahead on merit alone. As an agency of social discipline, the school, together with other elements in the tutelary complex, both reflects and contributes to the shift from authoritative sanctions to psychological manipulation and surveillance—the redefinition of political authority in therapeutic terms—and to the rise of a professional and managerial class that governs society not by upholding authoritative moral standards but by defining normal behavior and by invoking allegedly nonpunitive, psychiatric sanctions against deviance.

The extension of these techniques into the political realm transforms politics into administration and finally into another article of consumption. The growth of a professional civil service, the rise of regulatory commissions, the proliferation of governmental agencies, and the dominance of executive over legislative functions provide merely the most obvious examples of the shift from political to administrative control, in which issues allegedly too abstruse and technical for popular understanding fall under the control of professional experts. Governmental regulation of the economy has often been advocated with the explicit objective of insulating business and government against popular ignorance—as when George W. Perkins, one of the founders of Theodore Roosevelt's Progressive party and a leading champion of the regulatory commission, demanded that economic issues like tariffs and trusts be taken "out of politics," deplored the "shockingly incompetent manner in which our great business problems have been handled," and cited the "hullabaloo over the Sherman Law" as an example of the incompetence of politicians and their constituents. But even reforms intended to increase popular participation, such as the presidential primary, have had the opposite effect. Twentieth-century politics has come to consist more and more of the study and control of public opinion. The study of the "American voter" incorporates techniques first perfected in market research, where they served to identify the whims of the "sovereign consumer." In government as in industry, devices originally intended merely to register opinion—polls, samples, and balloting itself—now serve to manipulate opinion as well. They define a statistical norm, deviations from which become automatically suspect. They make it possible to exclude unpopular opinions from political discussion (just as unpopular wares are excluded from the supermarket) without any reference to their merits, simply on the basis of their demonstrated lack of appeal. By confronting the electorate with the narrow range of existing choices, they ratify those choices as the only ones capable of attracting support. Just as the interviews conducted at Hawthorne trivialized the workers' grievances, polls and surveys trivialize politics by reducing political choices to indistinguishable alternatives. In both cases, those in power invite popular "input" strictly on their own terms, under cover of scientific impartiality. The study of voting "behavior" becomes at the same time an important determinant of that behavior.

In industry, the exclusion of workers from control over the design of work went hand in hand with the rise of a new and profoundly undemocratic institution, the corporation, which has centralized the technical knowledge once administered by craftsmen. In politics, the exclusion of the public from political participation is bound up with the decline of a democratic institution, the political party, and its replacement by institutions less amenable to popular control. The policy-making function of the party has been taken over by the administrative bureaucracy; its educative function by the mass media. Political parties now specialize in marketing politicians for public consumption, and even here party discipline has broken down to a remarkable extent. The electorate is "no longer bound to party through the time-honored links of patronage and the machine," as Walter Dean Burnham points out. As a result, politics has become an "item of luxury consumption, . . . an indoor sport involving a host of discrete players rather than the teams of old."

The New "Personhood" The social changes so far summarized—the substitution of observation and measurement for authoritative, "judgmental" types of social sanctions; the transformation of politics into administration; the replacement of skilled labor by machinery; the redefinition of education as "manpower selection," designed not so much to instill work skills as to classify workers and to assign them either to the small class of administrators, technicians, and managers who make decisions or to the larger class of minimally skilled workers who merely carry out instructions—have gradually transformed a productive system based on handicraft production and regional exchange into a complex, interlocking network of technologies based on mass production, mass consumption, mass communications, mass culture: on the assimilation of all activities, even those formerly assigned to private life, to the demands of the marketplace.

These developments have created a new kind of selfhood, characterized by some observers as self-seeking, hedonistic, competitive, and "antinomian," by others as cooperative, "self-actualizing," and enlightened. By this time, it should be clear that neither description captures the prevailing sense of self. The first sees consumerism only as an invitation to self-indulgence. It deplores "materialism" and the desire for "things" and misses the more insidious effects of a culture of consumption, which dissolves the world of substantial things (far from reinforcing it), replaces it with a shadowy world of images, and thus obliterates the boundaries between the self and its surroundings. Critics of "hedonism" attribute its increasing appeal to the collapse of educational standards, the democratization of an "adversary culture" that formerly appealed only to the intellectual avant-garde, and the decline of political authority and leadership. They complain that people think too much about rights instead of thinking about duties. They complain about the pervasive sense of "entitlement" and the claim to unearned privileges. All these arguments invite the reply that although a democratic culture may offend "champions of public order and high culture," as Theodore Roszak calls them, it gives ordinary people access to a better life and a wider range of "options."

Neither party to this debate stops to question the reality of choices that have no lasting consequences. Neither side questions the debased conception of democracy that reduces it, in effect, to the exercise of consumer preferences. Neither side questions the equation of selfhood with the ability to play a variety of roles and to assume an endless variety of freely chosen identities.

Since the celebration of "personhood" seeks only to re-fute critics of selfishness and hedonism, it cannot come to grips with an argument that rejects the prevailing terms of debate. It can only elaborate ingenious variations on the same theme, constructing new typologies that express the same crudely conceived contrast between the old individual-ism and the "new social ethic," as Daniel Yankelovich calls it. Charles Reich's Consciousness II and Consciousness III, Gregory Bateson's Learning II and Learning III, Alvin Toffler's Second Wave and Third Wave all serve to label stylized cultural configurations and personality traits that have little reference to anything besides their own opposi-tion. Thus the new consciousness, according to Reich, affirms the "wholeness of self" and rejects the "aggressive, disciplined, competitive pursuit of definite goals." The old culture, on the other hand, rests—as Toffler explains it—on an exploitive attitude toward nature, an "atomic model of reality" that sees only the parts and misses the whole, a mechanistic view of causality, and a linear sense of time. Theodore Roszak, like many others, insists that the emerg-ing ethic of personhood should not be confused with narcis-sism, egocentricity, or self-absorption. Although a "yearn-ing for growth, for authenticity, for largeness of experience" sometimes takes the form of "brashness, vulgarity, and youthful impetuosity," these side-effects, for Roszak as for Peter Clecak, Daniel Yankelovich, and Paul Wachtel, repre-sent a passing phase in the development of a sensibility that will eventually reconcile self and society, humanity and na-ture. Critics of the new culture, according to Roszak, "mis-read the new ethos of self-discovery, mistaking it for the old vice of self-aggrandizement." They confuse the "sensitive quest for fulfillment with the riotous hedonism of our high consumption economy." They see another "revolt of the masses" in what is actually a "revolt of people *against* mas-sification in behalf of their embattled personhood."

In Wachtel's version of this argument, the decline of economic man and the rise of psychological man bode well for the future. Those who see this development as a decline, like Rieff, attribute to psychology in general bad effects that ought to be attributed only to psychoanalysis, which defines "grasping selfishness" as the basis of human nature and thus mirrors the capitalist ethic of competitive individualism. The new growth therapies and family therapies, on the other hand, offer a "healthy-minded" alternative to atomistic individualism. Far from encouraging "narcissism," they insist on the cultural determinants of personality and the importance, allegedly ignored by psychoanalysis, of transactions between the individual and his environment. They promote a "psycho-ecological point of view." "It is not psychology that is the problem," Wachtel argues; "it is the *wrong* psychology."

According to Morris Berman, the new "planetary culture" rejects "ego-consciousness" in favor of an "ecological sense of reality." Drawing on the "astonishing synthesis provided by the cultural anthropologist Gregory Bateson" —the "only fully developed articulated holistic science available today"—Berman announces the death of the Cartesian worldview and the emergence of a new sense of "cosmic connectedness." Verbal-rational learning (Learning II, as Bateson calls it) separates the individual from the environment and from his fellows, insists on a split between mind and body and between fact and value, and clings to a linear sense of time. Holistic consciousness (Learning III) reunites fact and value and dissolves the ego, the "independent self so dear to Western thought." The collapse of the mechanistic view of the world, Berman believes, heralds a "holistic society," "dreamier and more sensual than ours," in which the "body will be seen as part of culture," not as a "dangerous libido to be kept in check." The new society will value community more highly than competition. It will rest on extended families, not on the "competitive and isolating nuclear family that is today a seedbed of neurosis." Tolerant, pluralistic, and decentralized, it will concern itself with "fitting into nature rather than attempting to master it." The new consciousness leads to a "reenchantment of the world."

In order to contrast the new "personhood" with acquisitive individualism, its admirers argue that the cultural revolution, far from encouraging narcissism, puts an end to the narcissistic "illusion of self-sufficiency," as Philip Slater calls it. In passages reminiscent of Norman O. Brown, Slater contends that the illusion of "infantile narcissistic omnipotence" underlies competitive individualism, the achievement ethic, and the Promethean urge to dominate nature and "to extend oneself in a linear way into the environment." Now that the "disconnector virtues"—the "most treasured virtues of the past"—have lost their "survival value," a new ecological awareness has begun to take shape, which understands man's embeddedness in a larger system of life. The old culture rests on an "arrogant assumption about the importance of the single individual in society and the importance of humanity in the universe." The new culture, on the other hand, values the "humble virtues" that have taken on "higher survival value" in a world endangered by runaway technology, ecological disaster, and nuclear holocaust. "The conditions that gave competitiveness survival value have long since evaporated."

In Betty Friedan's *Second Stage*, the same slogans take on a feminist coloration. According to Friedan, the feminist movement has combined with a "quiet movement of American men" to produce an androgynous personality type that is already "humanizing" both the family and the corporation. She cites studies carried out by the Stanford Research Institute—the source of much optimistic assessment of the "changing image of man"—that allegedly document the transition from an authoritarian to a pluralistic style of corporate leadership. The Alpha style—another variation on the standard typologies—rests on "analytical, rational, quantitative thinking," in Friedan's words. It wrongly assumes that every choice leaves some people winners and others losers. It may have been an appropriate style for the "authoritarian and homogenous society" of the recent past; but the coming of a new kind of society in which the "main problems of economic and even physical survival have to do with the complex relationships, behavior and values of *people*, not things," requires a new kind of leadership. "Contextual," "relational," flexible, and tolerant, concerned with the "subtleties of human interaction" rather than with the imposition of uniform values, the Beta style is a feminine or androgynous style, the growing importance of which signals the obsolescence of "masculine, win-lose, zero-sum linear thinking." Its emergence, together with the religious revival, the human potential movement, and the general hunger "for larger purposes beyond the self," refutes social critics who make a speciality of "ranting and raving about the 'me generation' and the 'culture of narcissism.' "

In a book that grew out of the Stanford studies, *Voluntary Simplicity*, Duane Elgin summarizes the industrial worldview and the postindustrial worldview in parallel columns: "materialism" as opposed to "spirituality," "cutthroat competition" as opposed to cooperation, conspicuous consumption as opposed to conservation. Industrialism defines the individual as "separate and alone"; the new planetary perspective defines him "as both a unique *and* an inseparable part of the larger universe." According to Elgin, the environmental movement, the antinuclear movement, the counterculture, the human potential movement, the interest in Eastern religions, and the new concern with health add up to a "quiet revolution," an "awakening interest in the inner aspect of life." Marilyn Ferguson makes the same claims in *The Aquarian Conspiracy*, still another book directed against "social critics [who] speak from their own despair or a kind of cynical chic that belies [*sic*] their own sense of impotence." Criticism of the new consciousness, Ferguson maintains, rests on a "fear of the self" and a "cultural bias against introspection," according to which introspection is "narcissistic or escapist." In fact, the new culture repudiates "selfishness," in her view. It knows that "the separate self is an illusion." It reunites self and society, mind and body, science and mysticism. It rejects the materialistic conception of reality long upheld by Western rationalism. Reality is another rationalistic mirage, according to Ferguson. "If the nature of reality is . . . holographic, and the brain operates holographically, then the world is indeed, as the Eastern religions have said, *maya:* a magic show. Its concreteness is an illusion."

"Selfishness" or Survivalism? In its liberal use of labels, its addiction to slogans, its reduction of cultural change to simplified sets of opposite characteristics, and its conviction that reality is an illusion, this simpleminded case for "cultural revolution" betrays its affinity with the consumerism it claims to repudiate. The most glaring weakness of this argument, however—and of the whole debate in which it is immersed—is the equation of narcissism with "selfishness of an extreme form," in the words of Daniel Yankelovich. The terms have little in common. Narcissism signifies a loss of selfhood, not self-assertion. It refers to a self threatened with disintegration and by a sense of inner emptiness. To avoid confusion, what I have called the culture of narcissism might better be characterized, at least for the moment, as a culture of survivalism. Everyday life has begun to pattern itself on the survival strategies forced on those exposed to extreme adversity. Selective apathy, emotional disengagement from others, renunciation of the past and the future, a determination to live one day at a time—these

techniques of emotional self-management, necessarily carried to extremes under extreme conditions, in more moderate form have come to shape the lives of ordinary people under the ordinary conditions of a bureaucratic society widely perceived as a far-flung system of total control.

Confronted with an apparently implacable and unmanageable environment, people have turned to self-management. With the help of an elaborate network of therapeutic professions, which themselves have largely abandoned approaches stressing introspective insight in favor of "coping" and behavior modification, men and women today are trying to piece together a technology of the self, the only apparent alternative to personal collapse. Among many people, the fear that man will be enslaved by his machines has given way to a hope that man will become something like a machine in his own right and thereby achieve a state of mind "beyond freedom and dignity," in the words of B. F. Skinner. Behind the injunction to "get in touch with your feelings"—a remnant of an earlier "depth" psychology—lies the now-familiar insistence that there is no depth, no desire even, and that the human personality is merely a collection of needs programmed either by biology or by culture.

We are not likely to get any closer to an understanding of contemporary culture as long as we define the poles of debate as selfishness and self-absorption, on the one hand, and self-fulfillment or introspection on the other. According to Peter Clecak, selfishness is the "deficit side" of cultural liberation—an "unavoidable byproduct of the quest for fulfillment." It is a part of contemporary culture that must not be confused with the whole. "Though they are plausible to a degree, characterizations of America as a selfish culture typically confuse excesses with norms, by-products with central and on the whole salutary outcomes of the quest" for self-fulfillment. But the question is not whether the salutary effects of "personhood" outweigh hedonism and self-seeking. The question is whether any of these terms capture either the prevailing patterns of psychological relations or the prevailing definition of selfhood. The dominant conception of personality sees the self as a helpless victim of external circumstances. This is the view encouraged both by our twentieth-century experience of domination and by the many varieties of twentieth-century social thought that reach their climax in behaviorism. It is not a view likely to encourage either a revival of old-fashioned acquisitive individualism (which presupposed far more confidence about the future than most people have today) or the kind of search for self-fulfillment celebrated by Clecak, Yankelovich, and other optimists. A genuine affirmation of the self, after all, insists on a core of selfhood not subject to environmental determination, even under extreme conditions. Self-affirmation remains a possibility precisely to the degree that an older conception of personality, rooted in Judaeo-Christian traditions, has persisted alongside a behavioral or therapeutic conception. But this kind of self-affirmation, which remains a potential source of democratic renewal, has nothing in common with the current search for psychic survival—the varieties of which we must now examine in some detail.

II

The
Survival
Mentality

The Normalization of Crisis　In an uneasy age, still
secure in the enjoyment of material comforts unknown to
earlier ages yet obsessed by thoughts of disaster, the problem
of survival overshadows loftier concerns. The preoccupation with survival, a prominent feature of American culture
ever since the early seventies, takes many forms, grave and
trivial. It finds its most characteristic and insidious expression, its ultimate expression, in the illusion of winnable nuclear wars; but it by no means exhausts itself in the anticipation of earthshaking calamities. It has entered so deeply into
popular culture and political debate that every issue, however fleeting or unimportant, presents itself as a matter of life
or death.

A left-wing magazine, *Mother Jones*, advertises itself as a
"survival guide" to the "political Dark Ages" brought about
by the election of Ronald Reagan. A Los Angeles radio

station, hoping to spread "kindness, joy, love, and happiness," commends itself to its listeners as "your survival station of the eighties." Samsonite, a manufacturer of luggage, advertises its latest briefcase as "the survivor." A *New York Times* headline refers to an attempt to limit the substitution of recorded music for live performers, conducted by the American Federation of Musicians, as a "survival battle." An antifeminist tirade, published with the usual media fanfare, announces itself as *A Survival Guide for the Bedeviled Male.* A basketball coach praises one of his players for his capacity to learn from his mistakes and to "survive" them. The same sportswriter who reports this tribute muses about the "survival" of college basketball as a major spectator sport.

At Yale, a "Student Rescue Committee" urges parents to send their sons and daughters a "survival kit" ("nourishing snack foods in a humorously packaged box") to help them weather the "most crucial and nerve racking [*sic*] period of the entire academic year—Final Exams!" The American Historical Association publishes a pamphlet designed to help women overcome discrimination: *A Survival Manual for Women (and Other) Historians.* A patient suffering from herpes explains how he overcame his fear of the disease by confiding in fellow sufferers: "When you begin sharing with other people, it's like being with survivors of a flood or a POW camp." A review of Henry Kissinger's memoirs bears the predictable headline, "Master of the Art of Survival." Michael Sellers, son of the late actor Peter Sellers, tells reporters that "Dad clung frantically"—even after a heart attack in 1964—"to the belief that he was a survivor and . . . would live until he was seventy-five." Another actor, George C. Scott, speaks of himself as a "survivor" in a cutthroat calling. Jason Robards, Jr., having weathered alcoholism, a nearly fatal automobile crash, and a long period of critical neglect, wonders about the "mystery" as a result of which "people like George [Scott] and myself have survived." A drama critic acclaims revivals of Noël Coward's *Private Lives* and Herman Wouk's *The Caine Mutiny* in an article, "Survivors," that also acclaims the return of Elizabeth Taylor and Richard Burton to the Broadway stage.

Erma Bombeck introduces her latest collection of columns as a book "about surviving." Another book addressed to housewives—*Surviving as a Woman, or How to Keep Your Chin High, Your Courage Up, and Never Be Caught with Your Brioches Down*—adopts the same tone, depicting daily life as a succession of minor emergencies. "Whether they are squares or swingers," women have "one thing in common," according to Betty Canary. "And that is, they are determined to be survivors." Betty Friedan resorted to the same kind of rhetorical exaggeration in *The Feminine Mystique*, but without any humorous intent, when she called the middle-class household a "comfortable concentration camp." Those who take a more kindly view of domestic institutions nevertheless ask themselves whether the shrinking, beleaguered family still provides conditions "for the emotional survival of the individual in our mass society."

The trivialization of crisis, while it testifies to a pervasive sense of danger—to a perception that nothing, not even the simplest domestic detail, can be taken for granted—also serves as a survival strategy in its own right. When the grim rhetoric of survivalism invades everyday life, it simultaneously intensifies and relieves the fear of disaster. The victim of circumstances copes with crisis by preparing for the worst and by reassuring himself that the worst has a way of falling short of expectations. Bertolt Brecht once said that those who laugh have not yet heard the bad news. But laughter today—and this helps to explain why it often has a hollow sound and why so much contemporary humor takes the form of parody and self-parody—comes from people who are all too well aware of the bad news but have nevertheless made a determined effort to keep smiling. "Let a smile be your umbrella." Stanley Kubrick satirized this desperate good cheer in the subtitle of his film *Dr. Strangelove: How I Learned to Stop Worrying and Love the Bomb*. The editors of *Mad* satirized it, but also affirmed unfounded optimism as the only tenable attitude in a mad, mad, mad, mad world, when they set up as their spokesman the figure of Alfred E. Neumann, with his idiotic grin and his "What? Me Worry?"

Nothing is gained, after all, by dwelling on the bad news. The survival artist takes bad news for granted; he is beyond despair. He deflects reports of fresh disasters, warnings of ecological catastrophe, warnings of the probable consequences of the nuclear arms race by refusing to discriminate between events that threaten the future of mankind and events that merely threaten his peace of mind. He jokes about the unending outpouring of bad news on television and in the newspapers, complains that it depresses him, and thus absolves himself of the need to distinguish between various kinds and degrees of bad news. He protects himself from its impact, moreover, by dismissing those who bear it as prophets of gloom and doom—misanthropes and killjoys embittered by personal disappointments or an unhappy childhood, left-wing intellectuals embittered by the collapse of their revolutionary expectations, reactionaries unable to adjust to changing times.

The threat of nuclear war, the threat of ecological catastrophe, the memory of the Nazi's genocidal war against the Jews, the possible collapse of our entire civilization have generated a widespread sense of crisis, and the rhetoric of crisis now pervades discussion of race relations, prison reform, mass culture, fiscal management, and everyday personal "survival." A list of recent books on survival and survivalism would include books on ecology and nuclear war, books on the Holocaust, books on technology and automation, and a flood of "future studies," not to mention an outpouring of science fiction that takes a coming apocalypse as its major premise. But such a list would also include the huge psychiatric literature on "coping" and the equally enormous sociological literature on victims and "victimology." It would include books setting forth "survival strategies for oppressed minorities," "survival in the executive jungle" and "survival in marriage." Reinforced by other media—film, radio, television, newspapers, magazines—this propaganda of disaster has a cumulative effect almost exactly opposite to the effect ostensibly intended. The infiltration of everyday life by the rhetoric of crisis and survival emasculates the idea of crisis and leaves us indifferent to appeals founded on the claim that some sort of emergency commands our attention. Nothing makes our attention wander so quickly as talk of another crisis. When public crises pile up unresolved, we lose interest in the possibility that anything can be done about them. Then too, cries of crisis often serve merely to justify the claims of professional crisis-managers, whether they traffic in politics, war, and diplomacy or simply in the management of emotional "stress."

One reply to these claims insists that questions of genuine survival—energy policy, environmental policy, the nuclear arms race—ought to be decided politically, collaboratively, and democratically, instead of being treated as technical subjects understood only by a handful of specialists. It is more characteristic of the contemporary survival mentality, however, that it turns away from public questions and concerns itself with the predictable crises of everyday life, where individual actions still seem to have some minimal impact on the course of events. Everyday life has come to present itself as a succession of crises not necessarily because it is more risky and competitive than it used to be but because it confronts people with manageable stresses, whereas the hope of preventing public disaster appears so remote, for most people, that it enters their thoughts only in the form of a wistful prayer for peace and brotherhood.

Everyday Life Reinterpreted in the Light of Extreme Situations The word "survival" has taken on so many different meanings today—like "tradition," "problem," and "nostalgia," words that have undergone a similar expansion and debasement—that it takes a considerable effort merely to sort them out. Talk of survival can describe the difficulty of making ends meet. It can allude to the fear of aging, the fear of dying of cancer, the fear of succumbing to drugs, alcohol, or some other form of personal disintegration. It can allude to the difficulty of holding a marriage together. It can convey a sense of amazement that anything at all should last in a world of disposable goods. It can convey a vicarious identification with the survivors of Auschwitz and Treblinka, of the Gulag Archipelago, of Hiroshima and Nagasaki. It can express the perception that we are all survivors in the sense that we have lived through dark times and have emerged on the far side of the great historical divide, marked by the twentieth-century experience of mass murder, that already separates our epoch from earlier and more innocent ages.

The last of these meanings helps to explain the prevailing fear of nostalgia. Whatever can be said for or against our time, it is burdened with a knowledge unknown, if not entirely unsuspected, in earlier times: the knowledge that otherwise rational men will carry out the extermination of entire populations if it suits their purpose and that many good citizens, far from raising a wild cry of outrage and lamentation when confronted with these acts, will accept them as an eminently sensible means of shortening a war or establishing socialism in one country or getting rid of superfluous people. Seen through the prism of our contemporary knowledge of radical evil, as Hannah Arendt called it—evil so deep that it overflows any conventional category of sin and defeats attempts to fix responsibility or to imagine a suitable punishment—the past evokes nostalgia so intense that the emotion has to be fiercely denied, repressed, and denounced. Herman Kahn's question—"Will the survivors envy the dead?"—haunts our time, not only because it describes a possible future but also because it describes (though not intended in this way) our own relation to the past, whenever we allow ourselves to look into the fully documented horrors that have already taken place in the twentieth century, so much more difficult to live with, in the last analysis, than the horrors that may come.*

Our perception not only of the past and the future but of the present has been colored by a new awareness of extremes. We think of ourselves both as survivors and as victims or potential victims. The growing belief that we are all victimized, in one way or another, by events beyond our control owes much of its power not just to the general feeling that we live in a dangerous world dominated by large organizations but to the memory of specific events in twentieth-century history that have victimized people on a mass scale. Like the idea of survival, the idea of victimization, inappropriately applied to everyday misfortunes, keeps this memory alive and at the same time deadens its emotional impact. Indiscriminate usage broadens the idea of victimization until it loses its meaning. "In the times in which we live,

---

*Many people, of course, simply put all this out of mind. When reminded of it, they claim that our times are no more violent, bloody, and cruel than other times. Mass murder is nothing new, they insist. Every attempt to distinguish twentieth-century mass murder from the earlier record of war and oppression—by pointing out, for example, that it is often directed not against enemy nations or religious "infidels" or political opponents but against whole categories of persons declared superfluous, whose only offense lies in their existence—provokes the automatic rejoinder that it "romanticizes" the past.

One often encounters this Panglossian attitude among upwardly mobile academics, who are forever congratulating themselves on having escaped the narrow traditionalism of the village, the ethnic ghetto, or the middlebrow suburb. Here the refusal to look back comes not from the fear of homesickness but from complete indifference, coupled with a mindless faith in progress. Such absolute and unquestioning optimism, however, is gradually dying out. It demands a level of emotional shallowness and intellectual superficiality that most people, even academics, find it difficult to sustain over long periods of time.

everybody is exposed to the possibility of a criminal attack or incident of some kind," writes a specialist in victimology —a study he recommends as a "new approach in the social sciences." "The deepest human need," he continues, "is to survive, to live, work, and play together free from hurt. . . . The problem is that we are facing everywhere present and possible victimization, that we are living in the state or condition of being a victim of one sort or another." William Ryan proposes a similarly expansive definition of victimization in his well-known book, *Blaming the Victim*. In the preface to the revised edition, Ryan apologizes for devoting the first edition largely to the plight of black people and the poor. He has come to see that almost everyone is vulnerable to disaster: to "catastrophic illness"; to the "deliberate manipulation of inflation and unemployment"; to "grossly unfair taxes"; to pollution, unsafe working conditions, and the "greed of the great oil companies."

As these words suggest, the victim has come to enjoy a certain moral superiority in our society; this moral elevation of the victim helps to account for the inflation of political rhetoric that characterizes the discourse of survivalism. Many writers have adopted a "posture of accusatory public testimony," as Warner Berthoff notes in his study of postwar poetry and fiction. Identifying themselves with the underdog, straining to speak in the voice of victims or survivors—"persons living on after the decisive things have happened," in Berthoff's words—angry young men and angry women have exposed the injustices inflicted on oppressed and exploited minorities. Political spokesmen for these groups have assumed the same role. As they vie for the privileged status of victims, they appeal not to the universal rights of citizenship but to a special experience of persecution, said to qualify their people to speak about injustice with special authority and to demand not merely their rights but reparation for past wrongs. They claim—with good reason, in some cases—to be the victims, or survivors, of genocide. Rhetorical escalation transforms the meaning of injustice; it transforms the cause of oppressed minorities into a struggle for sheer survival. In the sixties, the shift from civil rights to "black power" announced the abandonment of efforts to create a multiracial society in favor of a strategy of black survival. Spokesmen for black power accused whites of plotting the destruction of the black race through birth control and racial intermarriage. In the seventies, radical feminists took up the cry of "gynocide." Instead of seeing the distinctive features of black culture or the distinctive pattern of historically conditioned femininity as "marks of oppression," in the manner of an earlier radicalism, or on the other hand as potential sources of a flourishing new cultural pluralism, spokesmen for disenfranchised minorities have reinterpreted their history in the light of the novel experience of genocide. Faced with a male-dominated society that plans the "technological elimination of women"—a "Final Solution to the 'problem' of Female Force"—radical feminists, according to Mary Daly, "have been developing new strategies and tactics for . . . economic, physical, and psychological survival. To do this, we have had to go deep inside our Selves." In something of the same way, reinvestigation of Jewish history has come to focus on the qualities that enabled the Jews to survive centuries of persecution. After the Holocaust, Jewish nationalism identified itself not with a transcendent moral mission but with the physical survival of the state of Israel. Pressure from Israel's neighbors and from the PLO, which based its program on the announced aim of liquidating the Jewish state, understandably intensified a commitment to the narrowest possible interpretation of Zionism. Meanwhile the Palestinians and their supporters in Western Europe and the United States claimed that they themselves were victims of Israeli "genocide."

Such exaggerations defeat their own purpose, of course.

Charges and countercharges of genocide make it hard to address the dangers that face mankind as a whole or even to alleviate the injustices suffered by particular groups. Too many "Final Solutions" have left us increasingly insensitive to this kind of appeal, even when such appeals deserve to be heard. The history of twentieth-century genocide, however, makes it inevitable that everyone with a claim to the honorable status of victim will model his plight on ultimate examples of victimization. Propaganda aside, it is no longer possible to think of victimization without thinking of the extermination of the Armenians, the kulaks, the Jews, and the people of Cambodia.

Large Organizations as Total Institutions The competitive free-for-all in large organizations provides many people with another occasion for the reassessment of ordinary experience in the light of extreme situations. The pursuit of success has been reconceived as a daily struggle for survival. According to a study conducted by the American Management Association, *The Changing Success Ethic*, Americans now see money not as a measure of success but as a "means of survival." Books addressed to executives, bearing such titles as *Survival in the Executive Jungle*, stress the importance of "street sense" or the "instinct for survival" and call attention to the low "survival rate of senior management." Recent success manuals compare large organizations to the Negro ghetto, where "survival . . . depends in large measure on the development of a healthy cultural paranoia." Those who offer their services as guides in the corporate wilderness, like Chester Burger and Michael Korda, recommend a "strategy for survival" based on watchfulness, suspicion, and distrust. "You need a long-range strategy precisely like a military battle plan. You need an analysis of where you stand and where the enemy stands. . . . Sometimes it's impossible to survive in your executive job, no matter what you do. . . . [But] in probably nine situations out of ten, survival is possible." According to Melville Dalton, "The individual in the large organization or mobile society, like the uncalculating animals, is also a defenseless creature who calculatingly practices deception for safety's sake against the invisible threats around him."

Social Darwinism long ago accustomed people to the idea that the fittest alone survive the rigors of modern business enterprise; but the twentieth-century awareness of a new dimension of organized brutality—of death camps and totalitarian political systems—has given a new direction to the fear of failure and provided a new source of imagery with which to elaborate the underlying perception of social life as a jungle.* The corporation takes on the appearance of a total institution, in which every trace of individual identity disappears. According to Erving Goffman, the sociologist of total institutions—systems of total control—there is a "tendency in the direction of total institutions" in "our large commercial, industrial, and educational establishments." During the student uprisings of the sixties, radical critics of the university repeatedly compared it to a detention camp or prison. Revisionist historians and critics of the public school system insisted on the prisonlike characteristics of the

---

*Under Reagan, social Darwinism has enjoyed something of a revival. The "dominant tradition of conservative ideology" holds that "those least able to survive should not be nurtured by the state," according to the liberal economist Robert B. Reich; and this type of conservatism, he argues, commends itself to Americans in the 1980s "because issues of survival have once again taken a central place in the nation's consciousness." Louise Kaegi rightly points out, however, that "survivalism is neither a 'conservative' nor a 'liberal' ideology." The left has developed its own version of social Darwinism, which exalts the survival of the species over the individual, promotes a lifeboat ethic under the slogan of "values clarification," and culminates in a "biological collectivism of eugenics and social prophylaxis," under which scientists and enlightened policymakers claim the right to allocate scarce resources and to pronounce on the survival value of competing ideas, beliefs, and social practices. "A survivalist strain," Kaegi writes, "underlies equally the economic-'libertarian' nightwatchman state, the 'conservative' national security state, and the 'liberal' therapeutic state."

common schools. A renewed interest in the history of Negro slavery, in the sixties and seventies, grew in part out of studies comparing plantation slavery to Nazi concentration camps. Sociologists subjected the prison to the same kind of reinvestigation, turning out books with titles like *Psychological Survival* and *The Ecology of Survival,* while popular interest in prisons fed on reports of prison riots and movements for prisoner's rights and on a stream of movies and television programs celebrating the resourcefulness of the prison survivor faced with an apparently irresistible environment.

The disposition to think of organizations as total institutions and of modern life in general as a succession of extreme situations can be traced to the death camps and concentration camps of World War II, an awareness of which has colored perceptions of social life far more deeply than has been understood. "The testimonies of the few who came through this experience alive are virtually bench marks on which other survival attempts in our time can be measured," write Stanley Cohen and Laurie Taylor in their study of long-term imprisonment. Unlike most students of survival, Cohen and Taylor take care to distinguish extreme situations from the everyday stresses that disturb our peace of mind but can be resolved "without profoundly affecting other parts of our life." In the same way, Goffman called attention to the differences between total institutions and organizations that claim only a part of the individual's attention for part of the day. He also called attention to their similarities, however; and the effect of his thinking as a whole, which combined a study of total institutions on the one hand with a study of everyday life on the other, unavoidably weakened the distinction between extreme situations and everyday emergencies. Once the imagery of total confinement and extreme situations took hold of the contemporary imagination, the temptation to extend this imagery to lesser forms of stress and hardship and to reinterpret every kind of adversity in the light of Auschwitz proved almost irresistible. An early study of the death camps announced in its title the question that has continued to absorb the late twentieth-century imagination: "How Did They Survive?" Answers to this question vary widely, as we shall see in the next chapter, but for the moment it is the question itself that concerns us. It is a question that runs through all our thinking about the Nazi death camps; but it also runs through historical investigations of other minorities subjected to persecution and discrimination, through the psychiatric literature on stress and "coping mechanisms," and through much of the popular writing on stresses experienced in the business world. Direct or vicarious exposure to extreme situations has surrounded not only oppression and hardship but everyday rivalry and competition with a new set of images and has thereby altered the way oppression, hardship, and competition are experienced. Adversity takes on new meanings in a world where the concentration camp stands as a compelling metaphor for society as a whole.

Competition, for example, now centers not so much on the desire to excel as on the struggle to avoid a crushing defeat. A willingness to risk everything in the pursuit of victory gives way to a cautious hoarding of the reserves necessary to sustain life over the long haul. The heroic rebel, warrior, or robber baron, earlier prototypes of successful competition, yield their place in the popular imagination to the wily veteran determined not so much to outstrip his opponents as to outlast them. The old code of combat, which stressed the dignity of death in the service of a worthy cause, loses its appeal under conditions—modern technological warfare and mass extermination—that make death neither sweet nor fitting. Survivalism leads to a devaluation of heroism. Extreme situations, wrote Goffman, clarify the "small acts of living," not the "grander forms of loyalty and treachery." Total institutions organize massive "assaults upon the self" but at the same time preclude effective resistance, forcing inmates to resort instead to "recalcitrance," ironic detachment and withdrawal, and the combination of conciliation and noncooperation Goffman referred to as "making out." Total institutions fascinated Goffman because—among other reasons—they force inmates to live one day at a time, since absorption in the immediate provides the best hope of long-term survival. Goffman's work on total institutions rested on the same premise that underlay his studies of the "presentation of self in everyday life": that people reveal themselves most fully, even under the most harrowing circumstances, in the unheroic events of everyday interchange, not in extraordinary feats of skill or courage. Total institutions—the death camps above all—have made us aware of the banality of evil, in Hannah Arendt's famous phrase; but they have also taught us something about the banality of survival. A growing belief that heroes don't survive informs the disenchantment with conventional codes of masculinity, alluded to in the previous chapter. It is not only masculinity that has lost its survival value, however, but the entire stock of allegedly outworn ideals of honor, heroic defiance of circumstances, and self-transcendence. As Vincent Canby noted in reviewing Lina Wertmüller's movie *Seven Beauties,* the survivor has discovered that "idealism is self-defeating."

The Cold-War Critique of Survivalism   This preliminary survey of survival themes might prompt the conclusion that our society suffers from a failure of nerve, that it needs to recover its sense of purpose and to rededicate itself to the ideals of freedom on which it was founded. The deterioration of Soviet-American relations since 1979, the escalation of the arms race, and the revival of the Cold War have given this kind of talk a certain plausibility. Thus Phyllis Schlafly condemns advocates of nuclear disarmament as people who can conceive of no higher object than mere survival. Norman Podhoretz deplores the "culture of appeasement" and the growing disinclination to defend American national interests and honor. Sidney Hook, in a bitter attack on the "strategy of ultimate surrender" allegedly advocated by Bertrand Russell and more recently by George F. Kennan, claims that it rests on the doctrine that "survival is the be-all and the end-all of life, the ultimate value." Rather than risk nuclear war, Russell and Kennan would "accept the certainty of communist domination," according to Hook. Quoting Alexander Solzhenitsyn—"To defend oneself, one must be ready to die"—Hook argues that "if we renew our moral courage, our dedication to freedom, we can avoid both war and capitulation in the days ahead." On the other hand, "Those who say that life is worth living at any cost have already written for themselves an epitaph of infamy, for there is no cause and no person that they will not betray to stay alive."

The peace movement has recently come under attack not only from the right but from a few critics on the left, who enter the same objection to a "zoological" conception of politics, as Cornelius Castoriadis calls it. "If nothing is worth dying for, . . . then nothing is worth living for," write Ferenc Feher and Agnes Heller in a recent issue of *Telos,* one of a series of issues devoted to unexpectedly virulent criticism of the movement for nuclear disarmament. Even though world peace becomes more desirable than ever in an age of nuclear weapons, "There is still a contradiction," according to Feher and Heller, "between a good life and a mere life." It follows that "violence and wars cannot be entirely eliminated from our actions if we seek something more than survival."

Both the substance of these arguments and the moral

fervor behind them recall attacks on appeasement by Lewis Mumford and Reinhold Niebuhr, among others, during the controversies about foreign policy that erupted on the eve of World War II. Niebuhr found it hard to understand, he said, "in what sense the peace of Munich is to be celebrated because 'at least it postponed the war.' Is it really true that to postpone a war is to add to the chances of its ultimate avoidance?" Pragmatic liberalism, as Mumford called it, had lost the "tragic sense of life." It refused to confront the reality of death, hoping that "science's steady advances in hygiene and medicine might postpone further and further that unpleasant occasion." In 1940, Mumford reported a conversation with a liberal who told him that he could not support a political decision that might lead to war and thereby bring about the death of other human beings. "When I objected that the failure to make such a decision in the existing international situation would certainly lead to the less fruitful death of these same human beings six months or six years hence, he confessed that for him any extra time spared for the private enjoyment of life seemed that much gained." This man had "ceased to live in a meaningful world," Mumford concluded. "For a meaningful world is one that holds a future that extends beyond the incomplete personal life of the individual; so that a life sacrificed at the right moment is a life well spent, while a life too carefully hoarded, too ignominiously preserved, is a life utterly wasted."

Today the peace movement invites a similar condemnation when it takes survival as its slogan—"Better red than dead"—or associates itself with an opposition to any form of personal sacrifice. This attitude reflects a widespread reluctance not merely to die in an unjust war but to die for any cause whatsoever. It reflects the refusal of moral and emotional commitments that identifies the survival mentality and the culture of narcissism. "To the narcissistic," Russell Jacoby writes, "sacrifice is a con-job, a loss with no benefits." Contemporary politics, to be sure, provides an abundance of realistic reasons for regarding sacrifice in this light. When political authorities exhort citizens to consume less heating fuel and utility companies respond by raising prices to compensate for lower demand, the perception that sacrifice is a swindle makes a good deal of sense. There is a difference, however, between the kind of political disaffection that rests on a realistic awareness that sacrifices usually fall on those who can least afford them and a loss of the very capacity for sacrifice, loyalty, and personal commitments. In the widely acclaimed film *Coming Home*, starring Jane Fonda and Jon Voigt—a film that captured the popular revulsion against war in the wake of Vietnam—a paraplegic Vietnam veteran lectures to a high-school assembly on the evils of war. The burden of his harangue is that those who go to fight in Vietnam will die there. Even though it can certainly be argued, once again, that the American cause in Vietnam—and in future police actions that may be undertaken for the defense of corporate interests or a misguided ideal of national greatness—did not justify the sacrifice of American lives, the attitude conveyed by this film goes beyond opposition to imperialism to an opposition to any form of sacrifice at all, an opposition based not on moral or political principle but on a deeper sort of refusal that clings to life at all costs. It is as if the makers of *Coming Home* were unable to imagine any form of loyalty that might justify the sacrifice of life. The character played by Voigt has come home from Vietnam with wounds deeper than those imagined by his creators, a paralysis of the moral will; and this example shows that although it is possible to distinguish analytically between a refusal to make sacrifices for an unworthy cause and a damaged capacity for sacrifice, historically they often prove inseparable. The kind of historical experience of which Vietnam represents the logical culmination—the ordering of our lives by others, without our consent—ends by depriving us of the very capacity to take responsibility for decisions that affect us or to adopt any stance toward life except that of victims and survivors. The experience of victimization, which justifies resistance, can also destroy the capacity for resistance by destroying the sense of personal responsibility. This is precisely the deepest injury inflicted by victimization: one finally learns to confront life not as a moral agent but solely as a passive victim, and political protest degenerates into a whine of self-pity. Witness the innumerable variations on the ever-popular leftist theme of the injustice of "blaming the victim."*

The antiwar movement and the environmental movement—closely associated with each other precisely in their growing insistence on the issue of survival—appeal to some of the worst impulses in contemporary culture when they proclaim that "nothing is worth dying for," in the words of a poster displayed at an antidraft demonstration in the late seventies. When Richard Falk demands a "moral commitment to survival" or when Paul Ehrlich and Richard Harriman call for a "survival movement" against military and corporate control, they dramatize the importance of ecological issues and make it more difficult than before to dismiss conservation as an issue that appeals only to sentimental

---

*In the early days of the Vietnam protest, a student at the University of Iowa interrupted a discussion of "our" foreign policy to deny the responsibility for the Vietnam War that seemed to be implied by the first-person pronoun. "It's not my war," she said. "It's *their* war; it's *their* country; and neither has anything to do with me." At the time, it seemed to me that this outburst represented a useful corrective to the kind of discussions conducted by "responsible" opponents of the war on the implicit assumption that such discussions should be confined to a policy-making establishment that includes intellectuals as a loyal opposition. I still think so. Subsequent events, however, have qualified this impression by suggesting that many radicals who rejected "their" war all too often rejected any other forms of loyalty as well. Many of them refused to assume responsibility for anything on the grounds that they had no control over the "decisions that affect our lives." In saying this, I do not mean to imply, of course, that opposition to the Vietnam War or to nuclear war today can be reduced to personal pathology.

nature-lovers and wilderness freaks. Unfortunately they also reinforce the habit of mind that regards the preservation of life as an end in itself, the same habit of mind that informs modern medical technology, for instance, in its zeal to extend life without any regard for its quality. "A number of things give us hope," write Ehrlich and Harriman in the conclusion to their environmentalist manifesto, *How to Be a Survivor,* a book full of alarming predictions of overpopulation, global wars, and ecological disasters. "The first is that survival itself is the issue. Once people understand that, they will fight like hell for it." On the contrary, people committed only to survival are more likely to head for the hills. If survival is the overriding issue, people will take more interest in their personal safety than in the survival of humanity as a whole. Those who base the case for conservation and peace on survival not only appeal to a debased system of values, they defeat their own purpose.

It would be a great mistake, however, to see in contemporary social movements nothing more than another expression of a contemptible disposition to cling to life at all costs. Solzhenitsyn's insistence that self-defense implies a willingness to risk death, as we shall see more fully in the next chapter, rests on a hard-earned understanding of the situation of individuals faced with extreme adversity; but it does not necessarily apply to the situation of nations faced with the prospect of nuclear war. Nor can the moral insights of Niebuhr and Mumford illuminate the international situation today unless we grasp the way it differs from the international situation before World War II. The prewar critique of appeasement was directed against the wishful thinking that a postponement of war would somehow enable the Western democracies to avoid a war altogether. The most important argument advanced by Niebuhr and Mumford was that a postponement of war would merely lead to the "less fruitful death of these same human beings six months or six years hence." Nuclear weapons, however, cut out the ground beneath such arguments. They have made the avoidance of all-out war a moral imperative, not just a pious hope. Even those who advocate a further buildup of nuclear arms defend this policy on the grounds that it will help to prevent a major war. Until recently at least, it was almost universally acknowledged that no one could hope to win a nuclear war and that the use of nuclear weapons either by the Russians or by the Americans would amount to national suicide. Such a conclusion rests not on a "zoological" morality, but on simple realism: on an acknowledgment that nuclear weapons cannot be used to advance any national purpose.

Mumford based his argument against survivalism, it will be recalled, on the premise that it failed to envision a "future that extends beyond the incomplete personal life of the individual." The advent of nuclear weapons, as he himself was one of the first to recognize, poses another kind of threat to the future. When it comes to nuclear war, no one can argue that a willingness to risk war today will save lives tomorrow. No one can accuse opponents of nuclear war, as Mumford accused opponents of war in 1940, of forgetting that a life sacrificed at the right moment is a life well spent. Sacrifice has no meaning if no one survives. It is precisely the experience of mass death and the possibility of annihilation, among other developments, that have discredited the ethic of sacrifice and encouraged the growth of a survival ethic. A desire to survive at all costs ceases to be wholly contemptible under conditions that call into question the future of humanity as a whole. The same conditions have made the idea of timely sacrifice untenable. To ask people to lay down their lives in a nuclear war, on the grounds that the future "extends beyond the incomplete personal life of the individual," is a moral absurdity.

Criticism of survivalism has a moral claim to our attention, in the 1980s, only if it identifies itself with the movement for nuclear disarmament and environmental conservation. Otherwise the defense of an allegedly higher morality —national honor, political freedom, the willingness to take risks and to make sacrifices for a worthy cause—will usually reveal itself, on closer examination, as another variant of the survival morality it appears to condemn. Those who refuse to rule out a resort to nuclear weapons, on the grounds that a Soviet attack on Western Europe could not be turned back without them, have had to argue that the United States could fight a nuclear war and actually "prevail." In 1960, Herman Kahn was one of the first to maintain that the United States could make preparations that would assure not merely the physical survival of the population, or a significant fraction of it, but the material and cultural resources necessary to rebuild the American way of life. Today this kind of thinking, which goes beyond deterrence and seeks to assure victory in a nuclear exchange, appears to have become official American policy. The survivors will envy the dead, in this view, only if Americans persist in the misguided belief that a nuclear war is unthinkable and that their efforts should therefore be directed toward preventing war instead of surviving it.*

*Ostensibly, the United States remains committed to a policy of nuclear deterrence. But Secretary of Defense Harold Brown announced ominously in 1980 that "we are necessarily giving greater attention to how a nuclear war would actually be fought by both sides if deterrence fails." In April 1982, Secretary of State Alexander Haig, in a speech at Georgetown University, argued that "deterrence depends upon our capability, even after suffering a massive nuclear blow, to prevent an aggressor from securing a military advantage and prevailing in a conflict." Until recently, deterrence was usually understood to depend on mutually assured destruction, not on the capacity to fight a nuclear war or to prevent the other side from "prevailing." Deterrence requires only the capacity to deliver a massive counterattack. It does not require parity between the Soviet Union and the United States; nor does it require any program of civil defense. On the contrary, policies that seek to make the nation invulnerable to nuclear attack or to enable it to survive a nuclear exchange, even to "prevail," undermine deterrence and make nuclear war more likely. In March 1983, President Reagan took a long step away from deterrence when he proposed a "space age" technological shield that would make it unnecessary to rely on the fear of retaliation to deter a Soviet

   The Cold-War critique of survivalism, which singles out the antiwar movement for special condemnation, ignores far more striking expressions of the survival ethic. It deplores the ordinary individual's understandable disinclination to die in a cause that has little meaning, only to hold out the possibility that superior individuals—those with the foresight to prepare for the worst and the moral fiber to "prevail"—will keep the world going after the apocalypse and even rebuild it on a new basis. Today the survival ethic appears in its most fully developed form not in the peace movement but in the preparations undertaken by those who pride themselves on their ability to think about the unthinkable—preparations ranging from the high-level search for an impenetrable system of defense, which would allegedly make it possible for the United States to launch a nuclear attack without fear of retaliation, to the construction of private shelters, well stocked with German air rifles, crossbows, radiation suits, storage tanks for water and fuel, freeze-dried foods, and automobile parts, in which a few individuals foolishly hope to carry on while civilization crumbles around them.

   Shedding It All: The Spiritual Discipline of Survival
Those who believe in getting ready for the worst and who carry this position to its logical conclusion condemn "peace movement thinking," as Doris Lessing calls it, not because it values survival too highly but because it allegedly embo-

---

attack. He presented this new policy as a "vision of the future which offers hope," when in fact it offers nothing but trouble: at the very least, an indefinitely protracted nuclear arms race.
   The only way "to free the world from the threat of nuclear war"—Reagan's announced objective—is to outlaw nuclear weapons. Even deterrence is unreliable, precisely because it is so difficult for policymakers to accept its limitations—to live with a strategy that makes nuclear weapons politically useless—and so tempting for them, therefore, to edge over into more aggressive strategies still advertised as "deterrence" but directed at some other, illusory, goal: victory, invulnerability, survival.

dies a "death wish." Few writers have articulated as clearly as Lessing the morality that defines survival as the highest good. Formerly an advocate of disarmament, she has come to think that a proper program of civil defense would "protect people against everything but a direct hit." "The expertise is there," she maintains in a recent interview. A "cool consideration of the facts" indicates that "we can survive anything you care to mention." She takes the position that human beings are "supremely equipped to survive, to adapt, and even in the long run to start thinking."

This would-be realism rests on the conviction that European civilization is finished; that its passing can be regarded, on the whole, without regret; and that in any case the hope of revitalizing it through political action is a delusion, "one of the strongest of the false ideas of that epoch"—our epoch, the Century of Destruction, seen now from the extraterrestrial perspective adopted in Lessing's recent "space fiction" because it enables us to look "from outside at this planet . . . as if at a totally crazed species." As the hope of political change recedes, attention turns to the "business of survival," Lessing says: to "its resources and tricks and little contrivances." Lessing's later work, like so much recent fiction, speaks to the prevailing sense of living in a world in which the demands of daily survival absorb energies that might once have gone into a collaborative assault on the common dangers confronting humanity. Like other anti-utopian fantasies, which a society capable of destroying itself has generated in ever-increasing abundance, Lessing's owes its power not so much to its horrifying and ambiguous vision of the future (ambiguous because it can be taken both as a warning and a welcome) as to its ability to capture the feel of daily life as already experienced by inhabitants of decaying northern empires, people fallen on hard times. "Yes, it was all impossible," says the narrator of *The Memoirs of a Survivor*. "But, after all, I had accepted the impossible." Like Herman

Kahn, Doris Lessing has learned to think about the unthinkable.

If the peace movement and the environmental movement have no monopoly on survivalism, neither do they monopolize a vision of impending collapse. Critics of the "millennial subculture," as Charles Krauthammer calls it in an article deploring the apocalyptic imagination of our times, have traced it to religious fundamentalism and to the secularized version of the apocalypse allegedly preached by such alarmists as Bertrand Russell, Jonathan Schell, Paul Ehrlich, Robert Jay Lifton, and the Club of Rome. According to Krauthammer, "doomsayers" who predict a nuclear holocaust or a deepening environmental crisis ignore "man's capacity for adaptation"—the "elasticity of human nature and the adaptability of human societies." Here again, the charge is misdirected. The apocalyptic vision appears in its purest form not in the contention that the nuclear arms race or uninhibited technological development might lead to the end of the world but in the contention that a saving remnant will *survive* the end of the world and build a better one. It is not the prediction of doom that characterizes the apocalyptic imagination, now or in the past, so much as the belief that a new order will rise from the ashes of the coming conflagration, in which human beings will finally achieve a state of perfection.

Particularly in its modern secular form, the apocalyptic vision of the future affirms the possibility of human survival and transformation precisely on the grounds that men and women are endlessly resourceful and adaptable. Thus in Lessing's work, the hope of survival—human or merely personal—rests on a reconstruction of the self, on the development of higher mental powers hitherto unexploited and the transcendence of ordinary biological limitations and ordinary human emotions. Martha Quest, the heroine of *The Four-Gated City*, begins the "creation" of a new self by getting up earlier in the morning, giving up brandy in the evening, and disengaging herself from her lover. "When it's a question of survival, sex the uncontrollable can be controlled." Her new regimen—the "machinery" of personal survival at the "lowest level"—protects her against the "rebirth of the woman in love," that "hungry, never-to-be-fed, never-at-peace woman who needs and wants and must have," and leads her on to higher feats of self-"programming." She goes without sleep, starves herself, strips and sharpens herself, and in this way gets ready to follow her lover's estranged wife into a controlled descent into madness. This "business of charting the new territory" gives her the knowledge to "use her body as an engine to get out of the small dim prison of every day." It provides her with the higher technology of awareness with which survivors of the coming "catastrophe"—as we learn in the appendix to this novel, the first of Lessing's apocalyptic glimpses into the near future—begin life over again and breed a higher race of mutants, supernaturally gifted children who "include [all of recent] history in themselves and who have transcended it."

Environmentalists and advocates of nuclear disarmament paint a dark picture of the future in order to call attention to the need for social and political change. The true millennarian, on the other hand, secedes from a social order doomed to destruction and strikes out on his own. "Survivalists don't involve themselves in national politics at all," says Kurt Saxon. "They know that, as part of an intelligent minority, their votes will be cancelled . . . by the ignorant." Hard-core survivalists like Saxon, Mel Tappan, and William Pier share none of Doris Lessing's Sufi mysticism, but they share her confidence in the human capacity to adapt to extreme hardship, her contempt for politics, and her belief in the need for a moral elite. "Survival is the most important subject today," Saxon writes in his monthly newspaper, but "only a few recognize it." The "ignorant masses" are "doomed" and "the more able locked into an interdependent technology." Only a self-chosen few have built shelters, put by provisions, and made themselves self-sufficient. Their foresight makes them members of an elite who command not only their own fate but the fate of humanity. "If you prepare to survive, you deserve to survive." On the other hand, "Those who can, but won't prepare, don't deserve to survive and the species would be better off without them."

Arch-individualists, Saxon and his kind would find little to admire in Doris Lessing's vision of a new order based on the understanding that the "individual does not matter"; but they hold much the same view of the spiritual discipline required for survival. Cut your ties; simplify your needs; get back to basics. "You can't waste time with friends who have little potential as allies," Saxon writes. "Survival is looking after Number 1." Lessing believes, on the contrary, that individuality is an illusion held by creatures that "have not yet evolved into an understanding of their individual selves as merely parts of a whole, . . . parts of Nature." Yet these opposing attitudes share an unsuspected affinity. Both repudiate ordinary human emotions and the ties of love and friendship that distract people from "higher" purposes. Both take the position, in effect, that the demands of survival leave no room for a personal life or a personal history. Survivors, after all, have to learn to travel light. They cannot afford to weigh themselves down with a family, friends, or neighbors, except for the kind of friends whose death requires no mourning and can be accepted with a shrug of the shoulders. Emotional baggage has to be thrown overboard if the ship is to stay afloat. "When you get to be middle-aged," Doris Lessing tells an interviewer, ". . . it is very common to look back and to think that a lot of the sound and fury one's been involved in was not that necessary. There is quite often a sense of enormous relief, of having emerged from a great welter of emotionalism." Middle age brings relief not only from sexual desire and emotional turmoil but from the delusion that "if one is in a violent state of emotional need it is our unique emotional need or state." In Lessing's view, which epitomizes the survivalist's false maturity and pseudo-realism, "It really is a most salutary and fascinating experience to go through, shedding it all."

Who Are the Doomsayers? What defines the dooms-day mentality, unfairly attributed to environmentalists and advocates of nuclear disarmament, is the injunction to prepare for the worst, whether by accepting it as the will of God or the culmination of some grand historical design, by digging in for a bitter but bracing season of adversity, or by escaping from a doomed planet to the new frontier of outer space. Those who plan for the end may seek salvation in old-time religion, in mystical traditions imported from the East, in a revival of nineteenth-century technology and nineteenth-century individualism, in a repudiation of individualism, or in space travel; but they all agree not only that the end approaches but that foresight and planning (both spiritual and technological) can transform the end into a new beginning. Those who argue, on the other hand, that mankind has no chance of surviving the end but still has a chance to avert it, by getting rid of nuclear weapons, devising less wasteful technologies, and adopting a less wasteful way of life, rightly refuse to console themselves with the fantasy of a new life after the apocalypse. Because they warn of the terrible consequences that will follow a failure to change our ways, environmentalists find themselves dismissed as doomsayers and apocalyptic visionaries; while the real visionaries, except when they adopt unacceptable right-wing ideologies, win praise for their realism and confidence.

It is the lure of new frontiers, spiritual or geographical, that underlies the appeal of this kind of thinking. Environmentalism is unpopular, in part, because it rejects the frontier psychology and the dream of unlimited expansion. Survivalism, on the other hand, revives the old imperial dream, the hope that a declining civilization can reinvigorate itself through conquest, expansion, and the harsh discipline of a primitive environment. Where Kurt Saxon advocates a return to wood stoves, candles, draught horses, muzzle-loaders, and herbal remedies, others hope to use modern technology in its most highly developed form—space travel—to achieve essentially the same result: "to enact a parallel with what happened in Europe when America was being colonized," as Stewart Brand puts it, when "new lands meant new possibilities [and] new possibilities meant new ideas." An unexpected convert to the campaign for space colonization, Brand, like Doris Lessing, has gravitated from an earlier commitment to peace and ecology to an enthusiasm for the technological conquest of space. As editor of the *Whole Earth Catalogue*, he once advocated homemade technologies in the hope of making people independent of the wasteful, destructive, exploitive machinery that depletes natural resources, pollutes the earth and its atmosphere, undermines initiative, and makes everyone more and more reliant on experts. Instead, the *Whole Earth Catalogue*s often led people to hole up in the mountains, not so much in the hope of demonstrating that they could live harmoniously with nature as in the hope of surviving the end of the world. Brand continues to oppose this kind of "paranoid" survivalism, as he explained in an interview in 1980, but he now rejects "self-sufficiency" only to embrace the more insidious escapism of space travel, the latest expression of the frontier psychology that runs through so much of Western culture.

In an editorial introducing space colonization to readers of *CoEvolution Quarterly*, a journal formerly devoted to conservation, voluntary simplicity, and labor-intensive technologies, Brand defends the idea of "free space" in language reminiscent of nineteenth-century populist demands for "free land." But where Kurt Saxon sees the challenge of extreme adversity as an opportunity to revive individualistic self-reliance ("the individual's best guarantee of survival"), Brand, like Doris Lessing, sees it precisely as an antidote to individualism. "The harshness of Space will oblige a life-and-death reliance on each other."

Other enthusiasts insist that space travel would encourage planetary consciousness, break down national barriers, and overcome the parochialism of a world divided into "island republics." They also argue, of course, that space colonies would solve the energy problem, relieve the pressure of surplus population, and provide new markets. "All the disasters we face, from nuclear war to ecological collapse to the tide of irrationality, have one factor in common: population pressure," writes Ben Bova in *The High Road*. The movement to colonize outer space represents a "crucial struggle against . . . hunger, poverty, ignorance, and death. We must win this race, for one brutally simple reason: survival." But it is the promise of a fresh start that makes the idea of space travel so attractive to people oppressed by a sense of the old order's exhaustion. As conceived by the Princeton physicist Gerard O'Neill and explained in his testimony before congressional committees, in talks to the World Future Society and other such organizations, and in his book *The High Frontier*, space colonies would revive the spirit of adventure. "The human race now stands on the threshold of a new frontier, whose richness surpasses a thousand fold that of the new western world of five hundred years ago." O'Neill adds that "civilization could tear itself apart with energy shortages, population pressures, and running out of materials. Everything could become much more militaristic, and the whole world might get to be more of an armed camp." Another advocate of space colonization, Eric Drexler, cites the "multitude of dangers to the survival of attractive soci-

eties and to the survival of civilization itself" and concludes
that although "space may not save us, it seems to offer a
greater hope." Space "waits for us," according to Drexler,
"barren rock and sunlight like the barren rock and sunlight
of Earth's continents a billion years ago. If there is a purpose
to evolution, that purpose says *go!*"

When Brand submitted O'Neill's design for space colonies to readers and friends of *CoEvolution Quarterly* and
asked for comments, he touched off a debate that helps to
distinguish survivalists, both inside the environmentalist
movement and outside it, from those who still believe in the
possibility of collaborative action designed to prevent the
collapse of civilization, not merely to enable a few survivors
to weather the storm. Lewis Mumford dismissed space colonies as "technological disguises for infantile fantasies." John
Holt took the position that "earth's major problems will
have to be solved on earth." In the same vein, E. F. Schumacher called attention to the "work that *really* needs to be
done, namely, the development of technologies by which
ordinary, decent, hardworking, modest and all-too-often-
abused people can improve their lot." Dennis Meadows, one
of the authors of the Club of Rome report, agreed that the
hope of "another frontier" blocked "constructive response
to problems here on Earth." George Wald argued that space
colonies would carry depersonalization to the "ultimate
limit." Wendell Berry saw them as a "rebirth of the idea of
progress with all its old lust for unrestrained expansion, its
totalitarian concentrations of energy and wealth, its oblivi-
ousness to the concerns of character and community." "Like
utopians before you," he wrote to Brand, "you envision a
clean break with all human precedent."

Those who supported the colonization of space argued
that "the alternative," as one reader put it, "is Apocalypse."
Paul and Anne Ehrlich accused environmentalists of short-
sightedness in "prematurely rejecting the idea of Space

Colonies." Others attributed the "outcry" against space travel to an "ideological" or "theocratic" commitment to small-scale technologies, to a doctrinaire belief in "finitude" as the "basic requirement for a good character," and to a "naive," "irresponsible," and "theological" pessimism. "In a time of challenge to the foundations of our industrial civilization," wrote T. A. Heppenheimer of the Center for Space Science in Fountain Valley, California, "it ill-behooves us to dismiss major technologies out of hand." Paolo Soleri saw space travel as a "new momentous step toward the spirit." Buckminster Fuller saw it as a natural extension of human growth, "just as normal as a child coming out its mother's womb, gradually learning to stand, then running around on its own legs." A number of readers expressed reservations about space travel but saw it as inevitable; "constructive criticism" from environmentalists, they believed, would help to "humanize" the program. Of those who replied to Brand's invitation for comment, only 49 opposed the proposal for space colonies outright, whereas 139 accepted it with various degrees of enthusiasm. One reader even managed to convince himself that the building of space colonies would "encourage folk life and country music and old-time religion."

Apocalyptic Survivalism and Ordinary Apathy　　The debate about space travel and other survivalist fantasies is a debate among people alarmed by the deterioration of social and physical conditions on this planet. It naturally holds no interest for those eternal optimists who see no cause for alarm, who close their ears to disturbing reports, or who cling to the hope that humanity will somehow muddle through. Nor does it hold any interest for the much larger class of people who regard the future as so deeply troubling that it hardly bears looking into at all and who prefer to concern themselves, accordingly, with more immediate and manageable issues. The ignorant masses, as Kurt Saxon calls them, remain indifferent to long-range planning for survival. They have never taken much interest either in a governmental program of civil defense or in privately constructed survival shelters, survival condominiums, survival collectives, or groups like Posse Comitatus or Survival, Inc. Neither have they taken a passionate interest in environmentalism. They support environmental legislation, but only as long as it does not threaten their jobs. Their "apathy" is the despair of environmentalists and survivalists alike. They care about survival only in the most immediate sense. Compared with the apocalyptic fantasies circulated by those who care about long-range survival, however, their "apathy" has a good deal to commend it.

The contrast between these two attitudes, the apocalyptic activism of a self-chosen survivalist elite and the ordinary citizen's indifference to ideologies, emerges very clearly from a recent film, Louis Malle's *My Dinner with André*. Two friends renew their acquaintance in a New York restaurant and defend the choices that have led them down divergent paths. André has traveled all over the world in search of spiritual enlightenment. Wally has stayed in New York, grubbing for work as a writer and actor and sharing a humdrum domestic existence with his girlfriend. He defends everyday comforts and conveniences against André's contempt for mindless materialism and mass culture. When he volunteers the information that he sleeps under an electric blanket, he provokes André's scorn. Turning on an electric blanket, according to André, is "like taking a tranquilizer or . . . being lobotomized by watching television." Wally replies that "our lives are tough enough as it is." "I'm just trying to survive," he says, ". . . to earn a living."

While Wally contents himself with small pleasures and small attainable goals, André pursues spiritual transcendence, higher states of consciousness. He experiments with

Eastern religions, mind-altering spiritual exercises, and communal retreats. He wants to wake up the world, or at least to save the best of our civilization when the rest of it collapses. Returning to New York after a long absence, he sees it as the "new model for the concentration camp"—a prison populated by "lobotomized people" and "robots." He and his wife "feel like Jews in Germany in the late thirties." They "have actually had this very unpleasant feeling that we really *should* get out"—"escape before it's too late." "The world now may very well be a self-perpetuating unconscious form of brainwashing created by a world totalitarian government based on money." Under these conditions, the only hope is that small groups of the elect will gather in "islands of safety where history can be remembered and the human being can continue to function, in order to maintain the species through a Dark Age."

The encounter between André and Wally juxtaposes two kinds of survivalism, both predicated on the unspoken, unexamined premise that the crisis of twentieth-century society has no collective or political solution. It juxtaposes the banality of everyday existence with the banality of stylish social criticism, which denounces a society of sleepwalkers and tries "to wake up a sleeping audience" with alarming reports of impending catastrophe. "We're living in the middle of a plague." Cancer—caused, André adds, by "what we're doing to the environment"—has reached "plague dimensions. . . . But is anybody calling it a plague? I mean, in the time of the Black Plague, when the plague hit, people got the hell out." One kind of survivalism takes refuge in the immediate; the other, in apocalyptic visions of things to come. Both have renounced hope. But whereas André longs to desert the sinking ship, Wally stays in the city he grew up in, a city saturated with memories. "There wasn't a street —there wasn't a building—that wasn't connected to some memory in my mind. There, I was buying a suit with my

father. There, I was having an ice cream soda after school."
André's disdain for ordinary life, on the other hand, springs
from a terrifying sense of its impermanence. "A baby holds
your hands, then suddenly there's this huge man lifting you
off the ground, and then he's gone. Where's that son?" The
contrasting circumstances of these friends' lives suggest that
although a sense of place and a respect for ordinary facts
may prevent the imagination from taking wing, they also
prevent it from consuming itself in flights of apocalyptic
fantasy. André himself detects in the new "monasteries,"
where survivors will gather to preserve what remains of
civilization, a "sort of self-satisfied elitist paranoia that grows
up, a feeling of 'them' and 'us' that is very unsettling" and
leads to a "kind of self-contained, self-ratifying certainty."
In such moods, he is "repelled by the whole story" of his
own quest for mystical transcendence.

The doomsday mentality makes ordinary everyday survivalism like Wally's look like a model of common sense and
democratic decency. Whatever its limitations, everyday survivalism retains a sense of place, a loyalty to familiar surroundings and their associations. It retains something of
what Hannah Arendt called a love of the world—the world,
that is, of human associations and human works, which give
solidity and continuity to our lives. But although it cherishes
personal memories, this attitude has little use for history or
politics, both of which appear to people like Wally to serve
merely as a theater for the play of competing ideologies. The
everyday survivalist has deliberately lowered his sights from
history to the immediacies of face-to-face relationships. He
takes one day at a time. He pays a heavy price for this radical
restriction of perspective, which precludes moral judgment
and intelligent political activity almost as effectively as the
apocalyptic attitude he rightly rejects. It allows him to remain human—no small accomplishment in these times. But
it prevents him from exercising any influence over the

course of public events. Even his personal life is sadly attenuated. He may reject the fantasy of escape to a mountain retreat or a desert island or another planet, but he still conducts his own life as if he were living in a state of siege. He may refuse to listen to talk of the end of the world, but he unwittingly adopts many of the defensive impulses associated with it. Long-term commitments and emotional attachments carry certain risks under the best of circumstances; in an unstable, unpredictable world they carry risks that people find it increasingly difficult to accept. As long as ordinary men and women have no confidence in the possibility of cooperative political action—no hope of reducing the dangers that surround them—they will find it hard to get along, in short, without adopting some of the tactics of hard-line survivalism in a milder form. The invasion of everyday life by the rhetoric and imagery of terminal disaster leads people to make personal choices that are often indistinguishable in their emotional content from the choices made by those who proudly refer to themselves as survivalists and congratulate themselves on their superior insight into the future course of history.

Everyday Survival Strategies The softer style of survivalism, precisely because it is unsupported by an ideology or a political program or even by a rich fantasy life (the most compelling fantasies in our time having been identified not with the realistic description of everyday life but with the vision of apocalyptic transformation), thus tends to give way in moments of personal stress or heightened imaginative awareness to a harder style. Everyday life begins to take on some of the more undesirable and ominous characteristics of behavior in extreme situations: restriction of perspective to the immediate demands of survival; ironic self-observation; protean selfhood; emotional anesthesia.

Whereas the hard-core survivalist plans for disaster, many

of us conduct our daily lives as if it had already occurred. We conduct ourselves as if we lived in "impossible circumstances," in an "apparently irresistible environment," in the "extreme and immutable environment" of the prison or the concentration camp. We share the prevailing disenchantment with the "romantic vision of extreme situations," as Cohen and Taylor call it in their study of long-term imprisonment, "in which the man who fights back, who overcomes his environment, who refuses to be beaten down, whatever the odds, is the hero." Some of this romanticism lingers among the visionary survivalists, but the rest of us ridicule the John Wayne ideal, without ridding ourselves, however, of the preoccupations that underlie the heroic style of survivalism. We deplore or laugh at those who try to arm themselves against the apocalypse, but we arm ourselves emotionally against the onslaught of everyday life.

We do this in a variety of ways: for example, by concentrating our attention on the small, immediate obstacles that confront us each day. "Successful people plan their lives for successful *days*," says Michael Korda. "Judge your performance by what you have done *today*, not what you did yesterday or what you plan to do tomorrow." Recent success manuals, unwittingly echoing studies of behavior in extreme situations, stress the importance of narrow, clearly defined objectives and the dangers of dwelling on the past or looking too far into the future. "In sensitivity training we concentrate on what we call the 'here and now.' " Such an approach, according to one author, promises "greater managerial competence through deeper self-understanding." Success manuals are not alone in urging people to lower their sights and to confine their attention to the immediate moment. The human potential movement, the medical and psychiatric literature on coping, the growing literature on death and dying all recommend the same strategy for dealing with the "predictable crises of adult life." A focus on the present serves not only as a requirement of successful "functioning" but as a defense against loss. The first lesson survivors have to master is letting go. A young poet describes his first book, aptly entitled *Reservations,* as a collection of "elegies for everything, including myself." His poems, he says rather ingratiatingly, reflect a self "with only a tenuous grip on its surroundings." They try "to arrest the moment long enough to say farewell, to let things go rather than be subject to their disappearance." The survivor cannot afford to linger very long in the past, lest he envy the dead. He keeps his eyes fixed on the road just in front of him. He shores up fragments against his ruin. His life consists of isolated acts and events. It has no story, no pattern, no structure as an unfolding narrative. The decline of the narrative mode both in fiction and in historical writing—where it has been displaced by a sociological approach that tries to reconstruct the details of daily life in earlier times—reflects the fragmentation of the self. Both time and space have shrunk to the immediate present, the immediate environment of the office, factory, or household.

Survivors have to learn the trick of observing themselves as if the events of their lives were happening to someone else. One reason people no longer see themselves as the subject of a narrative is that they no longer see themselves as subjects at all but rather as the victims of circumstance; and this feeling of being acted on by uncontrollable external forces prompts another mode of moral armament, a withdrawal from the beleaguered self into the person of a detached, bemused, ironic observer. The sense that it isn't happening to *me* helps to protect me against pain and also to control expressions of outrage or rebellion that would only provoke my captors into further tortures. Here again, a survival technique learned in concentration camps reappears in success manuals, where it is recommended as a reliable method of dealing with "tyrants." Chester Burger, author of *Executives under Fire* and *Survival in the Executive Jungle*, takes it for granted that resistance to overbearing superiors is out of the question; but he also advises his readers not to "toady to tyrants." Instead he urges readers to "try for a quality of detachment."

> You cannot allow yourself to take these situations [conflicts with jealous superiors trying to protect their "little empires"] personally. You have to stand back and see yourself objectively as a participant. . . . I try to function as if I were two people: the participant, and also the observer of the situation. . . . This technique enables me to minimize any emotionalism on my part that would trigger off something in the other guy.

Role-playing, another strategy repeatedly recommended by survival manuals, serves not only to project an appropriate image of energy and confidence but to protect the self against unseen enemies, to keep feelings in check, and to control threatening situations. "You have to *feel* self-assured to inspire confidence and be in control," according to Betty Harragan. "A commanding appearance starts by playing a role, a part in a play. . . . Self-assurance comes by practicing before every available audience." In "today's vast systems of rationality," according to Melville Dalton, people have to resort to what "biologists call 'protective mimicry.'" Survivalism encourages a protean sense of selfhood, which expresses itself in the routine advice to adopt the protective coloration of one's immediate surroundings but also, more broadly, in a growing rejection of the social roles prescribed by "traditional" cultural norms. Gender roles in particular have come under criticism as an arbitrary constraint on self-expression. The attack on sexual stereotypes, like so many other features of the contemporary cultural revolution, contains unsuspected ambiguities. On the one hand, it points to a broader definition of the self. It rightly insists on the undeveloped capacity for tenderness in men and for enterprise and self-reliance in women. On the other hand, it shrinks the self by conceiving of it purely as the product of cultural conditioning. Carried to its logical conclusion, it dismisses selfhood as an illusion. It reduces personal identity to the sexual and social roles imposed on people by conventions that can be subverted, presumably, by the simple act of assuming a new identity or "lifestyle."

A conception of endlessly adaptable and interchangeable identity can help to free men and women from outworn social conventions, but it can also encourage defensive maneuvers and "protective mimicry." A stable identity stands among other things as a reminder of the limits of one's adaptability. Limits imply vulnerability, whereas the survivalist seeks to become invulnerable, to protect himself against pain and loss. Emotional disengagement serves as still another survival mechanism. An ever-present undercurrent in recent success manuals, in much of the commentary on extreme situations (as we shall see in more detail in the next chapter), and in recent poetry and fiction is the insistent warning that closeness kills. Thus John Barth writes novels peopled by "performers who cannot feel a thing," as Josephine Hendin writes in her study of postwar fiction—characters driven by the "urge to kill any closeness in any encounter." In Robert Stone's novels, as Hendin notes, "Lovers and moralists are the first to go." When the protagonist of Stone's *Hall of Mirrors* identifies the body of his mistress, who has hanged herself, all he can think is: "I'm alive baby. . . . It was you who died. Not me. I don't need you. . . . I'm a survivor." On Kurt Vonnegut's imaginary planet, the inhabitants conduct "wars as horrible as any you've seen or read about. There isn't anything we can do about them so we simply don't look at them." When someone dies, the Tralfamadorians "simply shrug" and say, "So it goes." In Robert Heinlein's *Stranger in a Strange Land,* the hero, sole survivor of an Earth mission to Mars, comes back to Earth and is dismayed by the passionate emotion he finds everywhere. "How can these human brothers suffer intense emotion without damage?" The point, of course, is that they can't. Life is better on Mars because there is no emotion there and, above all, no sex. In the same vein, Richard Brautigan writes about men who stay as cool as trout, while William Burroughs eagerly looks forward, he says, to a "whole generation . . . that [will feel] neither pleasure nor pain."

The fading of the hope of an "antithetical collaborative order," according to the author of another study of postwar writing, Warner Berthoff, has produced a literature of "personal relief, survivor's indemnification," a literature "by, and for, and mostly about survivors." The world of the postwar writer, Berthoff points out, consists of an "immense, bureaucratized, conspiratorial *system* to which men and women are essentially enslaved, whether they know it or not, and from which no escape is possible except by a withdrawal of selfhood so absolute that its natural fulfillment is suicide." Suicide becomes the ultimate form of self-defense in a world perceived—not just by writers but by ordinary men and women or at least by those who instruct ordinary men and women in the everyday arts of survival—as a comfortable concentration camp.

III

The Discourse
on Mass Death:
"Lessons" of the
Holocaust

One "Holocaust" or Many?   The destruction of the
Jews of eastern Europe did not become a "holocaust" until
the mid-sixties. Who first proposed the term is unclear, but
it was adopted, in all likelihood—and not only by the Jews
—in the hope that it would distinguish acts of monumental
inhumanity from routine killing and warfare, even from
other incidents of mass murder. The label carries with it the
implication that what the Nazis did to the Jews remains
unique. It registers a protest against (even as it contributes
to) the debasement of political rhetoric, which turns every
injustice into another example of "genocide." "I know what
is a holocaust," Menachem Begin said in 1982, in reply to
those who applied the term, all too easily and predictably,
to the Israeli bombardment of West Beirut and the subsequent massacre of Palestinian refugees by the Christian
party in Lebanon. Begin's statement served, unfortunately,

not only to emphasize the peculiar horror of Nazism but to absolve his own government of responsibility for actions deplorable by any standard of international morality. Yet the impulse behind it—misguided as it may have proved in practice—ought to command respect. The Final Solution marked a turning-point in human affairs, the crossing of a hitherto unapproachable moral barrier; and the language that seeks to describe this appalling event and to capture its unparalleled, cold-blooded ferocity must not be allowed to become routine, lest cold-blooded killing become itself routine.

The trouble is, of course, that words fail in the face of evil on such a scale. As many survivors have argued, silence is the only fitting tribute to the three and a half million who died in concentration camps and death camps, to the two million exterminated by mobile killing units on the eastern front, and to the half million more who died in the ghettos of eastern Europe of hunger, disease, terror, and Nazi reprisals. Words fail, but it is nevertheless necessary to speak. Who can remain silent, having witnessed such events? But a language of extremity, the only language appropriate to extreme situations, soon loses its force through repetition and inflation. It facilitates what it seeks to prevent, the normalization of atrocity. The massacre of the Jews became a holocaust because the word "genocide," in an age of genocide, had already lost the capacity to evoke the feelings appropriate to the events it tried to characterize. Searching for a language still more extreme, historians of the Holocaust have themselves contributed to the debasement of "genocide." Thus one of them, Yehuda Bauer, has recently explained that "genocide" refers only to "forcible denationalization," as opposed to the "total murder of every one of the members of a community." Against the Poles and other captive peoples of eastern Europe, Hitler practiced what can be called genocide, according to Bauer. "Their institutions

of learning [were] closed, their political leadership deci-
mated, their language and national culture discarded, their
churches eliminated from a free exercise of their functions,
their wealth despoiled, and they were subjected to killings
of groups and individuals as the Nazis pleased." Only the
Jews experienced a holocaust, however.

We can agree that such distinctions seem essential, even
if they drain "genocide" of its accepted meaning; but we
shall nevertheless find it impossible to apply them with any
rigor. If numbers mean anything, the Holocaust was not
unique. Estimates of those who died in the forcible collectivization of Soviet agriculture range as high as twenty-two
million. If we include the victims of other policies pursued
by the Stalinist regime—the political purges, the massacre of
nationalities, the persecution of religious believers and other
dissidents, the slave labor camps—the figure reaches sixty
million, on a conservative estimate. If we pay less attention
to numbers, on the other hand, and emphasize the systematic destruction of a whole class or nation, we can hardly
ignore the holocaust inflicted by the Turks on the Armenians during World War I, which provided a foretaste of
twentieth-century genocide, or the extermination of the entire urban population of Kampuchea in 1975, which left two
million dead, according to the American estimate—as many
as three million, according to the Vietnamese—out of a total
Kampuchean population of seven million. Killing on such
a scale has prompted one authority, Richard L. Rubenstein,
to conclude that the upheavals associated with industrialism,
beginning with the enclosure movement in early modern
England, have created vast numbers of superfluous people
and that systematic extermination represents only the culmination of a long process of population removal, deportation,
harassment, and persecution. Hannah Arendt, another
thinker who saw the problem of superfluous populations as
endemic to modern society, regarded the "factories of anni-

hilation" constructed by Hitler and Stalin as an "attraction [as well] as a warning," since they "demonstrated the swiftest solution to the problem of overpopulation, of economically superfluous and socially rootless human masses."

Even the attempt to distinguish genocide from ordinary warfare encounters the difficulty that warfare is no longer ordinary, having itself taken on some of the characteristics of genocide. It is important to remind ourselves that the Nazis had no military or political reason for their extermination of the Jews; that modern totalitarianism distinguishes itself from earlier forms of tyranny in directing its violence not only against external enemies but against its own citizens; and that even these have perished, most of them, not because they were political enemies of the state but merely because they got in the way of some program of racial purification or forcible industrialization or population control—because, as it was said in Kampuchea during the ascendancy of the Khmer Rouge, "There is nothing to gain by keeping them alive, nothing to lose by doing away with them." The exigencies of war cannot explain such events; but neither can they provide a satisfactory explanation of Hiroshima and Nagasaki, the firebombing of Dresden, or strategic bombing in general, which makes no distinction between military targets and the extermination of civilians and serves more as an instrument of terror than as an instrument of warfare in any conventional sense. Historians of the Holocaust are right to insist that Auschwitz cannot be compared with Dresden or Hiroshima, either in terms of the numbers killed or the motives behind them. But if it is unwise and even morally obtuse to make facile comparisons, it seems equally unwise to ignore the growing destructiveness in modern society as a whole or the possibility that all these atrocities—however incommensurable in their origins and specific effects—prefigure even more radical atrocities, including, perhaps, the annihilation of humanity itself. By locating the Holocaust in the past, by reserving it for the Jews, and by associating it with insane racial policies now universally condemned (officially at least), the most sober and responsible historians of the Holocaust, seeking to prevent the routinization of the language of atrocity, unavoidably obscure the point that the United States and the Soviet Union, in pursuit of legitimate national goals, under the leadership not of criminals but of ordinary men in full possession of their mental faculties, even now prepare themselves to commit genocide against each other in the event of a nuclear war. As Jonathan Schell points out, nuclear war, like genocide, represents a "crime against the future," which attacks not merely "existing people and things but . . . the biological or the cultural heritage that human beings transmit from one generation to the next." Hitler's war of extermination against the Jews warns us that "gigantic, insane crimes are not prevented from occurring merely because they are 'unthinkable.'" The warning is lost, however, whenever we consider the "Holocaust"—however rightly —as a unique and unparalleled atrocity committed by a uniquely monstrous and criminal regime.

"Totalitarianism": From Radical Evil to Comparative Political Typology The attempt to understand Hitler's Final Solution of the Jewish problem confronts us, then, with a choice between equally compelling and equally unsatisfactory lines of explanation. If we insist on its uniqueness, we lose the ability to place it in a wider perspective. If we try to use it as the basis for larger generalizations about modern politics and culture, on the other hand, we obscure its particular horror.

Consider the concept of totalitarianism, the history of which illustrates the difficulty of doing justice to both sides of this question. It first took shape, in the late thirties, in the writings of those who had begun to question both the socialist credentials of the Stalinist regime and the Marxist interpretation of fascism as the final stage of capitalist decay. Thanks to the Moscow trials, the Spanish Civil War (in which the Soviet Union helped to abort a democratic revolution led by anarchists), and the Nazi-Soviet pact, George Orwell, Arthur Koestler, Franz Borkenau, James Burnham, and other former Marxists had come to see Stalinism as a new form of domination: neither a return to an older type of autocracy nor the perverted socialism described by Trotsky as bureaucratic collectivism but a system of total control that sought to regulate not only the individual's public life but his inner life as well, thereby abolishing the very distinction between the public and private realms and between society and the state. Meanwhile it was becoming increasingly clear that the Nazi regime in Germany could not be understood, as Orwell himself characterized it as late as 1939, during his brief flirtation with Trotskyism, as a further "development of capitalism" or even as a revival of old-fashioned autocracy. "The terrifying thing about modern dictatorships," Orwell wrote a few weeks later, "is that they are something entirely unprecedented." Not only did they enjoy a good deal of popular support, but their use of terror, culminating in systematic programs of mass murder, seemed to go far beyond anything required by the practical exigencies of gaining and holding power. One of the earliest students of National Socialism, Hermann Rauschning, described Nazism as a "revolution of nihilism," a movement without "fixed political aims" and based only on "impulse." This perception crystallized in the concept of totalitarianism advanced, for example, in Orwell's *1984*, which depicts a state that exercises total power for its own sake without even the pretense that its power serves the interests of humanity as a whole.

After publishing reports on the Nazi concentration camps by Bruno Bettelheim and Hannah Arendt, in 1945, Dwight

Macdonald wrote in his magazine *Politics* that "the extermination of the Jews of Europe was not a means to an end one can accept as even plausibly rational. . . . No military purpose was served by their extermination; the 'racial theory' behind it is scientifically groundless and humanly abhorrent and can only be termed, in the strictest sense of the term, neurotic." A growing fund of information on the Stalinist terror prompted a similar set of conclusions. In *1984*, totalitarian terror no longer serves even the rational objective of intimidating opponents, since it continues to flourish when opposition has been effectively silenced. According to John Strachey, Orwell's novels, *1984* and *Animal Farm*, suggested that communism, often misinterpreted as the "culmination of rationalism," had "lost almost all touch with objective reality and pursued psychopathic social objectives."

Hannah Arendt's *Origins of Totalitarianism*, first published in 1951, owed its remarkable hold over the postwar mind to the insight, sustained over five hundred pages and supported with a wealth of horrifying detail, that crimes on such a scale as those committed by Stalin and Hitler marked a decisive turning-point in history, "breaking down all standards we know" and signaling the arrival of a world to which the civilization of the past could no longer serve as a guide or even as a reliable moral standard by which to condemn it.* Neither a satisfactory explanation of the rise of Nazism and Stalinism nor a comparative analysis capable of doing justice to the difference between them, Arendt's book derived its value from its understanding of the mentality that "everything is possible." Totalitarianism differs from earlier forms

---

*Alfred Kazin, reviewing Elisabeth Young-Bruehl's recent biography of Arendt in the *New York Review*, writes: "What made Hannah Arendt's name a specter and a bugaboo to many, an everlasting consolation to a few, is that she invested her expressiveness . . . in the conviction that there *has* been a 'break' in human history. She lived this. That there has been a 'break,' that we live in truly 'dark times,' no one confronted by her was allowed to doubt. Arendt's greatest value, her distinct example, was that she could not accept this break, as most of us do."

of autocracy, according to Arendt, because it carries to its limit the logic that can dismiss whole categories of people as historically superfluous. Thus the death camp, the ultimate expression of totalitarianism, seeks not so much to exploit the labor of a captive population as to provide the most vivid demonstration of its dispensability. In her attempt to identify the "burden of our time"—as the book was called when it appeared in England—Arendt repeatedly emphasized the danger that "political, social, and economic events everywhere are in a silent conspiracy with totalitarian instruments devised for making men superfluous."

In a world of chronic unemployment, automation, and overpopulation, her warning remains just as important as ever. But it was exactly this element in Arendt's work—her insistence that totalitarianism represents a solution, however irrational, to the unsolved problems of industrial society—that was most quickly forgotten as the concept of totalitarianism began to work its way into political discussion in the 1950s. Arendt herself contributed to misunderstanding of her book by presenting it as a typology or anatomy of totalitarianism as a "novel form of government." Accordingly social scientists misread *The Origins of Totalitarianism* as a contribution to comparative political analysis and then proceeded to criticize it on the grounds that it failed to pursue the comparison with scientific rigor or to extend it to Fascist Italy, Communist China, or to the Soviet satellites in Eastern Europe. The work of a writer deeply at odds with the whole tradition of the social sciences, *The Origins of Totalitarianism* entered the mainstream of sociological discourse and became at once the inspiration and the target of a long series of studies attempting to strip the concept of totalitarianism of its "normative" and ethical implications, to "operationalize" Arendt's "findings," and to anatomize the general characteristics of "totalitarian democracy," as J. L. Talmon called it.

By generalizing the concept of totalitarianism in the hope of making it more systematic, social scientists obscured the original insight behind it. They made totalitarianism a synonym for revolutionary change or "direct democracy" and gave it a long history. Talmon traced its antecedents back to Rousseau. Karl Popper identified Plato as the first totalitarian, on the grounds that he founded the tradition of "Utopian social engineering." In *The Pursuit of the Millennium*, Norman Cohn took the tradition of "revolutionary chiliasm" back to peasant revolts in the late Middle Ages. "For all their exploitation of the most modern technology," Cohn argued, Hitler and Stalin revived a revolutionary "faith" that originated in the medieval dream of a world turned upside down and continued to lead a "dim, subterranean existence down the centuries, flaring up briefly in the margins of the English Civil War and the French Revolution, until in the course of the nineteenth century it began to take on a new, explosive vigor."*

---

*Arendt, on the other hand, went out of her way to point out that the social preconditions of totalitarianism "did not result from growing equality of condition, from the spread of general education and its inevitable lowering of standards and popularization of content." Orwell too took the position, even more emphatically, that the most effective defense against totalitarianism remained the egalitarian ideal, unrealized but still honored by the "whole English-speaking world." Both Orwell and Arendt directed their attack much more against the culture of intellectuals than against popular culture. Orwell's view of totalitarianism took shape in a period of his life when he was gaining new respect for the common sense and "common decency" of the ordinary Englishman. "My chief hope for the future," he wrote in 1940, "is that the common people have never parted company with their moral code." His insistence that "intellectuals are more totalitarian in their outlook than the common people" distinguishes his position from that of many of his admirers, including the *Partisan Review* intellectuals in New York, who promoted Orwell's work but found the counterweight to totalitarianism not in the good sense of the common man but in the "intellectuals' tradition" of critical modernism. For Orwell, the critical thinking on which the intelligentsia prided itself had become an automatic reflex, an expression of its "extraordinarily negative outlook, its lack of any firm beliefs or positive aims, and its power of harbouring illusions that would not be possible to people in less sheltered places." Similar views can be found in Arendt's *Origins of Totalitarianism*: for example, in her masterly account of the literary avant-garde in the Weimar Republic with its "protest against society," its cult of violence, its delight in unmasking hypocrisy, its "pas-

This kind of work succeeded only in demonstrating that the concept of totalitarianism had become completely useless for the purposes of historical analysis or for the comparative study of dictatorship. Even the more limited concept of fascism does not stand up to rigorous comparative analysis. The attempt to find fascist or totalitarian features in a variety of regimes stretches these terms so thin that they become meaningless. A typology of totalitarian regimes, moreover, obscures the very developments that Arendt wanted to call attention to in the first place: the disastrous collapse of political morality, the growth of moral and political nihilism, and the embodiment of this nihilism, this indifference even to elementary considerations of political utility and expediency, in the "death factories" set up under the Nazi and Stalinist regimes. Scholars who have tried to find totalitarian features in fascist and communist regimes of almost every description lose sight of the genocidal frenzy that most clearly defines the radical break between modern totalitarianism and old-fashioned autocracy. Indeed the concept of genocide does not figure in most of the comparative work on totalitarianism at all, even in the work of scholars —Carl Friedrich and Zbigniew Brzezinski, for example— who at least try to retain something of Arendt's sense of totalitarianism as "historically an innovation," in their words. If totalitarianism has the "purpose of affecting a total social revolution," as Brzezinski argues in one of his dubious formulations, totalitarian terror has to be seen merely as a means of getting rid of opposition. "Where total change is intended," Friedrich writes, "massive resistance is engendered; to break it, the adversaries of the regime have to be terrorized into submission." This kind of argument leads to

---

sion for anonymity and losing oneself," and its futile attempt to shock a bourgeoisie that "could no longer be shocked" and that applauded attacks on itself "because it had been fooled by its own hypocrisy for so long that it had grown tired of the tension and found deep wisdom in the expression of the banality by which it lived."

the absurdity that the Nazi campaign of extermination against the Jews, the most appalling and also the most important and characteristic feature of National Socialism, has to be dismissed as incidental. "The extermination of the Jews," according to Friedrich, ". . . had no function in the regime." The comparative study of totalitarianism thus fails to explain even the irrationality remarked on by so many observers of National Socialism. Vastly exaggerating the Nazis' commitment to the "destruction of the existing society," political scientists and comparative sociologists proceed to reduce their irrationality to the failure to observe the rules of pluralistic interest-group politics—to their "determination to achieve total change."

By the mid-sixties, even mainstream social scientists had to acknowledge the uselessness of their comparative typology of totalitarianism. Their reasons for rejecting it, however, were no better than the reasons behind its original acceptance. They objected that the term contained "pejorative and ideological overtones," as if moral passion were out of place in a discussion of unprecedented political savagery. They demanded that study of totalitarianism give way to the comparative study of "modernization." One critic, Benjamin R. Barber, even objected to the bias against "centralized political power." Meanwhile the left made its own contribution to the debasement of this debate. While mainstream social scientists redefined totalitarianism so as to exclude its most important features and finally rejected the term altogether, the left used it so recklessly that it lost its value even as a moral reference point. Justifiably uneasy about the increasingly facile equation of fascism and communism, writers on the left did not hesitate to characterize "Amerika" itself as a totalitarian society or to describe the treatment of blacks and other minorities as a policy of calculated genocide. "By virtue of the way it has organized its technological base, contemporary industrial society tends to be totalitarian," wrote Herbert Marcuse in *One-Dimensional Man.* "It thus precludes the emergence of an effective opposition against the whole." Such talk did nothing to clarify the nature of modern political systems; it merely contributed to the general air of crisis and to the impression that the "system" is infinitely evil but at the same time infinitely resistant to change. Nor did it even arouse moral indignation, as it was intended to do. By equating every instance of injustice with totalitarian genocide, it effectively annulled the horror of the events the memory of which it unceasingly evoked.

Auschwitz as an Image of the Modern Malaise   The agony of the Jews under Hitler is too important and too outrageous to be forgotten; yet it can be remembered, it seems, only in ways that distort its meaning and deny its importance. Both the nature of the Nazi regime and the suffering Hitler inflicted on his victims elude precise description. "Totalitarianism," a new word invented because none of the words in the existing vocabulary of political oppression could convey the systematic brutality practiced by the Nazi and Stalinist regimes, proved incapable of carrying the moral freight with which it was burdened. The same difficulty dogs the attempt to find a word—not just genocide but the "Holocaust"—with which to describe the anguish endured by the victims of totalitarian terror. The "unfathomable horror" of mass death, as Bruno Bettelheim calls it, exhausts our powers of emotional response and defies every attempt to make sense of it. The only appropriate response, in the end, is a collective commitment to peace and justice, to a world in which men and women can live in dignity. In recent years, however, the will to bring such a world into being has steadily weakened, even while the horrors of World War II and of the "Holocaust" in particular have become a public obsession. The Holocaust has come to serve not as a warning or as an incentive to social action but as a convenient symbol for the prevailing sense of helplessness. It has become a "Jewish catchword for all the things everyone [is] talking about," in the words of Jacob Neusner, "a kind of Jewish key word for the common malaise." A society made up of people who think of themselves as victims and survivors finds in "Auschwitz" the consummate mythology of victimization and survival. Rejecting the only lessons Auschwitz has to offer—the need for a renewal of religious faith, the need for a collective commitment to decent social conditions—it pores over the historical record in search of a lesson Auschwitz cannot possibly yield: how to survive a holocaust. The Final Solution has become a particular obsession of the Jews because the mythology of the Holocaust helps to maintain Jewish ethnic identity, as Neusner argues, in a period when Jewish identity is no longer defined by religion; but it has become a general obsession because it holds out the false but seductive promise of insights into the technology of survival.

"At first the testimony of survivors inspired awe and humility," writes Elie Wiesel. "But popularization and exploitation soon followed." The concentration camps lost their "mystery." "The Holocaust became a literary 'free for all.' . . . Novelists made free use of it in their work, scholars used it to prove their theories." This exploitation of the "Holocaust" can be charted in the growing preoccupation with survival strategies, in the recklessness with which commentators began to generalize from the concentration camps to normal everyday life, and in their increasing eagerness to see the camps as a metaphor for modern society. The first reports from survivors contained surprisingly little speculation along these lines. The most famous of these reports, Bettelheim's "Individual and Mass Behavior in Extreme Situations," set out to examine the methods used by the Nazis to "produce changes in the prisoners which would make them useful subjects of the Nazi state." Bettelheim showed how systematic terror can force men and women to "live, like children, only in the immediate present" and even to adopt some of the values of their oppressors, but he never raised the "question that haunts all who study the extermination camps," as he himself described it in a book written fifteen years later: the question, that is, of why "millions walked quietly, without resistance, to their death," why "so few of the millions of prisoners died like men." Nor did Bettelheim's original article generalize from the plight of the prisoners to the plight of modern man. "The concentration camp," he concluded, "has an importance reaching far beyond its being a place where the gestapo took revenge on its enemies"—but only because the concentration camp allegedly dramatized what "happened in less exaggerated form to most inhabitants of that larger concentration camp called Germany." The concentration camp "ought to be studied by all persons interested in understanding what happens to a population subject to the methods of the Nazi system."

Whether or not Bettelheim was correct in his interpretation of the concentration camp as a "laboratory" in which the Nazis learned how to terrorize an entire population, his first attempt to grasp the meaning of the Final Solution at least avoided the temptation to draw moral and political lessons from the prisoners' experience or to speculate about the qualities that might have enabled more of them to survive it or at least to bear it more heroically. By 1960, however, when Bettelheim published *The Informed Heart: Autonomy in a Mass Age*, a shift in the public mood had made these subjects central both to Bettelheim's work and (as we shall see a little later) to that of his critics. The concentration camps, Bettelheim now insisted, taught a "lesson" not just about German society under the Nazis but about the "influence of the environment on man" and the danger that "mass society" would extinguish the sense of individuality. If the

Nazis reduced individuals to a formless mass, "similar tendencies are present in any mass society and can be detected to some degree in our own time." A study of mass society, it appeared—of the psychology of conformity—led to important insights about survival. Deploring the popularity of *The Diary of Anne Frank*, Bettelheim argued that the Franks' attempt to carry on "business as usual" represented "neither a good way to live, nor the way to survive." "Extreme privatization" failed in the face of adversity. "Even all Mr. Frank's love did not keep [his family] alive." On the other hand, those who managed to escape from Europe or to survive the concentration camps understood that "when a world goes to pieces, when inhumanity reigns supreme, man cannot go on with business as usual." They understood, moreover, that even death is preferable to the passivity with which so many victims of Nazism allowed themselves to be treated as "units in a system." The concentration camps could not deprive courageous men and women of the freedom to die defiantly, "to decide how one wishes to think and feel about the conditions of one's life."

"Mere" Survival Criticized and Defended Another psychiatrist, Victor Frankl, offered a somewhat similar interpretation of the Final Solution—still not yet referred to as the "Holocaust"—in a book published in 1959, *From Death-Camp to Existentialism: A Psychiatrist's Path to a New Therapy*. Like Bettelheim, Frankl saw an existential affirmation of selfhood as the only proper response to extreme situations. Like Bettelheim, he tried to make connections between the Nazi terror and "mass society." But where Bettelheim stressed mass society's assault on individuality, Frankl stressed its assault on "meaning." Modern society, he argued, frustrates the "will-to-meaning." Automation deprives people of useful work and leaves them bored and restless. The erosion of religious belief and the triumph of

a scientific worldview create an "existential vacuum." "The average man of today seems to be haunted by a feeling of the meaninglessness of life." The Nazi death camps, according to Frankl, embodied this crisis of meaning in an extreme form. By depriving the prisoner of meaning, they threatened his very will to survive.

Without an "ultimate goal in life," Frankl believed, men and women have no reason to go on living. Many prisoners in the camps suffered a "kind of emotional death." They "ceased living for the future." An "unemployed worker," Frankl noted, finds himself "in a similar position." "His existence has become provisional and in a certain sense he cannot live for the future or aim at a goal." By intensifying this experience, the death camps threw prisoners back on their own resources. Only those who managed to accept imprisonment as a test of inner strength, even as an "opportunity to grow spiritually," managed to preserve their "inner liberty." Most "lost all scruples in their fight for existence," according to Frank. "They were prepared to use every means, honest or otherwise, even brutal force, theft, and betrayal of their friends, in order to save themselves." A few prisoners, however, chose existential freedom over survival. Instead of asking whether their survival would give meaning to the suffering inflicted on them, they asked whether their suffering would give meaning to their survival, "for a life whose meaning stands and falls on whether one escapes with it or not . . . ultimately would not be worth living at all."

Frankl's "logotherapy," based explicitly on the lessons of Auschwitz, attempted to extend those lessons from the concentration camp to the consulting room. According to Frankl, modern man has to learn, with the help of his psychiatrist, how to create his own meaning in a meaningless world. Psychiatry becomes a "medical ministry," the doctor a surrogate priest. The logotherapist tries to cure "existential frustration, this world-wide collective neurosis," not—it goes without saying—through any "imposition of the doctor's personal values on the patient" but through carefully planned attempts to get the patient to discover personal "values" of his own. Why these values are worth living or dying for, when they make no claim to represent the moral consensus of the community and can never be "imposed" on anyone else, Frankl never explains. He believes that every individual has to find his own personal truth, since "it is impossible to define the meaning of life in a general way." But if truth and meaning are entirely personal and subjective, if they have no reference to anything outside our own immediate experience, it is not clear why they should give us any strength or support when things go wrong. Like many other observers, Frankl notes that people with powerful religious convictions—Jehovah's Witnesses, for example —bore up better than most under the hardships of the concentration camps; but he ignores the possibility that these people found strength in the revealed word of an absolute, objective, and omnipotent creator, as they saw it, not in personal "values" meaningful only to themselves. If survival cannot be regarded as an end in itself, as Frankl maintains, then it must be some purpose outside ourselves that gives us a reason to live or die. Frankl's existentialism cannot provide such a purpose. It counters nihilism, the nihilism that seeks only to survive at all costs, with empty affirmations: moral freedom, "values," "humanism." Frankl insists that man is a free moral agent, not a "mere product" or "parallelogram of inner drives and outer forces"; but he cannot explain why any particular action or moral choice is better than any other. He can only affirm choice itself, the "last of human freedoms"—the freedom, which even the concentration camps could not annul, to "choose one's attitude in a given set of circumstances" not of one's making, even under "terrible conditions of psychic and physical stress."

Since the existential, humanistic critique of mere survival rests on flimsy premises, upholding the importance of "values" without providing any reason to accept their validity, it invites rebuttal in the form of an argument that dismisses outmoded humanistic slogans and every other metaphysical remnant and extols survival itself as the ultimate affirmation of life. In 1976, at the height of the vogue for sociobiology, Terrence Des Pres published *The Survivor: An Anatomy of Life in the Death Camps,* in which he argues that the drive to preserve life asserts itself even in the face of every reason not to go on living. Des Pres's book advances an ethic of survivalism based on respect for "life in itself." The death camps, Des Pres maintains, robbed death of its dignity and thus undermined the possibility of heroism, martyrdom, patriotism, and self-sacrifice. They dramatized the obsolescence of moralities based on personal responsibility. Under extreme conditions, the "honored forms of heroism fail as models for action and spiritual support." Conventional morality upholds the willingness to sacrifice your life and condemns the act of " 'merely' surviving, as if life in itself were not worth much; as if we felt that life is justified only by things which negate it." The survivors of the Holocaust have taught us, according to Des Pres, something of the "sustaining power which life itself provides when all else has been stripped away." They have showed us how to live without hope and without fear. In other words, their experience clarifies the condition under which all of us live today, which the death camps carried to extremes. Under extreme adversity, sanity depends "on always expecting the worst." The survivor rejects hope and thus also rejects despair. He is "glad to be alive"; this unconditional, "illogical, irrational" affirmation of life comes to stand as the "survivor's special grace, . . . the wisdom of Lear on the heath, stripped of everything but his pain."

Des Pres not only challenges the "bias against 'mere survival' " but tries to refute criticism of the Jews, advanced by Bettelheim and Hannah Arendt (in her book on Eichmann), for their failure to fight back against the Final Solution. He bases his argument partly on empirical grounds, citing instances of cooperation, mutual aid, and resistance among the prisoners. The main burden of his argument, however, is philosophical. "Bettelheim's critique of camp behavior is rooted in the old heroic ethic," according to Des Pres. Thus he upholds suicide as an isolated act of defiance. As the spokesman for an outmoded humanism, an outmoded system of metaphysics, Bettelheim extols the spirit over the body. He tries to keep "everything 'lower' out of sight." The experience of the death camps, however, redeems the "undramatic, unglorified sorrow of the body," commonly ignored "in favor of 'inner' suffering." It "inverts the values of civilization." It shows that "physical existence can no longer be dismissed as unworthy of concern." The survivor's "recalcitrance"—his refusal to give in to despair or to accept the role of a helpless victim of circumstance—reaffirms the " 'bio-social' roots of human existence." It testifies to the "stubbornness" of a "will impersonal and stronger than hope," that of "life itself." In a summary passage toward the end of his book, Des Pres argues that civilization, with all its achievements, has not

> defeated the body's crude claims. And this, again, is the survivor's special importance. He is the first civilized man to live beyond the compulsions of culture; beyond a fear of death which can only be assuaged by insisting that life itself is worthless. The survivor is evidence enough that men and women are now strong enough, mature enough, awake enough, to face death without mediation, and therefore to embrace life without reserve.

Like Bettelheim and Frankl, Des Pres rejects the behavioral view of personality, the view that "external forces shape internal being" and that "environment is omnipotent." The survivor's experience, he argues, refutes "current theories of victimhood." The survivors refused to accept the definition of themselves as victims. Their "recalcitrance" lay in their "refusal to be determined by forces external to themselves." This recalcitrance, however, derived not from "man's indomitable spirit," as humanists maintain, but from the "deeper knowledge" of the body, the "substratum of vital information biologically instilled." In the death camps, only the biological will to live could sustain life, since the brutal conditions of the camps effectively annulled the possibility that life has any higher meaning.

Des Pres recognizes, of course, that actions appropriate in a concentration camp might become highly inappropriate in normal life, and he rejects "invalid comparisons" between the concentration camps and the "predicament of modern man in 'mass society.'" The whole trend of his analysis, however, reinforces such comparisons. "The survivor is the man or woman who has passed through the 'crisis of civilization' we talk about so much," the collapse of "mythic structures" and the failure of "symbolism." Readers of *The Survivor* took it, with good reason, as a book about the modern predicament. Anatole Broyard, in an article significantly entitled "The Technology of the Soul," cited it as an example of the new trend in social thought that emphasizes man's strengths rather than his weaknesses. "We are becoming heroes again," Broyard wrote—"not the old heroes of myth and fable, not supermen, but heroes of the minimal, heroes of survival."

Survivor Guilt, Pro and Con Bettelheim has pointed out on a number of occasions—and "this cannot be stressed enough," he says—that prisoners in the concentration camps could do very little to assure their survival, except to hope for the victory of the Grand Alliance against Hitler. All they could do was to cling to selfhood—to fight off personal disintegration—so that some inner core of personal integrity would remain in the unlikely event any of them managed to escape with their lives. "My main problem," Bettelheim writes in *The Informed Heart*, "was . . . to protect my inner self in such a way that if, by any good fortune, I should regain liberty, I would be approximately the same person I was when deprived of liberty." Solzhenitsyn, another survivor of concentration camps, has made the similar observation that a prisoner must never say to himself, "I will survive at any cost." Even Des Pres concedes the importance of keeping "moral sense and dignity intact"; indeed he intimates at one point that "survival *depends* on staying human." He acknowledges, moreover, that "some minimal fabric of care, some margin of giving and receiving, is essential to life in extremity" and that in this sense, the "survivor owes his life to his comrades."

What Des Pres denies is that this "debt to the dead" gives rise to feelings of guilt. The issue of "survivor guilt" sharpens the conflict between two interpretations of the Holocaust, one of which sees it as a source of moral insight, the other as a source of lessons in the technology of survival. According to Bettelheim, Robert Jay Lifton, and Elie Wiesel, many survivors feel emotionally unworthy of the memory of the millions who perished, as if their own lives had been saved by the deaths of innumerable others. These authorities argue that an acknowledgment of his feelings of guilt, which establish a bond between the living and the dead, can become the survivor's first step toward the recovery of his humanity and toward the "death-haunted knowledge, even creative energy" that so many survivors, according to Lifton, have managed to salvage from their ordeal. "I live and therefore I am guilty," Elie Wiesel writes. "I am still here, because a friend, a comrade, an unknown died in my place." On this reading, the survivor's gratitude for life springs not merely from his awareness that life can no longer be taken for granted, as Des Pres maintains, but from his solidarity with the dead.

> One cannot survive the concentration camp [Bettelheim writes] without feeling guilty that one was so incredibly lucky when millions perished, many of them in front of one's eyes. Lifton has demonstrated that the same phenomenon exists for the survivors of Hiroshima, and there the catastrophe was short-lived—although its consequences will last a lifetime. But in the camps one was forced day after day, for years, to watch the destruction of others, feeling—against one's better judgment—that one should have intervened, feeling guilty for not having done so, and most of all, feeling guilty for having often felt glad that it was not oneself who perished, since one knew that one had no right to expect that one would be the person spared.

For Des Pres, guilt, like heroism and sacrifice, is another remnant of the morality of personal responsibility discredited by the death camps, which exposed the utter absurdity of thinking that anyone is responsible for his fate. The idea of "survivor guilt," he argues, can only discredit the survivor—and thus divert attention from the horrors to which he was exposed—by implying that he somehow deserved what happened to him. When the perpetrators of great evil so obviously felt no guilt, hiding instead, like Eichmann, behind the cloak of bureaucratic anonymity, the suggestion that survivors have any reason to feel guilty exemplifies the "blame-the-victim syndrome." It represents the final "slander against the decency of survivors" perpetrated by those who also claim that prisoners went meekly to their death, identified with their captors, and regressed to an infantile state of mind. All such ideas "reinforce our sense of impotence and despair," according to Des Pres. They imply that the "struggle to survive . . . does not count." "We cannot afford to believe" these libelous assertions, since they "confirm the prevailing sense of victimhood." Falling back on the humanistic slogans he elsewhere rejects, Des Pres accuses Bettelheim (as Bettelheim accuses Des Pres) of "fostering nihilism and radical loss of faith in our own humanness." Not content with this line of attack, he adds the *ad hominem* sneer that Bettelheim has no right to speak for the survivors at all, since he was confined to Dachau and Buchenwald, not to the Polish death camps, and managed, moreover, to secure his release after "only" a year's imprisonment. Here again, Des Pres tries to have things both ways: to challenge "current theories of victimhood" and to claim, at the same time, that only those who suffered the most extreme forms of victimization have a right to be heard.

Survivalism at Its Ugliest: Seven Beauties The glorification of victimhood by the victims of the "Holocaust" and their spokesmen (even by those spokesmen who object, with Des Pres, to the "prevailing tendencies in modern thinking that [have] accepted the condition of victimhood as final"); the unseemly eagerness to exploit the victims' suffering for polemical advantage; the refusal to let them rest in peace; the obsessive interest in documenting their ordeal down to the last detail; and the growing insistence that it offers exemplary moral and sociological insights provide an index of the steady decline of this discourse on mass death. In the years immediately following World War II, no one showed much inclination to make moral capital out of the fate of European Jews. There was little of "that obsession with 'the Holocaust,' " as Neusner puts it, "that wants to make the tragedy into the principal subject of public discourse with Jews about Judaism." Even those who argued that the concentration camps had an importance beyond themselves meant only that the concentration camp was more than a prison for political enemies, that it had to be seen as a systematic experiment in dehumanization. No

doubt this argument opened the door to the counterargu-
ment that "the 'experiment' did not succeed," as Des Pres
puts it; but these positions did not crystallize as poles in a
passionate conflict of ideologies until the 1960s, when the
studies of totalitarianism by Bettelheim and Hannah Arendt
began to be taken as a defamation of the victims requiring
a counterattack by their champions. Bettelheim and Arendt
tried to show that totalitarianism was something new; that
its victims failed to recognize it as such; and that they failed
to put up more resistance, during the initial period of the
Nazis' consolidation of power, because they could not believe that Hitler really intended to wipe out the entire Jewish population of Europe. In placing so much emphasis on
the question of resistance, however, they themselves introduced into the discussion a new element of moral censure
or seeming censure that prompted a long series of angry
rejoinders attempting to rehabilitate the victims, to dignify
their struggles, and finally to dignify survival as an end in
itself.

These counterclaims, these moral treatises on behalf of
survival, reach their nadir in a celebration of the "life force"
reminiscent of Nazism itself. In 1976—the same year Des
Pres published *The Survivor*, and a year after Elie Wiesel
complained about the way novelists and scholars had
"cheapened the Holocaust" and "drained it of its substance"
—Lina Wertmüller released her movie *Seven Beauties*, apparently a glorification of the anti-hero as survival artist.*
Exploiting the death camps as a source of black humor,
playing up to an audience beyond indignation or remorse,
Wertmüller seemed to suggest that men who opposed fas-

---

*"Apparently," I say, because Wertmüller, hedging her bets, built into the
movie a certain ambiguity, which made it possible for a number of reviewers to
interpret it as a condemnation, not as a glorification, of the man who will do
anything in order to stay alive. What is beyond ambiguity, however, is the underlying premise that only the ruthless survive.

cism perished ingloriously in the struggle, while Pasqualino, a petty gangster, rapist, and opportunist, survives imprisonment by sacrificing his friends, collaborating with the guards, and submitting to sexual relations with the loathsome, brutal woman who commands the camp to which he is consigned. "Your thirst for life disgusts me," says the commandant to Pasqualino. "You found strength for an erection. That's why you'll survive, and win in the end." Not only does Pasqualino survive the camps, he shows that he knows how to survive in the dog-eat-dog world of postwar Europe. He tells the whore he plans to marry: "No time to lose. I want kids, lots, twenty-five, thirty. We've got to defend ourselves."

Acclaimed by critics and reviewers, *Seven Beauties* showed that the "life force outruns ideas and ideals," in the words of Vincent Canby. Des Pres himself welcomed the film as another attack on the outdated morality of heroism, a celebration of the new man—"not a hero in the traditional sense"—who "prefers to live and carry the costs of that choice, rather than to remain uncompromised by that choice." Pasqualino "does not endure his fate passively," Des Pres observed. "His ordeal is painful and degrading, yet from it a modicum of dignity is born, if only because he comes to suffer the awareness of existence at its worst. . . . By the end of the film he has achieved a degree of moral awareness . . . which he entirely lacked at the start." Only later, after Bettelheim had denounced *Seven Beauties* for its false "lesson of survivorship"—"all that matters, the only thing that is really important, is life in its crudest, merely biological form"—did Des Pres decide that the movie should be taken as a description, not as an endorsement, of a "vile and loathsome man."

Comparative "Survivor Research": Extreme Situations and Everyday Stress   Once the concentration camps came to be seen as a source of moral enlightenment and "lessons," it proved increasingly difficult to sustain the distinction between survival strategies and actions intended to "give meaning to survival," as Bettelheim puts it. What Frankl and Bettelheim saw as a struggle against personal corruption becomes, in the eyes of observers further removed from direct experience of the camps, a struggle to stay alive in the face of "stress." Thus a growing body of comparative studies, in which the "Holocaust" serves merely as an extreme example of psychic stress, seeks to understand the psychology of victimization and survival and to apply this knowledge to everyday life. "Our ultimate aim," writes Henry Krystal in the introduction to a collection of essays entitled *Massive Psychic Trauma,* "is to learn from the extreme situations more about the handling and effect of trauma in everyday life." The "massive mistreatment" of the Jews may have surpassed anything else in our experience, but it is nevertheless comparable to the persecution of blacks and Indians in the United States and even to events in the history of a single family, "where the individual will assume an undesirable role unconsciously attributed to him by his parents, family, peers, or society." The "comparison of various groups permits us to isolate the particularly harmful effects" of victimization. "The applicability of our observations [of extreme situations] to everyday treatment and prevention becomes apparent in the fact that, in all cases, we find the psychic reality of the patient to determine the meaning and after effect" of persecution and the "severity of postpersecution pathology." Extremes illuminate the "psychopathology of everyday life."

A recent collection of essays on the Holocaust edited by Joel E. Dimsdale, *Survivors, Victims, and Perpetrators,* illustrates the growing confusion between the struggle to preserve personal integrity and the struggle for survival. It also illustrates the eagerness to base a technology of psychic survival on lessons learned from extreme situations. A number of contributors draw on the "relatively new concept of coping, which essentially focuses on how a person responds to stress," in order to explain not merely how prisoners in the camps sought to defend their dignity and autonomy against barbaric and brutalizing conditions but how some of them managed against all odds to survive. These psychiatrists warn against the conclusion that survivors had developed better coping mechanisms than those who perished. They remind themselves, from time to time, that survival in the concentration camps depended on circumstances over which individuals had little control. Yet the concept of coping, reinforced by a distinction between "effective" and "ineffective (counterproductive)" coping mechanisms, unavoidably encourages the conclusion that "effective coping can positively influence even the most severe criterion of adaptation, namely, survival itself." According to Patricia Benner, Ethel Roskies, and Richard S. Lazarus, "It is probable that people who engage in more effective coping actually experience less stress than do ineffective copers, both because they perceive fewer situations as threatening and because they can resolve those that appear so much more quickly and satisfactorily." The same writers reinterpret Bettelheim's essay, "Individual and Mass Behavior in Extreme Situations," as a survival manual. The testimony of Bettelheim and other survivors teaches us, they believe, that "denial and selective apathy were keys to survival" and that inmates' expectations had to be "adjusted downward to basic survival issues." "As time went on," they argue, "survival alone became a goal. Fighting for survival meant focusing on narrow, restricted goals." But "this restriction of perspective can occur in any extreme condition or when there are curtailed life expectancies."

Some of the contributors to the Dimsdale collection explicitly challenge the "widely held belief" that a prisoner in the concentration camps "was completely powerless to influence his fate," as Dimsdale puts it. Others challenge this belief only implicitly, in part by blurring the distinction between extreme situations and everyday life. In psychiatric practice, concepts like coping and "social competence" have come into use in the treatment of emotional distress resulting from sickness, old age, career crises, and other forms of stress. When extended to extreme situations, they give the impression that even a program of deliberate and systematic dehumanization can be countered by effective techniques of self-management. "Stress" comes to embrace a continuum of events ranging from the tortures inflicted by the SS to ordinary "stress-related transactions between person and environment." Even the "stress of a crying infant suffering with colic" poses a threat to "survival," if we believe a recent headline summarizing the latest medical research. According to Paul Chodoff, many "life situations within our society" contain "stresses found in the concentration camp": "malnutrition, physical abuse, deindividuation, dehumanization," and, more generally, all those stresses arising from the "individual's inability to manage his or her relationship with the environment, either because of severe internal conflicts or limited skills." It is not only in prisons, it seems, that "opportunities for acting upon the environment are . . . limited." Benner, Roskies, and Lazarus note that "variants of the coping strategies used by those in the concentration camps are evident in the lives of people facing the everyday stresses and strains of living." Statements of this kind undercut the occasional reminder that survival strategies effective in a concentration camp may not be altogether appropriate to the "regulation of distress" in everyday life. They leave the impression that everyday life has taken on many of the qualities of a struggle for survival, in which the best hope for men and women under siege is "to focus on those segments of reality that can be managed," to achieve a state of "psychic insensibility and resignation with regard to the unavoidable conditions," to suppress "self-evaluation, judgment, and self-reflective powers," and thus to effect a "robotization" or "automatization of functions dedicated solely to the task of survival."

Recent "survivor research" takes the narrowest possible view of the significance of the Holocaust. It is far more singlemindedly absorbed in the problem of survival than the firsthand accounts left by the survivors themselves. Common sense would lead us to expect the opposite. It would lead us to expect a gradual weakening of the survivor mentality, as the memory of the death camps recedes into the distance. It is the survivors themselves, Neusner writes, who ought to "see the world as essentially hostile," to distrust outsiders, and to "exhibit the traits of citizens of a city under siege, feeling always threatened, always alone, always on the defensive." The generation born since World War II, on the other hand, might be expected to "regard the world as essentially neutral, if not friendly, and should have the capacity to trust the outsider." In fact, the siege mentality is much stronger in those who know Auschwitz only at second hand than in those who lived through it. It is the survivors who see their experience as a struggle not to survive but to stay human. While they record any number of strategies for deadening the emotional impact of imprisonment—the separation of the observing self from the participating self; the decision to forget the past and to live exclusively in the present; the severance of emotional ties to loved ones outside the camps; the cultivation of a certain indifference to appeals from fellow-victims—they also insist that emotional withdrawal could not be carried to the point of complete callousness without damaging the prisoner's moral integrity and even his will to live. It is the survivors who try to "give meaning to survival," while those who come after them and live under conditions seemingly more secure see meaning only in survival itself. A heightened interest in the "Holocaust" coincides with a diminished capacity to imagine a moral order transcending it, which alone can give meaning to the terrible suffering this image is intended to commemorate. When Auschwitz became a social myth, a metaphor for modern life, people lost sight of the only lesson it could possibly offer: that it offers, in itself, no lessons.

IV

The Minimalist
Aesthetic:
Art and Literature
in an Age
of Extremity

The Roth-Cunningham Effect　Philip Roth once observed, before this kind of observation became a cliché, that the writer's imagination falters in the face of contemporary "actuality," which "is continually outdoing our talents." Newspapers and television news programs report events more grotesque and outlandish than the writer's wildest dreams. Our culture "tosses up figures almost daily that are the envy of any novelist." It "stupefies, it sickens, it infuriates, and finally it is even a kind of embarrassment to one's own meager imagination." In their bafflement and disgust, many writers turn away from the "grander social and political phenomena of our times," according to Roth, and "take the self as their subject": the "sheer fact of self, the vision of self as inviolate, powerful, and nervy, self as the only real thing in an unreal environment."

The bafflement of the moral imagination in the face of an

event like the Holocaust illustrates the difficulty that confronts anyone who tries to make sense of contemporary social life. When social reality becomes imaginatively unmanageable, the imagination takes refuge, as we have seen, in self-defensive survival strategies: exactly the kind of strategies also adopted by the contemporary writer and artist, according to Roth, in their attempt to keep the artistic enterprise alive in an age of extremity. Overwhelmed by the cruelty, disorder, and sheer complexity of modern history, the artist retreats into a solipsistic mode of discourse that represents "not so much an attempt to understand the self," in Roth's words, as an attempt "to assert it." He conducts his own struggle for survival as an artist, under conditions that have made it more and more difficult to transcribe any shared experience or common perceptions of the world, undermined the conventions of artistic realism, and given rise to a type of art that no longer seems to refer to anything outside itself. Instead of merely reporting it, the recent history of art and literature exemplifies the difficulty we have already analyzed in connection with writing about the Final Solution, the difficulty, that is, of formulating an imaginative response appropriate to extreme situations. Contemporary art is an art of extremity not because it takes extreme situations as its subject—though much of it does that too—but because the experience of extremity threatens to undermine the very possibility of an imaginative interpretation of reality.

The only art that seems appropriate to such an age, to judge from the recent history of artistic experimentation, is an anti-art or minimal art, where minimalism refers not just to a particular style in an endless succession of styles but to a widespread conviction that art can survive only by a drastic restriction of its field of vision: the radical "restriction of perspective" recommended by authorities on the subject as the survival strategy *par excellence*. Even the kind of embattled self-assertion envisioned by Roth as a typical artistic defense against an "unreal environment" has proved impossible to sustain. In the visual arts at least, the celebration of selfhood, as exemplified by abstract expressionism in the late forties and early fifties—the assertion of the artist as a heroic rebel and witness to contemporary despair—had already come under critical attack by the time Roth published his diagnosis of the literary malaise in 1961. An even earlier diagnosis, quite similar to Roth's in its intuition of the difficulties confronting imaginative activity but very different in its upshot, suggests why a minimal art rather than an expressive art has commended itself to those who despair of expressing the inexpressible. In 1952, the dancer Merce Cunningham urged artists to abandon effects based on "climax," on the alternation of tension and release. A society in crisis, he argued, did not require, as it might have appeared to require, an art concerned with crisis, an art dependent on the sense of climax. "Since our lives, both by nature and by the newspapers, are so full of crisis that one is no longer aware of it, then it is clear that life goes on regardless, and further that each thing can be and is separate from each and every other, viz.: the continuity of the newspaper headlines." Not a model of lucidity, this statement nevertheless stands today as a more accurate forecast than Roth's of the direction art would actually take in the coming years: an immersion in the ordinary, a deliberate effacement of the artist's personality, a rejection of clarifying contexts that show relationships among objects or events, a refusal to find patterns of any kind, an insistence on the random quality of experience, an insistence that "each thing can be and is separate from each and every other."

From Self-Assertion to Self-Effacement The statement that reality outruns the creative imagination conveys only part of the truth we need to grasp in order to understand the contemporary artist's predicament. Reality itself is no longer real in the sense of arising from a people's shared understanding, from a shared past, and from shared values. More and more, our impressions of the world derive not from the observations we make both as individuals and as members of a wider community but from elaborate systems of communication, which spew out information, much of it unbelievable, about events of which we seldom have any direct knowledge. Whether this information describes the doings of the rich and powerful or whether, on the other hand, it purports to describe the lives of average men and women, we find it hard to recognize our own experience in these curiously hypothetical representations of "reality." The only evidence that would confirm or refute our own experience is the evidence of people like ourselves, people who share a common past and a common frame of reference. The images transmitted by the mass media usually refer, on the other hand, either to celebrities admired precisely for their ability to escape the constraints of everyday existence (even though we are constantly told that they remain average men and women in spite of their celebrity) or to a hypothetical norm or average arising not from shared experience or even from the experience of "representative men" but from demographical analysis of a select statistical population, audience, or market. The mass media make an earnest effort to tell us who and what we are, indeed to generate a spurious sense of national identity, but they do this by telling us what programs we like to watch, what products we like to buy, what political candidates we plan to vote for, how many of us will marry and how many get divorced, how long we will live, how many of us will die of cancer, how many of us will die in traffic accidents on a holiday weekend, how many of us will die in a nuclear war, how many of us will survive a nuclear war if adequate precautions are taken. Demographic analysis is a poor substitute for reality, but since it is the only reality we have in common, we become increasingly reluctant to challenge it by citing our own singular, idiosyncratic perceptions of the world, let alone to hope that we can "impose" our idiosyncratic perceptions on others.

If the radio, the camera, and the television set merely usurped the representational function of the arts, as often alleged, it would be hard to account for the growing feeling that even an abstract and inward-turning art stands little chance of success in an environment already saturated with images and information. Modern recording equipment monopolizes the representation of reality, but it also blurs the distinction between reality and illusion, between the subjective world and the world of objects, and thus makes it increasingly difficult for artists to take refuge even in the "sheer fact of self," as Roth puts it. The self is no more a sheer fact than its surroundings. In recent poetry and fiction, the self "seems more and more deprived of assurance as to its basic purchase on life," in Warner Berthoff's words. An art of romantic egoism has proved as untenable as an art based on the conventions of realism.

A writer like Henry Miller stands in something of the same transitional position in the history of fiction that the New York School occupies in the history of art, a position midway between an older tradition of literary self-assertion and a newer literature of authorial self-abnegation. When Miller endorses Emerson's call for a literature of "diaries and autobiographies" instead of novels, when he seeks to open himself to the "whole damned current of life," and when he urges the artist "to overthrow existing values, to make of the chaos about him an order which is his own," he aligns himself with the long tradition of literary antinomianism in America, which affirms the inner light of selfhood against a world of darkness and deceit—a world characterized by Miller as a "mad slaughterhouse," a "cancer eating itself away," a "gray desert," and a "new ice age." But Miller strikes a new note, one not to be found in Emerson or Whitman, when he adopts the voice of a survivor who will do anything to stay alive.

> Somehow the realization that nothing was to be hoped for had a salutary effect upon me. . . . Walking toward Montparnasse I decided to let myself drift with the tide, to make not the least resistance to fate, no matter in what form it presented itself. . . . I made up my mind that I would hold on to nothing, that I would expect nothing, that henceforth I would live as an animal, a beast of prey, a plunderer. Even if war were declared, and it were my lot to go, I would grab the bayonet and plunge it, plunge it up to the hilt. And if rape were the order of the day then rape I would, and with a vengeance. . . . If to live is the paramount thing, then I will live, even if I must become a cannibal.

Even here, a certain biological core of selfhood remains, stripped of the spiritual illusions—falsely regarded as the "better part of [man's] nature"—that have so often betrayed humanity in the past, according to Miller. "I am only spiritually dead. Physically I am alive. Morally I am free," Miller insists—free, that is, to refuse either to assume moral responsibility for anything or to assign moral responsibility to anyone else. In Miller's successors, even the biological basis of selfhood comes into question. In the works of William Burroughs, a writer much indebted to Miller, metaphors of intoxication give way to metaphors of addiction. The self is no longer drunk with life; it is controlled by outside agents who exploit the addictive need for drugs, sex, and human contact in order to program a new race of robots. Miller celebrated the "furious ardor," as he called it, the "mystery about the phenomena which are labelled 'obscene.' " Burroughs sees human beings, on the other hand, as "Terminal Addicts of The Orgasm Drug." It is their love-and-need-disease, together with all the other drugs on which they depend, that exposes them to the machinations of the Nova Police, who first "create a narcotic problem" and then "say that a permanent narcotics police is now necessary to deal with the problem of addiction." Even words and images are drugs, according to Burroughs, by means of which unseen powers control a population of image addicts. "Images—millions of images—that's what I eat. . . . Ever try kicking *that* habit with apomorphine?" The romantic artist hurled words and images into the void, hoping to impose order on chaos. The postmodern, postromantic artist sees them as "mind screen movies," instruments of surveillance and control.

> The scanning pattern we accept as 'reality' has been imposed by the controlling power on this planet, a power primarily oriented towards total control. . . . At any given time recording devices fix the nature of absolute need and dictate the use of total weapons—Like this: Take two opposed pressure groups—Record the most violent and threatening statements of group one with regard to group two and play back to group two—Record the answer and take it back to group one—Back and forth between opposed pressure groups—This process is known as 'feed back.'

Described by a friend as a "writer who has gone through a long period of addiction and survived," Burroughs takes as his subject not the imperial self of an earlier literary tradition but the beleaguered, controlled, and programmed self. "I am primarily concerned with the question of survival," he has said recently, "—with Nova conspiracies, Nova criminals, and Nova police." The "tremendous range in which people can be programmed" calls the concept of human nature into question. "Your 'I' is a completely illusory concept." In the preface he wrote for the American edition of J. G. Ballard's *Love and Napalm*, Burroughs notes that "the line between inner and outer landscapes is breaking down." It is above all the profusion of images, he adds, that has produced this effect: in particular, the magnification of images to the point where they become "unrecognizable." Ballard's book, according to Burroughs, achieves the same effect that Robert Rauschenberg achieves in art, "literally *blowing up* the image."

The Imperial Ego Effaced by Images Ballard's novel invites comparison, in its own right, not only with *Naked Lunch* and *Nova Express* but with the long tradition of books on America by English writers—a tradition that includes D. H. Lawrence's *Studies in Classic American Literature*, H. G. Wells's *The New America: The New World*, and Aldous Huxley's *After Many a Summer Dies the Swan*—in which the brash exuberance and vulgarity of the American scene evoke mingled envy, admiration, and apprehension. Written at the height of the Vietnam war, *Love and Napalm*, pointedly subtitled *Export U.S.A.*, draws on familiar themes of literary anti-Americanism: the erotic feelings Americans invest in their machines, especially automobiles; the national passion for mechanized killing; the automobile as murder weapon; the multicar crash as the ultimate American orgy; the threat of an Americanization of the whole world. What distinguishes Ballard's book from earlier English attempts to capture the speed, frenzy, and menace of American life is the complete absence of the imperial ego, the endlessly acquisitive conquerer and pioneer that formerly played such a large part in this particular story. In *Love and Napalm*, human beings have shrunk to the point of invisibility, while the images they have made of themselves, grotesquely enlarged to gigantic dimensions and no longer recognizable as human images at all, take on a life of their own. "The serene face

of the President's widow, painted on clapboard four hundred feet high, moves across the rooftops, disappearing into
the haze on the outskirts of the city. There are hundreds of
the signs, revealing Jackie in countless familiar postures."
Magnified far beyond human scale, the body becomes a
landscape: "Marilyn's pitted skin, breasts of carved pumice,
volcanic thighs, a face of ash. The widowed bride of
Vesuvius." Fragments of the human face, disembodied and
blown up to enormous size, dwarf ordinary men and
women and cast a lurid glow over their infirmities. "An
enormous photograph of Jacqueline Kennedy had appeared
in the empty rectangle of the screen. A bearded young man
with an advanced neuro-muscular tremor in his lower legs
stood in the brilliant pearl light, his laminated suit bathed in
the magnified image of Mrs. Kennedy's mouth."

Ballard's otherwise uncharacterized protagonist—the
term is completely inappropriate here, of course, and even
his name varies from one chapter to the next as if to emphasize his lack of defining personal qualities—suffers from an
understandable obsession with the images surrounding him,
images of violent death and erotic arousal, and with the
possibility of rearranging them in some intelligible order.
"He wants to kill Kennedy again, but in a way that makes
sense." An image junkie, he pores over the documentary
record of contemporary chaos in the futile hope that it will
yield something more than a collection of fragments of sev-
ered and mutilated body parts. He studies, without ever
coming to any conclusions about them, an exhibition of
paintings of atrocities done by patients in a mental ward,
mock-ups of automobile crashes mounted by Ralph Nader
and his assistants, the Zapruder film of Kennedy's assassina-
tion, X-rays of exotic diseases, films of "neuro-surgery and
organ transplants, autism and senile dementia, auto-disasters
and plane crashes"—a "disquieting diorama of pain and
mutilation." Naturally he never finds whatever it is he is

looking for; nor is the situation clarified by the didactic commentaries of Dr. Nathan, who serves as a sort of substitute for a narrative voice, a tiresome voice-over whose monologues accompany and endlessly interpret without illuminating the endless procession of images. Even when Dr. Nathan seems to make sense, we find it hard to accept the validity of insights couched in a parody of psychiatric jargon, existential philosophy, and the other ready-made explanatory systems of an age never at a loss for explanations.

> Travers's problem is how to come to terms with the violence that has pursued his life—not merely the violence of accident and bereavement, or the horrors of war, but the biomorphic horror of our own bodies, the awkward geometry of the postures we assume. Travers has at last realized that the real significance of these acts of violence lies elsewhere, in what we might term 'the death of affect.' . . . What our children have to fear are not the cars on the freeways of tomorrow, but our own pleasure in calculating the most elegant parameters of their deaths.

Language like this becomes part of the background noise, as meaningless as Muzak, in a culture that finds silence unbearable and fills up every waking moment with prerecorded announcements. "You must understand that for Travers science is the ultimate pornography, analytic activity whose main aim is to isolate objects or events from their contexts in time and space. . . . One looks forward to the day when the *General Theory of Relativity* and the *Principia* will outsell the *Kama Sutra* in back-street bookshops." It is not that Dr. Nathan's pronouncements are necessarily wrong or even misleading; it is just that they have ceased in any important sense to matter. Commentary has become superfluous and self-defeating, Ballard implies, not because the images it seeks to elucidate are self-explanatory but because words have become images in their own right and have come to serve, like visual images, as instruments of psychological manipulation and control. The study of mankind has become another technique for dominating it. Scientific and sociological observation abolish the subject by making him the "subject" of experiments designed to elicit his response to a variety of stimuli, his preferences, and his private fantasies. On the strength of its findings, science constructs a composite profile of human needs on which to base a pervasive but not overtly oppressive system of behavioral regulations.

Ballard proposes, in effect, a theory of feedback even more nihilistic and paranoid in its implications than Burroughs's. Images control people, he seems to suggest, not merely by exploiting their addictions but by eliciting responses that are themselves recorded, photographed, X-rayed, measured, and minutely analyzed with an eye to the production of new images more precisely predictable in their effects. According to Ballard, dispassionate scientific studies—opinion surveys, polls, questionnaires, interviews, market research, psychological tests—serve the same purpose by giving people a choice of fantasies and thus making it possible for them to participate in the manufacture of the images best adapted to the regulation of their own emotional needs.

Studies were conducted to determine the effects of long-term exposure to TV newsreel films depicting the torture of Viet Cong: (a) male combatants, (b) women auxiliaries, (c) children, (d) wounded. In all cases a marked increase in the intensity of sexual activity was reported, with particular emphasis on perverse oral and ano-genital modes. Maximum arousal was provided by combined torture and execution sequences. Montage newsreels were constructed in which leading public figures associated with the Vietnam war, e.g., President Johnson, General Westmoreland, Marshall Ky, were substituted for both combatants and victims. On the basis of viewers' preferences an optimum torture and execution sequence was devised involving Governor Reagan, Madame Ky and an unidentifiable eight-year-old Vietnamese girl napalm victim. . . . The film was subsequently shown to both disturbed children and terminal cancer patients with useful results.

By turning horrible events into images, tearing these images out of context, rearranging them in new combinations, and characterizing the viewers' responses in the bland jargon of scientific neutrality, the technology of modern communications keeps people in line by making it easy for them to accept the unacceptable. It deadens the emotional impact of events, neutralizes criticism and commentary, and reduces even the "death of affect" to another catchword or cliché, one that reinforces the very condition it describes.

The Aesthetics of Exclusion In his attempt to capture the hallucinatory quality of a world in which images have replaced events, Ballard borrows heavily from recent experiments in the visual arts. As Burroughs notes, he tries to reproduce in words effects equivalent to those achieved by pop art. Practitioners of the pop and minimal styles, like Robert Rauschenberg, Andy Warhol, Roy Lichtenstein, Claes Oldenburg, Jasper Johns, and Robert Morris, address the same condition that underlies the passive, dreamlike atmosphere of Ballard's novels, the saturation of the environment by images and the consequent effacement of the subject. Adopting a style deliberately devoid of affect, they confront the spectator with familiar images and objects— comic strips, advertisements, movie posters, flags, hamburgers, toothpicks, drainpipes—blown up to monumental size or placed in unfamiliar contexts. They would take as a tribute the observation of a critic, intended as a reproach, that their isolation of everyday objects from everyday surroundings produces a "strange and almost hallucinatory effect" by draining objects of "sense and context." Their aim is precisely to encourage such effects and to blur the boundary between illusion and reality, art and everyday life. It is as if they had set out to document the arguments advanced by Walter Benjamin in his famous essay "The Work of Art in an Age of Mechanical Reproduction." According to Benjamin, who drew in turn on Marcel Duchamp and the theorists of dada, the mass production of images deprives art of its "aura" of mystery and uniqueness, makes it accessible to a wider public, and encourages a "mode of participation" in cultural life closer to the habitual use of old buildings by those who live in them than to the worshipful attention of the tourist. The same hopes were often expressed by those who revived Duchamp's work and reputation in the sixties and who proclaimed the death or suicide of the artist—his refusal to produce masterpieces carrying his personal signature in every detail of their coloring and composition—as the first step toward a society in which creativity would no longer be monopolized by "creative" individuals.*

Minimalism and pop art are not alone in their attempt to

*This protest against the deification of art might have desirable effects if it went along with a protest against the degradation of work and workmanship. It is because the taste for beauty and the "instinct of workmanship" no longer find satisfaction in the workplace that they have to seek an outlet in the modern religion of art. This was clearly understood by forerunners of the modernist movement like John Ruskin and William Morris, and even by early modernists like Walter Gropius, who commended Ruskin and Morris for seeking "to find a means of reuniting the world of art with the world of work" and deplored the "rise of the academies," which "spelt the gradual decay of the spontaneous traditional art that had permeated the life of the whole people." But Gropius went on to warn against "any recrudescence of the old dilettante handicraft spirit." "The division of labor," he thought, "can no more be abandoned than the machine itself. If the spread of machinery has, in fact, destroyed the old basic unity of a nation's production the cause lies neither in the machine nor in its logical consequence of functionally differentiated process of fabrication, but in the predominantly materialistic mentality of our age and the defective and unreal articulation of the individual to the demystify art and the cult of the artist. The same impulse informs most of the other schools and would-be schools of the sixties and seventies: systemic painting, optical art, process art, earth art, conceptualism. The "Minimalist Style," as John Perrault has remarked, is only one expression of a "larger tendency that might be termed the Minimalist Sensibility." This sensibility has shaped not only painting and sculpture but much of contemporary literature, music, and dance as well. Its hallmark is the deliberate depersonalization of the work of art, the elimination of craftsmanship, the elimination of the artist himself or at least a drastic reduction of his role as an interpreter of experience. The intentions attributed by Jasia Reickardt to the op artist Victor Vasarely can serve as a description of experimental art in general, in the age of the minimal self: "Vasarely is committed to the depersonalization of the artist's art—he feels that works of art should become available to all and discard their uniqueness."

The rapid succession of styles over the last twenty-five or thirty years can be seen as an attempt to find widely different

---

community." The Bauhaus, he added, "was anything but a school of arts and crafts, if only because a deliberate return to something of that kind would have meant simply putting back the clock."

The modernist movement in the arts has never questioned the reality of progress and the blessings of industrial technology. Even in the old days, when it still gave some thought to social issues, it aimed merely to get rid of predatory individualism and the "materialistic mentality" without also getting rid of the division of labor on which they rest. In the early days of modernism, architects like Gropius still claimed to build for the workers, but they took it for granted that they themselves knew best what the workers needed. Unable or unwilling to consider how the work process itself could be made more democratic and at the same time more artistic and playful, they put their hope in the illusion that advanced technology would eliminate drudgery altogether and free the workers for a life of leisure. Mechanization, said Gropius, would "abolish the individual's physical toil of providing himself with the necessities of existence in order that hand and brain may be let free for some higher order of activity."

In practice, this program comes down to control of production by the few—and of art as well—combined with a higher form of unemployment for the many, often with real unemployment as well.

means to the same end: the elimination of subjectivity. The minimalists sought a "minimum degree of self-expression," in Perreault's words, by doing away both with subject-matter and with subject—that is, with the controlling, ordering intelligence of the artist. What Barbara Rose called their "impersonality and self-effacing anonymity," which defined itself in opposition to the "self-indulgence of an unbridled subjectivity," led artists like Donald Judd, Carl Andre, Frank Stella, and Robert Morris to revive Duchamp's "ready-made" art, which confers artistic status on commonplace objects by the simple expedient of labeling them as art, or to work with mass-produced industrial materials (styrofoam, firebricks, florescent tubing), arranging them in rectangular or cubic forms deliberately divested of all metaphorical allusiveness and meaning. Pop art pursued the same objective, sometimes by using similar techniques, sometimes by making faithfully realistic representations of commonplace objects and images, themselves mass-produced, and by withholding any commentary, admiring or ironic, on their significance. Conceptual art, so-called, tried to eliminate the hand of the artist by planning every detail of the work before its execution, thereby "avoiding subjectivity," as Sol LeWitt explained. The idea behind a work, according to LeWitt, could serve as a kind of substitute for the artist, a "machine that makes the art." Some artists often spoken of as conceptualists welcomed completely random effects, on the other hand, as another way of reducing the artist's intervention in the creative process. Robert Barry, whose early work consisted of photographs recording the invisible movement of gases released into the air, explained, "I try not to manipulate reality. . . . What will happen, will happen. Let things be themselves." An "earth artist," Robert Smithson, spoke of his "earth maps" and "mirror displacements" of sunlight in much the same way, as an attempt not to manipulate the physical environment but to allow the viewer to sink into it and to experience a sense of timelessness and the "end of selfhood." The "existence of self," according to Smithson, is the root of the "expressive fallacy" in art. "As long as art is thought of as creation, it will be the same old story." Only an art that refuses to define itself in this way can bring about a state of mind, both in the viewer and in the artist himself, in which the "ego vanishes for a while."

Whether they embrace aleatory effects or go to the opposite extreme, planning everything down to the last detail, avant-garde artists since the mid-fifties have attempted to abolish interiority and to get beyond the "frenzy of individualism that has ravaged the West for centuries," as Jean Dubuffet once put it. In a lecture delivered in 1951, Dubuffet anticipated the main features of the minimalist sensibility by calling for the "complete liquidation of all the ways of thinking, whose sum constituted what has been called humanism and has been fundamental for our culture since the Renaissance." The artist should erase his personal signature from his work, Dubuffet insisted. If he paints a portrait, he should try to "relieve the portrait of all personal traits." A later generation has followed Dubuffet in his search for an impersonal art, though it has not shown much interest in his attempt to counter the Western tradition with the "values of savagery: instinct, passion, mood, violence, madness." Passion, violence, and madness are exactly what the new art seeks to escape. For this reason, it rejects primitivism, surrealism, and abstract expressionism with equal force. It seeks the antidote to romantic expressionism not in the "values of savagery" but in Islamic ornamentation or Zen Buddhism. Ad Reinhardt, another forerunner and theoretician of the expressionless art of the sixties and seventies, pointed out in 1957 that Islamic icons reduce figures to "formulas" instead of mistakenly trying to make them look like "everyday people"—the humanistic heresy that "came with the Renaissance." Reinhardt admired Buddhism for similar reasons, because of its "timelessness" and its willingness to go "over and over something until it disappears."*

Misleadingly identified by critics in the forties with the painters known as the New York School, Reinhardt had little patience with their subjectivity or their insistence on the importance of subject-matter. His own development took him in the opposite direction, foreshadowing the general revolt against abstract expressionism in the sixties. In the early fifties, he began to paint large, monochromatic canvases that deliberately defied interpretation or analysis of their "content." Whereas the New York painters—Mark Rothko, Clyfford Still, Barnett Newman, Willem de Kooning, Jackson Pollock—believed that "there is no such thing as good painting about nothing," in Rothko's words, Reinhardt, his biographer says, "made clear his opposition to any subject-matter." During the last ten years of his life, from 1957 to 1967, he painted nothing but compositions in black. "There is something wrong, irresponsible and mindless about color," he said in 1960, "something impossible to control. Control and rationality are part of any morality." His "Twelve Rules for a New Academy" (1957) set forth the principles of a new aesthetics of exclusion: no texture; no brushwork or calligraphy; no sketching or drawing ("everything . . . should be worked out in the mind beforehand");

---

*Others have found the same timelessness, eclecticism, and exteriority in the culture of modern Japan—reinterpreted, like so many other non-Western cultures, in the light of current preoccupations peculiar to the West. Donald Richie, an American who has lived for many years in Tokyo, author of books on Zen, Noh plays, and Japanese cinema, argues in a recent interview that Japan offers an antidote to the "falsehood" at the heart of Western culture, the belief in the self. "Japan is a country where you can't, in our sense, 'read' anything. . . . Appearance *is* the reality here. The ostensible is the real. . . . No matter how hard you look, the mask *is* the face. There is no notion of 'the real me,' a being somehow separate from the person. People here are what you can see, constructed from the outside. . . . The Japanese take what is well known and emblematic in the West and *own* it. And it's not a question of their being 'plastic' people, because everything here is 'plastic.' Of course, it is we who are living a falsehood in the West, with our absurd idea of 'the real me,' with our 'strong beliefs.' Oh, no! Plato and St. Paul really led us astray! And the Renaissance, of course. *Everything* here is presentational."

no forms, design, color, light, space, time, movement, size, or scale; "no object; no subject; no matter; no symbols, images, or signs; neither pleasure nor pain."

The Fusion of Self and Not-Self   The abstract expressionists revived a romantic conception of the artist as a man both of and against his time, who gives form to its innermost conflicts. They took the position that a violent age called for a violent art, as Adolph Gottlieb argued in 1943: "In times of violence, personal predilections for niceties of color and form seem irrelevant. . . . An art that glosses over or evades these feelings [of terror and fear, "experienced by many people throughout the world today"] is superficial and meaningless. That is why we insist on subject matter, a subject matter that embraces those feelings and permits them to be expressed." Mark Rothko, repudiating the label of "abstractionist," declared that he was "interested only in expressing basic human emotions" and in communicating them to others. The New York painters turned away from representational art not in order to shed subjectivity but precisely in order to explore its inner dimension. "In trying to probe beyond the ordinary and the known," said Arshile Gorky, "I create an inner infinity." The postromantic artist, on the other hand, seeks to cast off the burden of selfhood and to "survive only in the shallows," as Wylie Sypher puts it. A comparison of Reinhardt's black paintings with Rothko's seemingly similar series of paintings in black shows the difference between an art that, having renounced the hope of imposing the artist's order on the world, nevertheless clings to selfhood as the only source of continuity in an otherwise chaotic environment and an art, on the other hand, that renounces the very possibility of an interior life.

Rothko's black paintings [writes Eliza E. Rathbone] . . . continue to concern themselves with a humanly felt experience.

Even in those cases where Rothko seems closest to denying color, the most austere works are rich in felt permutations. . . . Reinhardt's choice of black was the ultimate step in an avoidance of any use of color—contaminated, as it were, by associations, or enlivened by vibrations of hue. . . . Reinhardt believed 'black is interesting not as a color but as a non-color and as the absence of color.' . . . Rothko's single idea is an experience that may expand in the response of the viewer, whereas Reinhardt's refutes any such exchange or interpretative possibilities. . . . All tension is resolved, eliminated.

Another critic, Nicolas Calas, has written more brutally of Reinhardt and his followers that Reinhardt's "last paintings have become icons for agnostics who prefer veils covering the obvious to signs indicating the presence of an enigma."

In its purest form, of course, the minimalist sensibility no longer finds it necessary even to disguise the obvious. It loudly proclaims the obvious, sticks to the surfaces of things, and refuses to look beneath them. "What you see is what you see," says Frank Stella of his work, most of which consists of paintings of stripes. "It is part of the vulgarism of our culture," according to the minimalist sculptor Carl Andre, to ask, "What does it mean?" A work of art means what it appears to mean and nothing more. According to Clement Greenberg, whose ideas influenced so many artists in the sixties and seventies, art should make no attempt to refer to anything outside itself. Painting is a form of communication only in the sense that it consists of "talk about line, color and form." "Let painting confine itself to the disposition pure and simple of color and line and not intrigue us by associations with things we can experience more authentically elsewhere." Paintings should insist on their two-dimensionality, in Greenberg's view, instead of struggling to create the illusion of a third dimension, the illusion of depth. A critic less friendly to minimalism, Peter Fuller, explains the "emergence of 'flatness' as a credo in the Fine Arts"—a development he deplores—as a response to a "certain urban experience which emphasizes the superficial rather than the physical, which denies interiority." In a modern city, Fuller argues, "one tends to live in a world of surfaces. . . . If you go to Times Square in Manhattan, or drive along almost any American highway, you see a constant stream of advertising images which . . . appear almost more real than reality itself. You have the impression of a physical world where things have been dematerialized or reduced to surfaces."

As Fuller points out, an art that concerns itself with surfaces not only denies the reality of inner experience but denies the reality of surrounding objects as well. It annihilates the subject and the object alike. In her survey of the art scene of the late sixties and early seventies, Lucy Lippard sees this "dematerialization of the art object" as a salutary fresh start, the production of art-objects having reached a "very important ending point" in Reinhardt's identical black-square paintings. Carl Andre advances a similar argument in explaining why he seeks flatness rather than "volume" in his sculpture, which consists of piles of bricks, boulders laid out in rows, or cinder blocks arranged in a single line on the floor. Our culture contains too many objects already, Andre argues, and now "requires significant blankness, . . . some *tabula rasa*, . . . some space that suggests there is a significant exhaustion. When signs occupy every surface, then there is no place for the new signs." Gregory Battcock, in his introduction to a collection of essays on minimalism, sees it as a virtue of recent sculpture, including Andre's, that it goes out of its way to emphasize its own impermanence. "We no longer subscribe to the sort of permanence [the absence of which is lamented by cultural reactionaries], and we prefer to make sure that our modern monuments *don't* last. In this way at least, there is less likelihood that they will obstruct the new of the future, as monuments of the past . . . seem to obstruct the new today." The "deemphasis on material aspects" of art, as Lippard puts it, leads to a repudiation of "uniqueness, permanence, decorative attractiveness." "The outcome of much of the 'conceptual' work of the past two years," two theorists of conceptualism announced in 1970—somewhat prematurely, as it turned out—"has been to carefully clear the air of objects."

The minimalist sensibility originates in a mood of retrenchment. It reflects a feeling that there is no place left to go in art and that modern society, like modern art, is approaching the end of the road. "I posit that there is no tomorrow," says Robert Smithson, "nothing but a gap, a yawning gap." With such a view of the future, it is no wonder that artists renounce the hope of permanence. Overwhelmed by a chaotic and overcrowded environment, by the profusion of images and objects, by an art-historical tradition perceived as overshadowing and oppressive, by the endless succession of styles and avant-gardes; overwhelmed also by the turmoil within, which answers to the turmoil without and threatens to engulf anyone who looks too deeply into the human interior (as it engulfed the abstract expressionists, whose careers ended all too often in alcoholism, despair, and suicide), the artists of the sixties and seventies felt the need to "narrow their operations," as Andre puts it, "to shut down a log of pointless art production [and] to concentrate on a line which was worthwhile." Andre told Peter Fuller that "minimalism means tightening up ship, for me." For others, it means withdrawal into a self-protective silence. Minimalism finds its most fitting expression, perhaps, in Adrian Piper's announcement that a refusal to exhibit any works at all constitutes a "protective measure."

> The work originally intended for this space has been withdrawn. The decision to withdraw has been taken as a protective

measure against the increasingly pervasive conditions of fear. Rather than submit the work to the deadly and poisoning influence of these conditions, I submit its absence as evidence of the inability of art expression to have meaningful existence under conditions other than those of peace, equality, truth, trust and freedom.

Notwithstanding its self-imposed ban on self-expression, late modernist art unmistakenly expresses the "numbed emotional aura" of the age, as Carter Ratcliff writes in an essay on Robert Morris: the "stasis or numbness induced by the refusal to risk the pains of self-revelation." When Morris posed for an exhibition poster in Nazi helmet and chains (1974) or exhibited a series of drawings and sculptures collectively entitled "In the Realm of the Carceral" (1979), he confirmed the suspicion that the boxes, mirrors, and labyrinths that figure in so much of his work, ostensibly devoid of any expressive content or anthropomorphic allusions, actually represent "human images imprisoned in catatonic reductivism." From the beginning, Ratcliff points out, Morris set himself up as an "administrator of confining possibilities." In 1961, he exhibited the "proto-typical minimalist work" (as Carl Andre later called it), a box containing a tape recording of the sounds of its own construction. "The thoroughness with which the recording is boxed in," Ratcliff writes, "joins with the isolated persistence of its sound to symbolize . . . an escape-proof situation." Morris's labyrinths and mirrors produce the same claustrophobic effect. They abolish the "residual distinction between images of self and of not-self"—the "differentiation upon which all subsequent distinctions are modeled"—and thus imply a world in which everything is interchangeable, in which "self-definition has been reduced to the play of self-image" and the inner self appears only as a "function of outward signs which are either beyond one's control or mutable at will." "It seems fair to extend the phrase, 'In the Realm of the Carceral,' . . . to his entire output." Morris's work reaches its logical culmination, according to Ratcliff, in drawings executed while he wore a blindfold or followed instructions issued by a blind man. The spectacle of a "visual artist equating sight with blindness, as if he didn't conceive the latter as a loss," conveys the "pain of deprivation . . . and also the deprivation of his inability to feel that pain."

Ratcliff argues that "of all the practitioners of reductive modernism, Morris is the only one who casts that pervasive anticreed in terms of imprisonment, of removal from a larger, richer reality." In doing so, however, Morris's work, it seems to me, makes explicit what is only implied by other work in the minimalist vein, that modernism in its most "advanced" form no longer explores new frontiers of sensibility, new dimensions of reality, but, on the contrary, undertakes a strategic retreat from reality and a regression into a realm, as Ratcliff says of Morris's imprisoned art, "in which mental and perceptual operations are so basic that they can't sustain any but the most undifferentiated emotions." It is hardly necessary to add that "advanced" art thus embodies the survival mentality characteristic of those faced with extreme situations: a radical reduction of the field of vision, a "socially approved solipsism," a refusal to feel anything, whether pain or pleasure. The artist has adopted the voice and eyes—or blindfold—of a survivor, not because he wishes to enter imaginatively into the survivor's ordeal but because he already experiences his own version of it in the collapse of the artistic traditions on which he depends, including the tradition of modernism itself. The survival of art, like the survival of everything else, has become problematical, not of course because art can have no "meaningful existence under conditions other than those of peace, equality, truth, trust and freedom," nor because mass communications have usurped the representational function of art, nor even because reality outstrips the artistic imagination, but because the weakening of the distinction between the self and its surroundings—a development faithfully recorded by modern art even in its refusal to become representational—makes the very concept of reality, together with the concept of the self, increasingly untenable.

The Strategic Retreat into Paranoia When Alain Robbe-Grillet issued his call for a "new novel," in essays written in the late fifties and early sixties, he defended a move beyond realism on the grounds that it would bring fiction even closer to "reality." One of those essays, in fact, bore the title "From Realism to Reality." Today it would be difficult to find an experimental writer who would admit so readily to an interest in reality. In turning away from the interior world, literature, like art, has also turned away from the world outside the self. Having renounced the "old myths of 'depth'," as Robbe-Grillet called them, novelists have discovered that everything else appears illusory as well. All that remains is literature itself—the only "subject" of advanced writing today, as art and art history present themselves as the only subjects for advanced artists.

Robbe-Grillet, not seeing the dead end to which it would quickly lead, gave the same advice to writers that Jean Dubuffet gave to painters: stick to the surface. Instead of "burrowing deeper and deeper to reach some ever more intimate strata, to unearth some fragment of a disconcerting secret," the writer should master the lesson of Samuel Beckett's plays, that "everything that is *is here*." There is no reality, in other words, beneath or beyond what meets the eye, no heaven or hell, no inner depths and no transcendent heights, no utopia in the future, nothing except this moment. Beckett's characters, according to Robbe-Grillet, "have no other quality than to be present." They live without a past and with no future except the certainty of death.

Their world—our world—lacks the consolation not only of religion but even of psychology. "Not only do we no longer consider the world as our own, our private property, designed according to our needs and readily domesticated, but we no longer even believe in its 'depth'. . . . The *surface* of things has ceased to be for us the mask of their heart, a sentiment that led to every kind of metaphysical transcendence."

So much has been said about the modern artist's "journey into the interior" that we tend to overlook the contrary movement, the flight from selfhood, that has characterized art and literature since the 1950s. In literature, the rejection of interior depth is easy to miss, because much of it continues to exploit the conventions of an earlier modernist tradition—the interior monologue, the glorification of the artist and the artistic sensibility—and to concern itself, moreover, in a way that recent painting and sculpture do not, with the depiction of inner states of mind. What Nathalie Sarraute said in 1950 can still be said, with an important qualification, of a great deal of the fiction published today: "A constantly rising tide has been flooding us with . . . novels in which a being devoid of outline, indefinable, intangible, and invisible, an anonymous 'I,' who is at once all and nothing, . . . has usurped the role of the hero [and at the same time reduced the other characters] to the status of visions, dreams, nightmares, illusions, reflections, quiddities or dependents of this all-powerful 'I.'" Today, however, this "I" is far from powerful; he no longer includes the whole of experience in himself, nor does he withdraw from the outside world in order to rediscover his own inner resources, to listen to the voice of memory, or to open himself to the buried depths of his unconscious being. "In contemporary American writing," Tanner observes, "the retreat into the self seems a more defensive, less assured, and less creative move." It takes the form of an "organized screening out" of experience, in the words of Susan Sontag's protagonist in *Death Kit*, or as Vonnegut's Tralfamadorians say, of a decision to "concentrate on the happy moments of life, and to ignore the unhappy ones." Instead of trying to sharpen his perceptions, the writer-hero now tries to blunt them or to apply them to problems that take him outside himself without leading him any closer to reality, as when Thomas Pynchon's Herbert Stencil tries to unravel an elaborate historical conspiracy rather than admit that "there is more accident to [life] than a man can ever admit to in a lifetime and stay sane."

In an earlier tradition of literary modernism, the interior monologue still presupposed an intelligible outer world. The writer stripped away surface illusions in the hope of finding the truth hidden beneath them, even if it took him on a journey into the heart of darkness. In recent fiction, the inner journey leads nowhere, neither to a fuller understanding of history as refracted through a single life nor even to a fuller understanding of the self. The more you dig the less you find, even though the activity of digging, pointless as it is, may be the only thing that keeps you alive. Pynchon's ambitious but intentionally inconclusive novels, like so much recent fiction, dramatize the difficulty of holding the self together in a world without meaning or coherent patterns, in which the search for patterns and connections turns back on itself in tightening solipsistic circles. His protagonists—Stencil, Tyrone Slothrop, Oedipa Maas—each attempt to unravel the secret history of modern times, relying, in the absence of more reliable data, on "dreams, psychic flashes, omens, cryptographies, drug-epistemologies, all dancing on a ground of terror, contradiction, absurdity." Surrogates—what else?—for the writer in search of a subject, these characters see "plots" everywhere and pursue their investigations with fanatical energy, only to see them dissolve into thin air. Each is gifted or cursed with the ability to imagine himself in a variety of situations and to adopt a variety of identities—a necessary defense against introspection, Pynchon implies, even though it leads only to pointless activity, never to any clear insights into the "ultimate Plot Which Has No Name." Stencil's impersonations and his habit of referring to himself in the third person serve "to keep Stencil in his place: that is, in the third person." "It would be simple," Pynchon says, ". . . to call him contemporary man in search of an identity. . . . The only trouble was that Stencil had all the identities he could cope with conveniently right at the moment: he was quite purely He Who Looks for V. [that is, for the "Big One, the century's master cabal"] (and whatever impersonations that might involve)." Without V., the mysterious woman whose trail promises to lead into the inner secrets of history but who becomes in the end a "remarkably scattered concept," Stencil would be left with an insupportable inner vacuum. Paranoia keeps him sane, as it keeps Slothrop and Oedipa Maas in a semblance of sanity. In *Gravity's Rainbow*, Pynchon describes Slothrop's fear of losing his mind. "If there is something comforting—religious, if you want—about paranoia, there is still also anti-paranoia, where nothing is connected to anything, a condition not many of us can bear for long." Paranoia serves as a substitute for religion because it provides the illusion that history obeys some inner principle of rationality, one that is hardly comforting but that is preferable, after all, to the terrors of "anti-paranoia."

The underlying kinship of madness and art is an old idea, but it has taken on a meaning in contemporary literature very different from the meaning it had in the nineteenth century or even in the early part of the twentieth century. For the romantic artist, it meant that the unsocialized self is the real self and that when art strips away the accumulated layers of civilized conventions and common sense, it reveals the authentic core of personality. For Pynchon, it means that art fabricates an illusion of meaning—a "plot" in which "everything fits"—without which the burden of selfhood becomes unbearable. Paranoia is the "discovery that *everything is connected.*" But Pynchon's own art—like contemporary art in general—simultaneously undercuts this "discovery." His "plots" lead nowhere. Stencil never finds V., any more than Oedipa uncovers the secret system of underground communication that "connects the world of thermodynamics to the world of information flow." Nor does Slothrop uncover the "mega-cartel" that operates the modern war machine. Instead, his pursuit of the sinister and elusive "Firm" only strengthens the suspicion that we live in a world where nothing is connected, a world without agency or control or discernible direction, in which "things only happen" and history consists of isolated " 'events,' newly created one moment to the next." Pynchon parodies the romantic quest for meaning and selfhood. His protagonists vaguely recall earlier American seekers—Henry Adams, Isabel Archer, Captain Ahab—only to call attention to the far more desperate predicament of the contemporary seeker after truth, who has begun to understand not only that history has no inner secrets but that the search for hidden meanings, even though it keeps him from disintegrating, may grow out of the same impulse to control and dominate, the same destructive will-to-power that has given rise to the war machine itself and to its most terrifying expression, the gravity-defying guided missile. If art shares with technology the irrational compulsion to escape from the natural law of entropy, as Pynchon implies, the only feasible alternative to paranoia seems to be a resigned acceptance of irreversible decline: the gravity that pulls everything irresistibly down into nothingness.

Modernism's Dead End   Pynchon first presents characters living in a state of siege, controlled and victimized by unseen powers and by the "culture of death" that pervades the modern world; then he denies even that they are victims of a conspiracy, at the same time implying that paranoia, the illusion of a conspiracy or "plot" that makes history intelligible, provides the only tenable basis of selfhood. It is hard to see how fiction could go much further in subverting the very possibility of selfhood or the possibility of fiction, for that matter. As John W. Aldridge observes in his study of the contemporary novel, the "breakdown of connection between the self and an engageable social milieu, the fading into each other of subjective perception and objective reality," induces "extreme feelings of anxiety and paranoia"— the feelings depicted over and over again in recent novels, paintings, and sculptures, even when these works claim not to depict any feelings at all. The "disappearance of all other modes of authoritative measure" outside the self, according to Aldridge, has left the artist "encapsulated in a bubble of self-awareness afloat in a void." Ad Reinhardt paints this void in the form of interchangeable black squares and rectangles. Pynchon uses a very different technique to achieve the same end. He fills the void with an overflowing abundance of historical scenes and allusions that have the same flavor of unreality, however, as the stage settings from old Hollywood extravaganzas and the "historical restorations" of old buildings on which Pynchon's own reconstructions of historical scenery—the British empire in decline, Southwest Africa under German rule, the siege of Malta in World War II, World War II in general—seem to be consciously modeled, as if to remind us, once again, that history consists of fictions and that historical characters represent so many "impersonations." The attempt to capture even a little of the flavor of history, if not the texture of historical experience, makes Pynchon stand out among serious contemporary novelists, most of whom long ago gave up any effort to convey a sense of our common life; but this evidence of a residual awareness of a world beyond the self only makes all the more poignant, therefore, his failure to find any meaning or substance in it beyond the familiar perception that all things run to ruin.

Notwithstanding its inventive brilliance, Pynchon's fiction finally leaves something of the same impression as Reinhardt's paintings, that of hiding the obvious behind a veil of obscurity. The same thing can be said of contemporary fiction as a whole, much of which, indeed, never even reaches Pynchon's level. There is no shortage of first-rate writers, but they satisfy themselves too easily with the repetition of stock themes that are no longer shocking or even mildly disconcerting: the impossibility of an objective understanding of events, the impossibility of moral discriminations in an age of atrocities, the impossibility of writing fiction in a world in which everything is possible and newspaper headlines outstrip the writer's imagination. The best writing today has the effect of removing history from the realm of moral judgments. It sees history as a system of total control that makes it as pointless to assign moral responsibility as to resist the flow of events. Whether the system of bureaucratic, conspiratorial, totalitarian control is conceived as the invisible government of corporate wealth or military-industrial collaboration, as an international system of espionage and counterespionage, as a criminal underworld, as an international traffic in drugs, as an international war machine that swallows up competing nationalisms and makes war not as a means of resolving national differences but as an end in itself, or as a far-flung stellar empire that has colonized the universe and rules it through invisible technologies of mind control and behavioral programming as well as through spectacular star wars, the underlying attitude stays the same. Since the individual appears to be programmed by external agencies—or perhaps by his own overheated imagination—he cannot be held accountable for his actions. Strictly speaking, he cannot act at all; his only hope of survival lies in flight, in emotional disengagement, in a refusal to take part in any form of collective life or even in the normal complications of everyday human interchange. The writer saves his skin by retreating into an imaginative world of his own but eventually loses the power even to distinguish this inner realm from the world around him.

If experimental fiction leads to the same solipsistic dead end as experimental art, the realistic novel hardly fares any better. The decay of authoritative sanctions against nonconformity and the emergence of a far more elusive system of social controls, which seeks not to enforce a moral consensus but to replace moral judgment with sociological surveys, public opinion polls, and therapeutic counseling, deprives the realistic novel of its satirical targets: hypocrisy, pomposity, misguided idealism, self-deception. When almost every institution has fallen into discredit, the novelist still moved by a sense of social injustice has to concern himself not so much with injustice itself—with the misuse of the power vested in persons of authority—as with the indignities suffered by their victims. If a contemporary writer tries to resurrect the conventions of social realism in order to marshal moral indignation on behalf of a specific group of victims, he usually finds it difficult to establish an independent basis for moral judgment outside the victim's own special experience. If he counts on a recital of the wrongs inflicted on women or blacks or mental patients or old people or Indians to awaken sympathy and compassion, he finds himself unable to explain what makes those indignities illuminating or representative. On the contrary, he usually ends up by taking the position that a long experience of victimization makes oppression unintelligible to outsiders. A white man can no more get inside the mind of a black man, he tells us, than a man can understand what it means to be a woman. The literature of social exposure and accusation, no less than the literature of solipsistic withdrawal, reduces experience to a form of programming that precludes imaginative identification. If people programmed as white Anglo-Saxon Protestants cannot enter vicariously into the lives of people programmed as blacks or Indians or Chicanos, experience loses the quality of contingency not only in the sense that cultural "conditioning" rules out freely initiated actions but in the sense that one person's experience no longer connects in any way with another's. The realistic novel thus arrives at the same conclusion reached earlier by the experimental novel: that, as Burroughs says, "there is no point in saying anything."

Modernism, a movement that once thrived on shock, has become as predictable in its negativism as Victorianism, at its worst, was predictable in its moral optimism and uplift. Formerly anti-academic, modernism has congealed into a new academicism, a set of critical dogmas as stifling to the creative imagination as the dogmas they replaced. Functionalism has hardened into formalism, the interior monologue into solipsism. The current notion of postmodernism expresses the growing consensus that the modernist impulse has exhausted itself but hazards no predictions about where our culture is going or what will take modernism's place. In the period of its creative vigor during the first half of this century, by contrast, the modernist movement did not hesitate to proclaim itself as the art of the future, even when it did not identify itself specifically with futurism. Not only did the early modernists believe that the twentieth century might still end more brightly than it had begun, they believed that modern art and literature, modern music, modern architecture conveyed intimations of a better future, indeed that it actively helped to create the future. Artists, according to Walter Gropius, were destined to become "architects of a new civilization." Modern art assigned to itself, even at its most negative and gloomy, nothing less than the task of humanizing the industrial order. Art would chasten the spirit of materialism and acquisitiveness and release unsuspected creative energies in society as a whole.

The fading of these hopes has destroyed the modern artist's confidence in his power even to understand history, let alone to change it. It has left him with the passive, spectatorial, and voyeuristic attitude toward history so characteristic of survivors. "We have learned to stand outside our history and watch it, without feeling too much," says a character in *Gravity's Rainbow*; and the same thing can be said of contemporary artists and writers. They can offer eminently plausible representations of the world around us; they can offer vivid accounts of a certain kind of inner experience; but what they seldom manage is to connect the two. When they try to revive the techniques of realism, they provide, at best, reports of reality that convey nothing of the experience of reality. When they reject realism, they convey the contemporary experience of helplessness, victimization, and paralyzing self-consciousness but without connecting it to any larger social life outside the self. The only experience they convey with any conviction, in short, is the experience of unreality—whether "paranoid" or "anti-paranoid" hardly matters.

V

The Inner History of Selfhood

Oneness and Separation The fundamental importance of the distinction between self and not-self—the source of all other distinctions, it has rightly been said— might suggest that it serves as the first principle of mental life, the axiomatic premise without which mental life cannot even begin. In fact, however, it is a distinction that is accepted, in the infancy of life, only with the greatest reluctance, after fierce inner struggles to deny it; and it remains the source of our existential uneasiness, as well as the source of our intellectual mastery of the world around us.

Mental life in the broadest sense—as opposed to the life of the mind—begins not with a clear understanding of the boundaries between the self and the surrounding world of objects but, on the contrary, with the blissful feeling of "oceanic" peace and union, as Freud called it. Selfhood

presents itself, at first, as a painful separation from the surrounding environment, and this original experience of overwhelming loss becomes the basis of all subsequent experiences of alienation, of historical myths of a lost golden age,
and of the myth of the primary fall from grace, which finds
its way into so many religions. Religion, like art at its best,
seeks precisely to restore the original sense of union with the
world, but only after first acknowledging the fact of alienation, conceived as original sin, as *hubris* followed by divine
retribution, as existential loneliness and separation, or in the
arts (especially in music, which conveys these experiences at
their deepest level), as the rhythm of tension and release,
conflict followed by inner peace.

What distinguishes contemporary art from the art of the
past, at least from the art of the nineteenth and early twentieth centuries, is the attempt to restore the illusion of oneness without any acknowledgment of an intervening experience of separation. Instead of trying to overcome this
separation and to win through to a hard-earned respite from
spiritual struggle, much of the literature and art of the present age, and much of our "advanced" music as well, simply
denies the fact of separation. It sees the surrounding world
as an extension of the self or the self as something programmed by outside forces. It imagines a world in which
everything is interchangeable, in which musical sounds, for
example, are experienced as equivalent to any other kind of
sound. It abolishes selfhood in favor of anonymity. As the
avant-garde composer Christian Wolff put it in 1958, in an
article called "New and Electronic Music," this new music
embodies a "concern for a kind of objectivity, almost anonymity—sound come into its own. The 'music' is a resultant
existing simply in the sounds we hear, given no impulse by
expressions of self or personality." Music, like the other arts,
thus frees itself from "artistry and taste." It excludes "personal expression, drama, psychology." In the same vein,

John Cage, acclaiming Edgar Varèse as the founder of the new music, notes that Varèse "fathered forth noise into twentieth-century music" but deplores his "mannerisms," which "stand out as [personal] signatures." Cage exhorts composers to "let sounds be just sounds" and to surrender any attempt to impose order on them, "giving up control so that sounds can be sounds."

The avant-garde artist advocates a suspension or abolition of conscious control, as we have seen, not in order to open himself to the promptings of his unconscious thoughts and desires but in order to extinguish every suggestion of his own personality. This is why Cage goes to such elaborate lengths—tossing coins, consulting the *I-Ching,* using a stop-watch to determine the time of performance—in his pursuit of random effects. He does everything he can to remove the possibility of an unconscious determination of his musical ideas. An inner agenda nevertheless underlies much of contemporary music, art, and literature, one that seeks to recapture a sense of psychic oneness without taking any account of the obstacles, psychic or material, that lie in the way of that oneness. The same thing can be said of many of the religious cults that flourish today, along with a profusion of therapeutic cults and movements, experiments in psychic healing, and self-proclaimed countercultures. They seek the shortest road to Nirvana. Whereas the world's great religions have always emphasized the obstacles to salvation, modern cults borrow selectively from earlier mystical traditions in the West, from ill-digested Oriental traditions, from mind-cure movements and various expressions of "New Thought," and from an assortment of therapies in order to promise immediate relief from the burden of selfhood. Instead of seeking to reconcile the ego and its environment, the new cults deny the very distinction between them. Though they claim to extend consciousness into areas hitherto unexplored, they promote a radical contraction of consciousness. They are founded on the need not to know, the psychic sources of which must now be considered in some detail.

Early Fantasies of Reunion   The pain of separation originates in the prolonged experience of helplessness in infancy, one of the circumstances that most clearly distinguishes human beings from other animals. The human infant is born too soon. He comes into the world utterly unable to provide for his biological needs and therefore completely dependent on those who take care of him, whom he endows in his unconscious imagination with superhuman powers. The experience of helplessness is all the more painful because it is preceded by the "oceanic" contentment of the womb, which we spend the rest of our lives trying to recapture. The trauma of separation begins at birth and recurs every time the child is left alone by its mother or feels the pangs of hunger, terrifying because they are experienced as a threat to its very existence. Because the "young child actually perishes when not adequately protected and taken care of," as Bettelheim observes, "there is no greater threat in life" than the threat of desertion. Much of the unconscious mental life of infants, it appears, and of children and adults, for that matter, consists of defenses against the fear of desertion and its attendant feelings of helplessness and inferiority.

In the womb, we lived in a state of blissful contentment, undisturbed even by desire, which, it could be argued, already presupposes the experience of frustration. The transposition of bodily needs into the register of desire, which seems so characteristic of humans and so foreign to other animals, begins only with birth, when we begin to experience instinctual demands not as needs inseparable from their fulfillment but as a clamorous assault on the lost equilibrium we seek to restore. The womb gave us an unforgettable experience of absolute oneness with the world—the basis of all our intimations of immortality and of the infinite, subsequently reformulated as religion. At the same time, it gave us a taste of complete self-sufficiency and omnipotence. Our original relation to the universe was both solipsistic and symbiotic. Self-contained and therefore independent of the need for any external source of care and nourishment, we nevertheless flowed indistinguishably into our surroundings.

Birth puts an end to the experience of narcissistic self-sufficiency and union with the world, even though most parents manage for a time to recreate something of the safety and contentment of the womb and even though the infant himself recreates the atmosphere of the womb, moreover, by going to sleep for long stretches at a time. The newborn experiences hunger and separation for the first time and senses its helpless, inferior, and dependent position in the world, so different from its former omnipotence. Repeated experiences of gratification and the expectation of their return gradually give the infant the inner confidence to tolerate hunger, discomfort, and emotional pain. But these same experiences also reinforce its awareness of separation and helplessness. They make it clear that the source of nourishment and gratification lies outside itself, the need or desire within. As the infant learns to distinguish itself from its surroundings, it understands the extent of its dependence on those who take care of it. It begins to understand that its own wishes do not control the world. The illusion of omnipotence, tenable as long as need and gratification were perceived as emanating from the same source, gives way to a painful sense of dependence on external sources of gratification. The separation of birth, in short, is followed by further experiences of separation, which underlie both the discontents to which humans are uniquely susceptible and the creativity to which they alone are able to rise. Premature birth and prolonged dependence are the dominant facts of human psychology.

"Before birth," writes Béla Grunberger in his study of narcissism, the infant "lived in a steady stable state of bliss," but his expulsion from the womb confronts him with "over-whelming changes that are continually deluging him and destroying his equilibrium." "Assailed by excitation," he seeks to restore the lost illusion of self-sufficiency, for example, by refusing to acknowledge in his unconscious fantasies what experience forces him to acknowledge in his conscious thoughts. Grandiose fantasies of omnipotence, as Géza Ró-heim once wrote, represent an "attempt to find the way back" to a primal sense of union with the outer world. Only a complete disavowal of experience, however, can protect such fantasies against the reality of helplessness and dependence; and a schizophrenic withdrawal from reality not only incapacitates a person for ordinary life but brings a new set of terrors all its own.

Another kind of unconscious fantasy seeks to allay frustration and the fear of separation not by denying the fact of dependence but by refusing to recognize that the adults on whom the child depends can frustrate as well as gratify his desires. The child idealizes his mother (and later his father as well) as a source of unending, unambiguous gratification. In doing so, he also disavows his own desire to injure those who frustrate or disappoint him. Unfortunately, overideali-zation of objects often gives way, when the idealized parents continue to interfere with the child's pleasure, to a "catastrophic devaluation of the object," as Otto Kernberg puts it. In the same way, grandiose fantasies of omnipotence, hard to sustain in the face of frustration and dependence, can alternate with feelings of complete insignificance and abject inferiority.

In another kind of defense, the child's fantasies dissociate the frustrating from the pleasure-giving aspects of the adults who take care of him. In his fantasies, the child refuses to admit that pleasure and frustration come from the same source. Thus he invents idealized images of the breast, side by side with images of omnipotent, threatening, and destructive maternal or paternal authority: a devouring vagina, a castrating penis or breast. The child needs not only the mother's nourishment but the unconditional, enveloping security with which it is associated. It is because the biological need for nourishment is suffused with desire that the infant's greed is insatiable; even the temporary absence of the mother gives rise to frustration and to feelings of rage. According to Melanie Klein and her followers, the young child envies the mother's power to give and withhold life and projects this resentment in the form of threatening figures, images of the "child's own hate, increased by being in the parents' power." But the attempt to restore a euphoric sense of well-being by splitting images associated with frustration from gratifying images arouses painful fears of persecution and, indeed, even spoils the capacity for pleasure and enjoyment. "Greed, envy, and persecutory anxiety, which are bound up with each other, inevitably increase each other." It is not for nothing that envy ranks among the seven deadly sins. Klein went so far as to suggest that "it is unconsciously felt to be the greatest sin of all, because it spoils and harms the good object which is the source of life." The associations between envy and the fear of retaliation are expressed, in another religious tradition, in the Greek concept of *hubris*, usually translated as pride but better understood as a form of envy and greed, rooted in the infant's total dependence on its caretakers and its overwhelming need for the warmth and nourishment they provide. "*Hubris* grasps at more," according to Gilbert Murray, "bursts bounds and breaks the order: it is followed by *Dike*, Justice, which reestablishes them." The Greek idea of justice, which punishes *hubris*, expresses more or less what is expressed by the psychoanalytic concept of the superego. The superego represents internalized fear of punishment, in which aggressive impulses are redirected against the ego. The superego—the primitive, punitive part of the superego, anyway—represents not so much internalized social constraints as the fear of retaliation, called up by powerful impulses to destroy the very source of life.

Gender Differences and the "Tragedy of Lost Illusions"
Early fantasies of reunion center on the incorporation of external goods on which the infant depends, in other words on oral desires associated with experiences of sucking, biting, and swallowing. As the child begins to discover other parts of his body, oral fantasies come to be overlaid with anal and genital fantasies, in which, for example, the child repossesses the mother and thus restores the sense of primal oneness through the agency of his phallus.* When oral fantasies

---

*I use the masculine pronoun, here and throughout this essay, trusting to the context to indicate when it is used as a generic pronoun and when it refers to males alone. This long-established usage seems preferable to the clumsy "he or she," to such recent coinages as "he/she" and "s/he," or to the use of the feminine pronoun as a generic—ideologically correct but intellectually useless expressions that serve only to announce a commitment, often a token commitment, to sexual equality. It goes without saying that sexual equality in itself remains an eminently desirable objective: one that is not likely to be achieved, however, by a freer use of feminine pronouns.

In the present context, where the masculine pronoun is used once again in its generic sense, I admit that it may give rise to genuine confusion. The assertion that little girls dream, like little boys, of becoming a husband to their mothers seems to contradict common sense. But this state of affairs no longer seems so farfetched when we remind ourselves that the phallus, as Juliet Mitchell explains in *Psychoanalysis and Feminism*, "is not identical with the actual penis, for it is what it signifies that is important." What it signifies, of course, is potency. In the child's unconscious fantasy-life, it appears to confer on its possessor undivided ownership of the mother and at the same time a certain independence from her. For girls as well as boys, it assures possession of the mother without the helpless dependence of infancy.

Annie Reich describes a number of women, whose mothers had treated them as substitutes for an absent or unsatisfactory husband, who reported fantasies traceable to the childhood wish to serve as the mother's missing phallus. One woman, having enjoyed some success as an actress, spoke of the euphoria of being

break down in the face of experience (though of course they never fully die, living on in the subterranean reaches of the mind), the child has to find new forms of wish-fulfillment, only to discover, in the course of time, that his genital equipment is unequal to the task assigned to it by his unconscious desires. At every point in his development, disappointment and frustration impel the child into a new stage of self-awareness. The failure of oral fantasies to sustain the illusion of self-sufficiency causes the child to take a livelier interest in the rest of his body, while the conflicts that grow out of the fantasy of sexual intercourse with the mother precipitate the Oedipus complex—an event that has to be understood, accordingly, as another variation on the underlying themes of separation, dependence, inferiority, and reunion.

Psychoanalytic theory since Freud has based its greatest advances on Freud's discovery of a more deeply buried, "Minoan-Mycenean" layer of psychic conflict underlying the Oedipal conflicts that had dominated earlier psychoanalytic speculation and on the suggestion—thrown out at the end of *The Ego and the Id* and developed at greater length in *Inhibitions, Symptoms, and Anxiety*—that "anxiety due to separation from the protecting mother" is the original source of mental conflict. It now appears that it is the child's growing awareness of the disparity between his wish for sexual reunion with the mother and the impossibility of

---

admired by an audience as an "intense excitement experienced over the entire body surface and a sensation of standing out, erect, with her whole body. Obviously," Reich adds, "she felt like a phallus with her whole body." Another said that "during intercourse she felt as though she were the man with the phallus-like body making love to her self, the girl." Joyce McDougall calls attention to the following passage in Violette Leduc's novel, *Thérèse et Isabelle*, which expresses very clearly the little girl's fantasy of serving as her mother's sexual partner. "So mother is getting married! . . . I used to say I was her little fiancé and she would smile . . . Now I shall never be her man. . . . She has smashed everything; she has all she needs—a married women. She has put a man between us. Yet we were sufficient to each other; I was always warm in her bed. . . . She wants a daughter and a husband. My mother is a greedy woman."

carrying it out that precipitates the Oedipus complex. As poets, philosophers, and theologians have often pointed out, human beings are cursed with imaginative powers that outrun their bodily capacities. Psychoanalytic theory restates this insight when it insists that the precocity of the child's mental and emotional development, the precocity of his sexual fantasies in comparison to his physical capacities, holds the key not just to the Oedipus complex but to much of his later development as well. The Oedipus complex confronts the child once again with the "discrepancy between his incestuous wishes," in the words of Janine Chasseguet-Smirgel, "and his ability to satisfy them, a discrepancy which springs from man's biological chronology. . . . Helplessness is at the heart of the problem." Freud himself noted that the "early efflorescence of infantile sexuality" is "doomed to extinction" not only because the father forbids sexual intercourse with the mother but because the child's wishes are "incompatible" with the "inadequate stage of [physical] development the child has reached." According to a number of recent analysts, these observations point to the need to reinterpret other elements in Freudian theory. Penis envy, for example, should be interpreted quite literally as a wish to appropriate the father's penis, so much better suited to its purpose than the child's. It occurs in boys as well as girls and signifies not a shocking recognition of the biological and social inferiority of women, as Freud thought, but an intensified awareness on the part of the child that his grandiose fantasies of sexual union with the mother, constructed in the first place as a defense against feelings of helplessness, are completely unrealistic after all and that the child continues to occupy a dependent, inferior position in relation to his parents. Penis envy embodies the "tragedy of lost illusions," as Chasseguet-Smirgel puts it. She goes on to argue that because we can never completely reconcile ourselves to the abandonment of those illusions, we continue to elaborate fantasies that deny any knowledge of sexual differences. Freud's own theory of sexual monism, she points out, itself incorporates elements of such a fantasy by insisting that children have no knowledge of the vagina, although in fact that knowledge is repressed, according to Chasseguet-Smirgel, only when it becomes evident to the child that he himself (or she herself) lacks a phallus capable of entering it and of thereby recapturing the primal state of oneness.

The well-known fantasy of the phallic mother, first analyzed in an essay by Ernest Jones, serves the same need. By equipping the mother with a phallus, the child unconsciously denies the knowledge that she needs that of her husband. The child denies, that is, that "what he wishes were true will never be true," as Joyce McDougall puts it: "that the secret of sexual desire lies in the mother's missing penis; that only the father's penis will ever complete her genital, and that he [himself] will be forever alienated from his primary sexual desire and his unfulfilled narcissistic wishes." The fantasy of the phallic mother announces, in effect: "It is not true [that] the sexes are different; my father is of no importance either to me or my mother. I have nothing to fear from him and besides my mother only loves me."

Origins of the Superego   A different kind of defense against the same sense of inadequacy is the devaluation of feminine characteristics. In order to deny the extent of his continuing need for the mother and everything she represents, the Oedipal child may withdraw libidinal investment from maternal organs and qualities or "project her power on to the father and his penis," as Chasseguet-Smirgel puts it. Hyper-masculinity, raised to a cultural norm, serves not only as a personal defense against feelings of helplessness and dependence but as a collective fantasy that expresses deeply rooted attitudes characteristic of pioneering societies and of industrial societies in general, which disavow their dependence on nature (our collective mother) and attempt through the technological conquest of nature to make themselves self-sufficient. Men (and women too, of course) who feel an overwhelming need to deny dependence on maternal support, and later to deny any form of dependence at all, become pioneers rather than explorers, in Melanie Klein's resonant terminology—exploiters of nature rather than loving cultivators of nature.

Because psychoanalysis has so often been accused of perpetuating cultural prejudices against women, it is important to note that the psychoanalytic tradition, taken as a whole, gives little comfort to the notion that contempt for women is ever natural in adults or that men achieve autonomy only by extinguishing every trace of femininity in themselves. The development of psychoanalytic theory and practice since Freud tends to confirm the view, expressed in Freud's very last paper, that a fear of dependence and passivity in men often becomes the "bedrock" of therapeutic failure in psychoanalysis. "At no other point in one's analytic work," Freud wrote, "does one suffer more from an oppressive feeling that all one's repeated efforts have been in vain, and from a suspicion that one has been 'preaching to the winds,' than . . . when one is seeking to convince a man that a passive attitude . . . does not always signify castration and that it is indispensable in many relationships in life." Later analysts have gone even further. Contempt for women, according to Chasseguet-Smirgel, "reveals personal uncertainty about one's own self-worth." "Underlying this scorn," she adds, "one always finds a powerful maternal imago, envied and terrifying."

These observations point to the more general conclusion that feelings of dependence and inferiority not only help to precipitate the Oedipus complex but play an important part in its resolution. Acknowledgment of such feelings and of the continuing need for mothers makes it possible to surrender the dream of sexual union with the mother without denying the emotional need behind it. The psychoanalytic tradition has been accused of holding up a relentlessly patriarchal model of psychological development, according to which a proper resolution of the Oedipus complex depends on total separation from the mother, fear of castration, and submission to the patriarchal reality of sexual repression and alienated labor, internalized in the form of a punishing superego. But in Freud's later writings, it is the ego, not the superego, that serves as the "representative of the external world, of reality," while the superego—the "heir of the Oedipus complex," as Freud called it in *The Ego and the Id* —"stands in contrast to it as the representative of the internal world, of the id." It is true that the superego consists of parental introjects; but Freud's later work and the work of his followers make it clear that these internalized images of parental authority bear little resemblance to the actual figures of the parents. For this reason, the superego cannot be understood to serve as the representative of established morality, as Freud had once assumed and as many commentators on Freud continue to assume (especially those who see psychoanalysis as the last bastion of patriarchal morality or, on the other hand, as the basis of a sweeping critique of patriarchal morality). On the contrary, the superego consists of the individual's own aggressive impulses, directed initially against his parents or parental surrogates, projected onto them, reinternalized as aggressive and domineering images of authority, and finally redirected in this form against the ego. Images of destructive and punitive parental authority originate not in the parents' actual prohibitions but in the unconscious rage of infancy, which arouses unbearable anxiety and therefore has to be redirected against the self. The more the individual "checks his aggressiveness" toward others, according to Freud, the more his superego's "inclination to aggressiveness against his ego" exposes the ego to a relentless flood of condemnation.*

If the superego merely carried out the demands of reality in censoring antisocial impulses, it would be hard to understand why it condemns the ego so unfairly, with such "extraordinary harshness and severity" and with so little regard either for the practical requirements of social conformity or for the individual's actual inclination to flout them. Freud's curious statement that the superego represents a "pure culture of the death instinct" seems to imply an archaic origin of the superego and even to qualify the view that it represents the heir of the Oedipus complex. The same discoveries that led Freud for the first time to give formal expression to the theory of the Oedipus complex seem to diminish the decisive and determining importance he assigned to it. They indicate that the Oedipus complex has to be regarded as the culmination of a long series of earlier conflicts that help to predetermine its outcome. Instead of saying that the Oedipus complex bequeaths to the child a punitive superego based on the fear of castration, we might say that castration anxiety itself is merely a later form of separation anxiety, that the archaic and vindictive superego derives from the fear of maternal retaliation, and that, if anything, the Oedipal experience tempers the punitive superego of infancy by adding to it a more impersonal principle of authority, one that is more "independent of its emotional origins," as Freud

*The terminology associated with Freud's structural theory of the mind carries with it the risk that those who use it begin to think of the id, ego, and superego —and now of narcissism and the ego ideal as well—as actual entities, each with a personality and a mind of its own. It is therefore necessary to remind ourselves that these terms refer to different forms of mental activity: desire, self-censorship, self-defense, and so on. The danger of reifying these mental "agencies" should not prevent us from seeing why they are so useful. They call attention to the way in which the mind is divided against itself. The objection that they lead us to confuse mental activities with actual things, well taken in itself, often carries with it a deeper, unspoken objection to the very hypothesis of unconscious mental conflict and suffering. It carries with it, that is, a wish to see the mind as whole and happy.

puts it, more inclined to appeal to universal ethical norms, and somewhat less likely, therefore, to associate itself with unconscious fantasies of persecution. We might speculate further that the Oedipal superego—the "loving and beloved superego," as Roy Schafer calls it—rests as much on the wish to make amends as on the fear of reprisals, though even here it is apparent that feelings of gratitude—the most important emotional basis of what is called conscience—first arise in connection with the mother.

Psychoanalytic theory leads, on the whole, to the conclusion that normal psychological development cannot be understood simply as the substitution of patriarchal authority for the pleasure principle or as an absolute separation from the mother. It leads to the conclusion, in other words, that a satisfactory resolution of the Oedipus complex accepts the father without betraying the mother. Increasingly elaborate analysis of early defenses against the fear and pain of separation makes it clear that these defenses, Oedipal and pre-Oedipal alike, share a common impulse. They all seek to dissolve the tension between the desire for union and the fact of separation, either by imagining an ecstatic and painless reunion with the mother or, on the other hand, by imagining a state of complete self-sufficiency and by denying any need for external objects at all. The first line of defense encourages a regressive symbiosis; the second, solipsistic illusions of omnipotence. Neither solves the problem of separation; instead, both deny its existence. The best hope of emotional maturity, then—or if this phrase seems to imply too sanguine an estimate of the prospects for such an outcome or too sharp a distinction between pathology and normal development, the best hope of ordinary unhappiness, as opposed to crippling mental torment—appears to lie in a creative tension between separation and union, individuation and dependence. It lies in a recognition of one's need for and dependence on people who nevertheless remain separate from oneself and refuse to submit to one's whims. It entails a rejection of the illusion that "I exist only through those who are nothing apart from the being they have through me," as Jean Genet once put it, in a statement that manages to combine symbiotic and solipsistic conceptions of the self in a single sentence.

The Ego Ideal   The significance of the Oedipus complex, then, lies in its destruction of the infantile illusion of omnipotence. The narcissistic longing behind this illusion lives on, however, in the form of the "ego ideal," which Freud once referred to as the heir of primary narcissism. Later analysts have based a growing body of theory on his insight. But whereas Freud himself proceeded to ignore it and to use "superego" and "ego ideal" as interchangeable terms, many analysts now argue that the ego ideal has distinctive attributes of its own and a distinctive history. Descriptions of this agency vary so widely, however, that they make it difficult, at first, to find any agreement about its properties or development. In general, the ego ideal, like the superego, consists of internalized representations of parental authority; but the superego internalizes the forbidding aspect of that authority, whereas the ego ideal holds up admired, idealized images of parents and other authorities as a model to which the ego should aspire. Because the ego ideal helps to sublimate libidinal impulses into a desire to live up to the example of parents and teachers or a striving for ethical perfection, some analysts see it as a more highly developed and mature formation than the superego, better integrated and closer to reality. According to Ernest Jones, the ego ideal is conscious, the superego unconscious. According to Erik Erikson, the "sense of ego identity" rests on the "accrued experience of the ego's ability to integrate" childhood identifications with the "vicissitudes of the libido, with the aptitudes developed out of endowment, and with the opportunities offered in social roles."

Other observers, however, insist that the ego ideal is more primitive than the superego, both in its origins and in its addiction to magical thinking and "hallucinatory wish-fulfillment." According to Annie Reich, "The formation of the superego is based upon acceptance of reality," whereas the ego ideal grows out of a "denial of the ego's, as well as of the parents', limitations" and on a desire "to regain infantile omnipotence by identifying with the idealized parents." John M. Murray points out that "anxiety related to the loss of the ego ideal [that is, to the loss of one's good opinion of oneself] . . . is clearly related to the primary fear of the loss of mother." He and many others have called attention to the regressive features of the ego ideal: its grandiose fantasies of omnipotence, its sense of "narcissistic entitlement," its reversion to oral patterns of dependency, its hope for "return to the lost Shangri-La with the childhood mother." Freud's own formulation—the heir of primary narcissism—suggests a similar interpretation.

In view of the lack of agreement about its properties and development, the ego ideal might appear to be a nebulous and useless concept. But if we pursue the problem a little farther, we see that the difficulty in characterizing the ego ideal indicates precisely why the concept is indispensable. It calls attention to the links between the highest and lowest forms of mental life, between the most exalted aspirations for spiritual transcendence and the earliest illusions of omnipotence and self-sufficiency. It shows how the impulse to restore those illusions expresses itself in regressive fantasies of a magical symbiosis with the world or of absolute self-sufficiency but also in a loving exploration of the world through art, playful scientific curiosity, and the activities of nurture and cultivation. The ego ideal is hard to define because, more than any other psychoanalytic concept, it catches the contradictory quality of unconscious mental life.

In the words of Samuel Novey, it refers to "that particular segment of introjected objects whose functional operation has to do with proposed standards of thoughts, feeling, and conduct acquired later than the Oedipal superego, but having its roots in the early pregenital narcissistic operations against [separation] anxiety." Simultaneously advanced and regressive,

> the ego-ideal spans an orbit that extends from primary narcissism to the 'categorical imperative,' from the most primitive form of psychic life to the highest level of man's achievements. Whatever these achievements might be, they emerge from the paradox of never attaining the sought-after fulfillment or satiation, on the one hand, and of their never-ceasing pursuit, on the other. This search extends into the limitless future that blends into eternity. Thus, the fright of the finity of time, of death itself, is rendered non-existent, as it once had been in the state of primary narcissism.
>
> Potentially, the ego-ideal transcends castration anxiety, thus propelling man toward incredible feats of creativity, heroism, sacrifice, and selflessness. One dies for one's ego-ideal rather than let it die. It is the most uncompromising influence on the conduct of the mature individual.

The concept of the ego ideal thus helps to remind us that man belongs to the natural world but has the capacity to transcend it and, moreover, that the capacity for critical self-reflection, adherence to the most demanding standards of conduct, and moral heroism is itself rooted in the biological side of man's nature: in the fear of death, the sense of helplessness and inferiority, and the longing to reestablish a sense of primal unity with the natural order of things.

Partial descriptions of the ego ideal, in the psychoanalytic literature, result from a failure to grasp its contradictory qualities and to entertain both sides of the contradiction at the same time. Some writers idealize the ego ideal, seeing only its mature and mitigating features. Others see only its regressive side. Seeking reunion with the mother yet constantly thwarted in this search, the ego ideal can become the basis of later identifications founded on a loving acceptance of the world rather than on the fear of punishment. On the other hand, it can also encourage highly regressive solutions to the problem of separation. "In order to be again united with the ego," writes Chasseguet-Smirgel in the definitive study of this subject, the ego ideal "can choose either the shortest route, the most regressive one, or the evolutionary one." Desire feeds on obstacles, and frustration may impel the child into the Oedipus complex, in which the desire for symbiosis associates itself with the newly conceived fantasy (itself destined for dissolution) of incestuous reunion with the mother. On the other hand, "If the mother has deceived her son by making him believe that with his (pregenital) infantile sexuality he is a perfect partner for her, . . . his ego ideal, instead of cathecting a genital father and his penis, remains attached to a pregenital model." Rather than accept the evidence of our dependence and helplessness, even when this evidence becomes almost impossible to ignore, we cling as long as possible to the illusion of self-sufficiency. Even the fear of castration is preferable to an acknowledgment of our own insignificance. According to Grunberger, the fantasy of forbidden incest serves to prevent or postpone the recognition that our own inadequacy, not the paternal threat of castration, prevents us from rejoining our mother in a euphoric approximation of the womb. Fear is easier to bear than a feeling of impotence. Here again, psychoanalytic theory finds confirmation in the observations of poets and philosophers. "If each of us were to confess his most secret desire," writes the essayist E. M. Cioran, "the one that inspires all his deeds and designs, he would say, 'I want to be praised.' Yet none will bring himself to confess, for it is less dishonorable to commit a crime than to announce such a pitiful and humiliating weakness arising from a sense of loneliness and insecurity, a feeling that afflicts both the fortunate and the unfortunate, with equal intensity."

Narcissism as Opposed to Ordinary Egoism If the search for self-esteem and lost perfection leads to contradictory results, this reflects the contradictory quality of narcissism itself, an overwhelming desire to live in a state of ecstatic freedom from desire. Grunberger argues in his study of narcissism that because it is rooted in experiences that antedate the awareness of separation, narcissism should be distinguished both from libidinal instincts and from the instinct of self-preservation and understood as a separate "system" altogether independent of the instinctual desire for bodily gratification. Narcissism evinces a certain indifference to bodily desires. It wishes "to exist on this earth free from both desire and body." For this reason, Grunberger rejects Freud's definition of narcissism as a libidinal counterpart of the self-preservative instinct. Narcissism precedes the emergence of the ego, which originates in an awareness of individuation. In its original form, narcissism is oblivious to the self's separation from its surroundings, while in its later form, it seeks always to annul awareness of separation. It has only "contempt," Grunberger writes, for the "puny and timorous" ego. In its ceaseless search for perfect equilibrium and union with its surroundings, it resembles not so much a libidinal investment of the ego as that elusive "Nirvana principle" Freud tried to capture in his dubious formulation of the death instinct. Except that it is not an instinct and that it seeks not death but everlasting life, narcissism conforms quite closely to Freud's description of a longing for the complete cessation of tension, which seems to operate independently of the pleasure principle ("beyond the pleasure principle") and follows a "backward path that leads to complete satisfaction." Narcissism longs for the absence of longing, the absolute peace upheld as the highest state of spiritual perfection in so many mystical traditions and also upheld, as we have seen, in so much contemporary art and literature. It seeks to free itself from the prison of the body, not because it seeks death—though it can lead people to commit suicide—but because it has no conception of death and regards the bodily ego as a lower form of life, besieged by the clamorous demands of the flesh. It follows a "backward path" to a lost paradise, but it can also become the basis of a mature idealism so exalted that it will sacrifice bodily comfort for a cause, even life itself, preferring death to dishonor.

Its scorn for the body's demands and for the ego that has to respond to them, while at the same time holding them in check, distinguishes narcissism from ordinary egoism or from the survival instinct. Having no understanding of death, narcissism is indifferent to the issue of survival.* The awareness of death and the determination to stay alive presuppose an awareness of objects distinct from the self. The

---

*In clinical practice, according to Grunberger, "one often finds that an individual's pursuit of a highly valued narcissistic ideal outweighs all his ego interests, a situation that can, through a systematic series of acts that are hostile to the ego, ultimately result in its total suppression (by death)." Here is another reason to reject the first of the two conceptualizations of narcissism offered by Freud: libidinal investment of the ego, a turning away from an erotic interest in others. In his essay, "On Narcissism," and in later writings, Freud offered two quite different ways of thinking about narcissism, as Jean Laplanche points out, and it was the second that eventually won out. This second thesis, in Laplanche's words, "would reconstitute the evolution of the human psyche starting from a kind of *hypothetical initial state in which the organism would form a closed unit* in relation to its surroundings. This state would not be defined by a cathexis of the ego, since it would be prior even to the differentiation of an ego, but by a kind of stagnation . . . in a biological unit conceived of as not having any objects [italics in the original]." Sleep, then, is the prototypical narcissistic state, not excessive self-admiration or a lack of interest in others (except insofar as this too is implied by sleep). As for dreams, they arise, according to Grunberger, not only out of a conflict between forbidden wishes and the censoring superego but out of an even deeper conflict between the narcissistic longing for equilibrium and imperious instinctual desires, which disturb this equilibrium. As Freud pointed out, dreams not only serve as wish-fulfillments, they also preserve sleep.

ego's separate existence and its helpless dependence for life on caretakers outside itself underlie the fear of mortality. Since narcissism does not acknowledge the separate existence of the self, as distinguished from the bodily ego, it has no fear of death. Narcissus drowns in his own reflection, never understanding that it is a reflection. He mistakes his own image for someone else and seeks to embrace it without regard to his safety. The point of the story is not that Narcissus falls in love with himself, but, since he fails to recognize his own reflection, that he lacks any conception of the difference between himself and his surroundings. "What held him enchanted over the water's surface," Grunberger writes, "—beyond his own face—was a return to the amniotic fluid, profound narcissistic regression."

A study of narcissism confirms the observation that the distinction between the self and the not-self is the basis of all other distinctions, including the distinction between life and death. We have already seen that the narcissistic longing for fusion leads to a denial of both sexual and generational differences. The infant's narcissism tells him that he is a perfect match for his mother, whom he equips, moreover, with a phallus of her own, in order to deny her need for a husband. An equivalent fantasy in little girls—who also dream, for that matter, of impregnating the mother—takes the form of a wish to become pregnant without any paternal intervention. In both sexes, narcissism rejects the Oedipal solution to the problem of separation, in which the child renounces the fantasy of an immediate reunion with the mother in the hope of growing up into adult roles that promise something of the same potency once associated with the infantile illusion of self-sufficiency. In narcissistic fantasies of reunion, which deny the need for fathers, "non-recognition of the difference between generations," according to Chasseguet-Smirgel, "is intimately connected to the non-recognition of the difference between the sexes." Narcissism lives by illusions, at least in its more regressive forms. "Non-recognition" defines its characteristic stance toward its surroundings. Yet it can also serve as the basis of an ego ideal that seeks to restore the sense of wholeness not through illusions of omnipotence and self-sufficiency but precisely through a disinterested pursuit of truth.

Childhood in a Narcissistic Culture If the designation of contemporary culture as a culture of narcissism has any merit, it is because that culture tends to favor regressive solutions instead of "evolutionary" solutions, as Chasseguet-Smirgel calls them, to the problem of separation. Three lines of social and cultural development stand out as particularly important in the encouragement of a narcissistic orientation to experience: the emergence of the egalitarian family, so-called; the child's increasing exposure to other socializing agencies besides the family; and the general effect of modern mass culture in breaking down distinctions between illusions and reality.

The modern family is the product of egalitarian ideology, consumer capitalism, and therapeutic intervention. In the nineteenth century, a combination of philanthropists, educators, and social reformers began to uphold bourgeois domesticity as a corrective both to fashionable dissipation and to the "demoralization" of the lower classes. From the beginning, the "helping professions" sided with the weaker members of the family against patriarchal authority. They played off the housewife against her husband and tried to make women the arbiters of domestic morality. They championed the rights of children, condemning the arbitrary power parents allegedly exercised over their offspring and questioning their competence as well. One result of their efforts was to subject the relations between parents and children to the supervision of the state, as executed by the schools, the social work agencies, and the juvenile court. A second result was to alter the balance of forces within the family. Men lost much of their authority over children to their wives, while children gained a certain independence from both parents, not only because other authorities asserted jurisdiction over childhood but because parents lost confidence in the old rules of child-rearing and hesitated to assert their own claims in the face of professional expertise.

In the twentieth century, the advertising industry further weakened parental authority by glorifying youth. Advertising, like the service professions, insisted that parents owed their children the best of everything while insisting that they had only a rudimentary understanding of children's needs. Advertising also promoted the "emancipation" of women from household drudgery and Puritanical sexual repression. In general, the culture of consumption promoted the idea that women and children should have equal access, as consumers, to an ever-increasing abundance of commodities. At the same time, it reduced the father's role in the family to that of a breadwinner.

These changes hardly add up to a "matriarchal" revolution, as antifeminists have sometimes claimed; nor did they even create a child-centered family in the sense of giving children a veto over their parents' authority. They freed women and children from patriarchal despotism in the home but did very little to strengthen their position in the outside world. In the case of children, the decline of parental supervision—however oppressive parental supervision may have been in the old days—turned out to be a dubious blessing. Not only did it deprive children of parental guidance, it went hand in hand with a second pattern of long-term historical change, the partial replacement of the family by other socializing agencies, which exposed children to new forms of manipulation, sexual seduction, and outright sexual exploitation. The school system, the child-care professions, and the entertainment industry have now taken over many of the custodial, disciplinary, and educative activities formerly carried out by the family. Their attentions to the child manage to combine the worst features of earlier systems of child-rearing. On the one hand, they reinforce the social segregation of the young that has always been so characteristic of bourgeois society, thereby depriving children of exposure to adult conversation, of practical experience of the world, and of participation in the community's work life. On the other hand, they expose the child all too early to the sexual life of adults, sometimes in the misguided hope of spreading a scientifically based sexual enlightenment, sometimes (as in the case of the mass media) with the deliberate intention of titillating a youthful audience. In many preindustrial societies, children are similarly confronted very early with the "facts of life," but seldom with such complete disregard for their capacity to absorb them. The promiscuous sociability described by historians of the old regime in Europe may have awakened a precocious sexual curiosity in children, but modern education and mass culture probably go much further in plunging children into the sexual dimension of adult experience before they are ready to understand it or deal with it. Nor does this sexual indoctrination succeed in its object—the object avowed by educators, anyway—of easing the child's transition into the adult world. As Bruno Bettelheim explains in his book on fairy tales, misguided attempts to substitute a more realistic and enlightened morality for the vindictive, punitive sense of justice embodied in fairy tales or to overcome fairy tales' loathsome picture of adult sexuality by propaganda about "healthy" sex actually increase the emotional distance between children and adults. To confront children with information for which they are emotionally unprepared, according to Bettelheim, undermines children's confidence in adult authority. "The child comes to feel that he and they live in different spiritual worlds." Premature exposure to modern scientific rationalism and to adult sexuality "makes for a discontinuity between the generations, painful for both parent and child."

If Bettelheim is right, the question of whether children suffer from a "new precocity" or from an unnecessarily prolonged period of economic and emotional dependence— equally plausible interpretations of contemporary child-hood, advanced by critics of current child-raising practices —is probably misconceived. Neither way of thinking about the condition of children captures the quality of childhood in a society that appears indifferent to the needs not merely of children but of future generations in general. The neglect of children is part of a broader pattern of neglect that in-cludes the reckless exploitation of natural resources, the pol-lution of the air and water, and the willingness to risk "lim-ited" nuclear wars as an instrument of national policy.

A recent report in the Toronto *Globe & Mail*, announc-ing that the "parenthood mystique has gone into an irrevo-cable decline," catches the flavor of the prevailing attitude toward children. A schoolteacher, quoted in this report, notes that "children can be fun, in small doses, but they can also be unrelentingly demanding. They don't have much time for anyone's fantasies but their own." A university instructor points out that children "turn your partner into a mother, one of the most depressing forms a human being can assume." Such statements, together with an abundance of other evidence, suggest that children have paid a heavy price for the new freedom enjoyed by adults. They spend too much time watching television, since adults use the television set as a baby-sitter and a substitute for parental guidance and discipline. They spend too many of their days in child-care centers, most of which offer the most perfunc-tory kind of care. They eat junk food, listen to junk music, read junk comics, and spend endless hours playing video games, because their parents are too busy or too harried to offer them proper nourishment for their minds and bodies. They attend third-rate schools and get third-rate moral advice from their elders. Many parents and educators, having absorbed a therapeutic morality and a misplaced idea of egalitarianism, hesitate to "impose" their moral standards on the young or to appear overly "judgmental." According to a psychiatric study cited by Marie Winn in her book *Children without Childhood*, "The majority of the parents shy away from firmly stating that they, rather than the children, should set the rules, and some parents state that *everyone* should be equal." The parents of an eleven-year-old boy who pushed his mother into a door, broke one of the bones in her back, and kicked her in the face while she lay on the floor told an interviewer who asked for a moral judgment on the child's action, "It was neither right nor wrong."*

---

*Needless to say, these attitudes are by no means universal. In a comparative study of day-care centers, Valerie Polakow Suransky includes a chapter on a low-income nursery school that caters largely to black children, where the black teachers, assisted by three grandmothers, practice a "traditional discipline of firmness and love," as the director puts it. Their supervision combines physical affection and unambiguous moral guidance. The adults do not hesitate to break up fights among the children, to label actions right or wrong, or to insist on the respect due themselves as adults; but neither do they hold themselves pedagogically aloof from the children or attempt to set a model of emotional restraint. The following scene provides a vivid glimpse of a moral atmosphere worlds apart from the atmosphere that prevails in many middle-class households:

"One morning Cedric and Benjamin were hitting each other, pulling hair and punching hard. They were left to 'fight it out.' However, when the fight escalated, Teacher Pat walked to the closet and brought out a box of beanbags. She threw one at each child and said: 'Here, throw this at each other.' Within minutes the children were laughing, engaged in a boisterous 'beanbag fight.' They were joined by other children, partitions were drawn back, and soon all thirty children, the staff, and three seventy-five-year-old grandmothers were ducking, throwing, and whooping with laughter."

Compare the contrasting situation Suransky found in a Summerhillian school, where the children are allowed to bully each other and the teachers and where, accordingly, "the 'survival of the fittest' appeared to be the norm." Dogmatically committed to "creativity" and "free expression," the adults in this experimental, progressive school never offer an opinion of their own or even an emotional response that might help the children find their bearings in a confusing world. These adults "appeared to be intimidated," Suransky writes, by their anti-authoritarian ideology.

An even more disturbing sign of the prevailing indifference to the needs of children is the growing inclination to exploit them sexually in movies and advertising, perhaps also in actual practice. There is some evidence that incest is on the rise. Whether it is or not, "a whole flock of sex researchers, academic sexual radicals, and other influential individuals and groups have been pushing the idea," as Vance Packard notes in *Our Endangered Children*, that incest may lead to "real intimacy within the family at a time when our world is becoming increasingly depersonalized" and that "antiquated ideas about incest today are comparable to the fears of masturbation a century ago." Packard rightly regards the idea of "salutary incest" as one of the most revealing signs of the fatalism about children that runs through our culture today: the feeling that adults are helpless in dealing with children, powerless to offer them a sheltered space to grow up in or to protect them from the devastating impact of the adult world, and therefore not responsible for failing to protect them or even for exploiting them in ways that make nineteenth-century child labor look almost benign by comparison.

Man-Made Objects and Illusions   Sweeping generalizations about the psychological implications of all this would be unwise, but it is not hard to believe that many children today encounter less and less cultural opposition to fantasies of sexual and generational interchangeability—the most important psychological defenses, as we have seen, against an acknowledgement of their weakness and dependence. Indeed these fantasies have acquired a kind of cultural sanction. They are bound to be strengthened by early exposure to sexual images of all kinds, including the display of precocious sexuality itself; by the misguided attempt to introduce children to scientifically sanitized information about sex at the earliest possible age; and more generally by the pretense of children's equality with adults. Our culture surrounds children with sexually seductive imagery and information; at the same time, it tries in every possible way to spare them the experience of failure or humiliation. It takes the position that "you can be anything you want to be." It promises success and gratification with a minimum of effort. Adults spend a great deal of energy trying to reassure the child of his importance and of their own love, perhaps in order to allay the suspicion that they themselves have little interest in children. They take pains not to remind the child of his immaturity and dependence. Reluctant to claim the authority of superior experience, parents seek to become their children's companions. They cultivate a youthful appearance and youthful tastes, learn the latest slang, and throw themselves into their children's activities. They do everything possible, in short, to minimize the difference between generations. Recently it has become fashionable to minimize gender differences as well, often—once again—with the best intentions.

The combination of sexual seduction and the pretense of generational equality helps to confirm the young child, in all likelihood, in the illusion of his own sexual potency, the illusion he wishes, for his own reasons, so desperately to maintain. These developments in contemporary culture reinforce the family pattern so often observed in narcissistic and schizophrenic patients, who regularly describe their fathers as "ciphers" while characterizing their mothers as both seductive and "mortally dangerous." "They might all have been children of the same family," writes Joyce McDougall of her patients in psychoanalysis. "The overall picture was invariably of a father who failed to fulfill his paternal functions—and a mother who more than fulfilled hers." In such families, the mother conveys to the child that she has no sexual need of her husband. Often she upholds another masculine model—a favored brother or friend, or her own father

—and encourages the child to take his place. "It is astonishing to learn how long these children have been able to believe that they would one day have sexual relations with her." Annie Reich has described narcissistic women who conceive of their whole body as a phallus with which to take the place of an absent male and to satisfy the mother. Such fantasies protect the child against the inevitable disillusionment that normally accompanies the Oedipus complex but in our culture often seems to come much later, even in adolescence, and to be administered by the mother herself, when she thoughtlessly disparages the child's sexual powers, thrusts the child belatedly out of her bed, has another baby, takes another sexual partner, or in some other way indicates that the child is not after all to remain her partner for life.

The emotional absence of the father has been noted again and again by students of the modern family; for our purposes, its significance lies in the removal of an important obstacle to the child's illusion of omnipotence. Our culture not only weakens the obstacles to the maintenance of this illusion, it gives it positive support in the form of a collective fantasy of generational equality. Beyond this, it supports illusions in general, promotes a hallucinatory sense of the world. The emergence of mass culture—the third line of historical development referred to earlier—has weakened the very distinction between illusions and reality. Even science, which takes as its task precisely the disenchantment of the world, helps to reactivate infantile appetites and the infantile need for illusions by impressing itself on people's lives as a never-ending series of technological miracles, wonder-working drugs and cures, and electronic conveniences that obviate the need for human effort. Among the "external forces which stimulate the old wish to bring the ego and the ego ideal together by the shortest route," and which contribute to the "changes in pathology we observe today," Chasseguet-Smirgel reserves the most important place for "those factors which tend to take progress in science as a confirmation of the possible and immediate reuniting of the ego and the ego ideal," that is, of the reestablishment of infantile illusions of omnipotence. Science adds to the prevailing impression that everything is possible. Like modern art, modern communications, and the production of consumer goods, it has "cleared the air of objects," thus allowing fantasies to flourish unchecked by a sense of the intractability of the material world around us.

The culture of narcissism is not necessarily a culture in which moral constraints on selfishness have collapsed or in which people released from the bonds of social obligation have lost themselves in a riot of hedonistic self-indulgence. What has weakened is not so much the structure of moral obligations and commandments as the belief in a world that survives its inhabitants. In our time, the survival and therefore the reality of the external world, the world of human associations and collective memories, appears increasingly problematic. The fading of a durable, common, public world, we may conjecture, intensifies the fear of separation at the same time that it weakens the psychological resources that make it possible to confront this fear realistically. It has freed the imagination from external constraints but exposed it more directly than before to the tyranny of inner compulsions and anxieties. The inescapable facts of separation and death are bearable only because the reassuring world of man-made objects and human culture restores the sense of primary connection on a new basis. When that world begins to lose its reality, the fear of separation becomes almost overwhelming and the need for illusions, accordingly, more intense than ever.

Perhaps the most suggestive analysis of the links between psychology and culture is D. H. Winnicott's theory of "transitional objects." It is well known that blankets, dolls, teddy bears, and other toys provide children with libidinal gratification and serve as substitutes for the mother's breast. But Winnicott challenges the psychoanalytic reductionism that regards such objects as nothing more than substitutes. In his view, transitional objects also help the child to recognize the external world as something separate from, yet connected to, himself. "The object is a symbol of the union of the baby and the mother"; but it is also an acknowledgment of their separation. "Its not being the breast (or the mother) . . . is as important as the fact that it stands for the breast (or mother)." Symbolism serves to invest external objects with the erotic gratification and security formerly associated with the mother, but it originates in a certain disillusionment: the discovery that the outside world does not obey the infant's whim and is not subject to his omnipotent control. The symbolism of transitional objects occupies the borderland between subjectivity and objectivity. "The object represents the infant's transition from a state of being merged with the mother to a state of being in relation to the mother as something outside and separate." Eventually the child outgrows the need for transitional objects, but only because the "transitional phenomena have become diffused, have become spread out over the whole intermediate territory between 'inner psychic reality' and the 'external world as perceived by two persons in common,' that is to say, over the whole cultural field."

Winnicott's theory calls attention to the importance of play in the development of a sense of selfhood. It shows the connections between play and art—hitherto demoted by psychoanalysis to the status of another substitute-gratification—and gives psychological support to the argument, advanced by Johan Huizinga and others, that not only art but all forms of culture contain an important admixture of play. "On the basis of playing is built the whole of man's experiential existence," Winnicott argues. "We experience life in

the area of transitional phenomena, in the exciting inter-
weave of subjectivity and objective observation, and in an
area that is intermediate between the inner reality of the
individual and the shared reality of the world that is external
to individuals." Culture mediates between the inner world
and the outer world; and the "interplay between originality
and the acceptance of tradition," a feature of every form of
cultural activity, strikes Winnicott as "just one more example . . . of the interplay between separateness and union."

It is the intermediate realm of man-made objects, then,
that threatens to disappear in societies based on mass production and mass consumption. We live surrounded by
man-made objects, to be sure, but they no longer serve very
effectively to mediate between the inner world and the outer
world. For reasons explored in an earlier chapter, the world
of commodities takes the form of a dream world, a prefab-
ricated environment that appeals directly to our inner fantasies but seldom reassures us that we ourselves have had a
hand in its creation. Commodities cannot take the place of
hand-made objects any more than science can take the place
of practical worldly experience. Neither contributes to a
sense of exploration and mastery. We may take some vicarious, collective pride in scientific achievements, but we cannot recognize those achievements as our own. The world of
commodities has become a kind of "second nature," as a
number of Marxist thinkers have pointed out, no more amenable to human direction and control than nature herself. It
no longer has the character of a man-made environment at
all. It simply confronts us, at once exciting, seductive, and
terrifying. Instead of providing a "potential space between
the individual and the environment"—Winnicott's description of the world of transitional objects—it overwhelms the
individual. Lacking any "transitional" character, the commodity world stands as something completely separate from
the self; yet it simultaneously takes on the appearance of a

mirror of the self, a dazzling array of images in which we can see anything we wish to see. Instead of bridging the gap between the self and its surroundings, it obliterates the difference between them.

VI

The Politics
of the Psyche

Contemporary Cultural Debate: An Ideal Typology
Since the argument I have advanced in the foregoing pages
cuts across conventional political boundaries, it will seem
confusing to readers who rely on familiar ideological land-
marks to keep their intellectual bearings. But it is not my
argument alone that resists easy political classification.
Long-established distinctions between left and right, liberalism and conservatism, revolutionary politics and reformist
politics, progressives and reactionaries are breaking down in
the face of new questions about technology, consumption,
women's rights, environmental decay, and nuclear arma-
ments, questions to which no one has any ready-made answers. New issues give rise to new political configurations.
So does the growing importance of cultural issues. The new
left, the women's movement, and the environmental movement defy conventional categorization, in part, because they

insist that the "personal is political," whereas earlier political movements paid little attention to the political implications of family life, gender arrangements, and sexuality.

For many purposes, psychoanalytic terminology now provides a more reliable guide to the political landscape than outmoded distinctions between left and right, not because controversies about contemporary culture are necessarily conducted in psychoanalytic language—though they often are—but because they address issues best illuminated by Freud and his followers. In order to provide ourselves with an accurate map of the geography of cultural politics, we can distinguish three positions, each with its own diagnosis of the cultural malaise, its own set of remedies, and its own affiliation with one or another among the psychic agencies distinguished by Freud in his structural theory of the mind. A broad sketch of these positions can hope only to suggest their general outlines, not to capture every nuance of cultural debate. No one has formulated arguments that conform perfectly to any of the following descriptions. These guidelines provide an ideal typology of debates about contemporary culture rather than an exhaustive historical transcript of everything people are saying. They represent the terrain in bold relief, missing many of the finer details. They represent it more faithfully, however, than obsolete labels derived from nineteenth-century political alignments.

Those who take the first of these positions see the crisis of contemporary culture, in effect, as a crisis of the superego. They regard a restoration of the social superego and of strong parental authority as the best hope of social stability and cultural renewal. According to partisans of the second position, on the other hand, it is the ego, the rational faculty, that needs to be strengthened. Our society needs moral enlightenment, they argue, not a forbidding structure of moral prohibitions and commandments. It needs people with the inner strength to make discriminatory judgments among a plurality of moral options, not people who slavishly follow orders or conform unthinkingly to received moral dogmas.

The first position obviously has an affinity with the conservative tradition and the second with liberalism, but neither coincides exactly with those categories. The party of the superego, as we might call it, does not by any means include everyone who calls himself a conservative today; nor, on the other hand, does it include political conservatives alone. On the spectrum of current political opinion, it comes closest to describing the position of those labeled neoconservatives, many of them former liberals dismayed by the moral anarchy of the sixties and seventies and newly respectful of the values of order and discipline. The second position represents what I take to be the essence of the liberal, humanist tradition, with its respect for human intelligence and the capacity for moral self-regulation. It is a position that appeals not only to liberals, however—to those liberals, that is, who still keep the old faith—but also to democratic socialists and even to many revolutionary socialists. It is the position of the old left as opposed to the new; and it is precisely their deep disagreement about culture and morality, as we shall see, and not some disagreement about abstruse points of Marxist doctrine, that most clearly distinguishes these two movements.

The third position, the one that corresponds, more or less, to the thinking of the new left or at least to those who advocate a "cultural revolution" not merely against capitalism but against industrialism in general, is the most difficult to describe and the easiest to caricature. For this reason, I shall devote most of my attention to it, but only after sketching in the other two, since it is their inadequacies that have given rise to the critique and rebuttal mounted by the new left.

The Party of the Superego   Those who adhere to the first of these positions attribute the disorder and confusion of contemporary culture to the collapse of moral inhibitions, the climate of permissiveness, and the decline of authority. They deplore hedonism, the "me-first mentality," and the widespread sense of "entitlement"—the belief that we ought to enjoy happiness, personal success, admiration, and respect without earning these things, as if they were part of our birthright. An "adversary culture," according to this assessment, has popularized attitudes formerly held only by alienated intellectuals: disrespect for institutions, authority, and tradition; rejection of society's claims on the individual; hatred of the bourgeoisie; demands for unlimited sexual freedom, unlimited freedom of expression, unlimited access to experience. A kind of principled negativism; a transvaluation of all values; an unmasking of the base motives underlying claims of moral rectitude: these habits of thought, hallmarks of the modernist sensibility, have allegedly filtered down to students, Hollywood scriptwriters, commercial artists, and writers of advertising copy, with the result that our entire culture now reverberates with the rhetoric and imagery of Dionysian revolt. The combination of "modernism in the streets" (as Lionel Trilling referred to the youth movement of the sixties), an "antinomian" cult of the self, and a therapeutic, remissive morality threatens to dissipate the last shreds of social obligation. Only a revival of the "transgressive sense," as Philip Rieff calls it—a "renascence of guilt" —will stem the rising tide of impulse.

In order to understand this position, we must be careful not to accept the characterization offered by its opponents. Those who see a strong social superego as the only reliable defense against moral anarchy—Rieff, Daniel Bell, and Lionel Trilling, to name only three of the most prominent exponents of this position—stress the importance of moral consensus and the internalization of moral constraints. They do not advocate a repressive apparatus of laws and moral dogmas designed to enforce moral conformity. They have little confidence in external controls, laws against pornography and abortion, or the restoration of the death penalty, except as symbolic expressions of shared beliefs strong enough to influence conduct without the constant threat of punitive sanctions. They advocate positions usually identified with conservatism, but they do not stand mindlessly for law and order. They stand for the superego: that is, for a morality so deeply internalized, based on respect for the commanding moral presence of parents, teachers, preachers, and magistrates, that it no longer depends on the fear of punishments or the hope of rewards. It is for this reason that the party of the superego does not coincide with the contemporary political right, though it includes people on the right. Many right-wingers have no faith in the superego at all. Either they seek simply to enforce moral and political conformity through outright coercion or, in the case of many free-market conservatives, they take the same libertarian view of culture that they take toward economics, asking only that everyone enjoy the freedom to follow his self-interest. The first approach relies not on conscience but on pure compulsion. The second cannot properly be called conservative at all, since it traces its intellectual roots back to nineteenth-century liberalism. A truly conservative position on culture rejects both enforced conformity and laissez-faire. It attempts to hold society together by means of moral and religious instruction, collective rituals, and a deeply implanted though not uncritical respect for tradition. It stresses the value of loyalty—to one's parents, one's childhood home, one's country. When it speaks of discipline, it refers to an inner moral and spiritual discipline more than to chains, bars, and the electric chair. It respects power but recognizes that power can never take the place of authority. It defends minority rights and civil liberties. In this respect, cultural conservatism is compatible with political liberalism, even with democratic socialism. Thus Bell describes himself as a cultural conservative, a political liberal, and a socialist in economics.

When I say that the conservative critique of modern culture rests on respect for the superego, I do not mean to imply that it draws on psychoanalysis or even that it accepts the validity of psychoanalytic methods and concepts. On the contrary, many conservatives regard psychoanalysis as one of the cultural influences that have undermined respect for authority, contributed to a therapeutic morality, and exposed "all justifications as ideologies," in Rieff's words. Nevertheless it is possible to state the conservative position in psychoanalytic terms without doing violence to it, as a number of theorists have already demonstrated when they criticize American culture as a culture in which the id has triumphed over the superego. In his psychoanalytic exploration of contemporary society, *The Dying of the Light*, Arnold Rogow includes a chapter called "The Decline of the Superego" in which he deplores the "flight from the superego" and the "breakdown of social controls" and insists that "those who value a civilized way of life must ultimately choose between the superego and the superstate." A few years ago, Henry and Yela Lowenfeld presented a similar argument in a paper entitled "Our Permissive Society and the Superego." "The youth of today are being deserted by their parents in regard to the superego development," they write. "The social superego is also ineffectual and its representatives give no support." The "decline of the superego," together with the growing "hostility against the culture which forces the individual to restrict his libidinal and aggressive drives," threatens the foundations of social order, according to the Lowenfelds.

These explicitly psychoanalytical formulations of the conservative position alert us to its principal shortcoming: its overestimation of the superego. According to the conservative indictment of modern culture, society's failure to uphold authoritative moral commandments or "interdictions," to use one of Rieff's favorite terms, opens the gates to a riotous horde of impulses demanding immediate gratification. In fact, the superego never serves as a reliable agency of social discipline. It bears too close a kinship to the very impulses it seeks to repress. It relies too heavily on fear. Its relentless condemnation of the ego breeds a spirit of sullen resentment and insubordination. Its endlessly reiterated "thou shalt not" surrounds sin with the glamor and excitement of the forbidden. In our culture, the fascination with violence reflects the severity with which violent impulses are proscribed. It also reflects the violence of the superego itself, which redirects murderous resentment of authorities against the ego. The superego, at least in its more primitive form, exemplifies a type of authority that knows only how to forbid. Careful study of its operations confirms the political truism that authority betrays its weakness when it seeks to rule by means of intimidation and threats of retaliation. It is never enough for authorities to uphold ethical norms and to insist on the obligation to obey them. Unless those norms are rooted in an emotional identification with the authorities who uphold them, they will inspire no more than the perfunctory obedience that fears punishment. Political theory and moral philosophy have always recognized that conscience rests not on fear but on the more solid emotional foundation of loyalty and gratitude. If the "transgressive sense" is breaking down in our society, the reasons for this lie not only in authorities' failure to insist on firm moral guidelines but in their failure to provide the security and protection that inspire confidence, respect, and admiration. A government that maintains a deadly arsenal of nuclear weapons and talks casually about "winnable" nuclear wars in which millions would be incinerated can no longer claim very plausibly to protect its citizens against foreign invasion.

A government that preaches law and order but fails to guarantee public safety, to reduce the crime rate, or to address the underlying causes of crime can no longer expect citizens to internalize respect for the law. From top to bottom of our society, those who uphold law and morality find themselves unable to maintain order or to hold out the rewards formerly associated with observance of social rules. Even middle-class parents find it increasingly difficult to provide a secure environment for their offspring or to pass on the social and economic advantages of middle-class status. Teachers can no longer claim that education promises upward social mobility. In many schools, they find themselves hard pressed even to keep order in the classroom. Authorities can promise neither the security of inherited customs and social roles, the kind of security that used to prevail in preindustrial societies, nor the opportunity to improve one's social position, which has served as the secular religion of egalitarian societies. The fiction of equal opportunity—the basis of what used to be called the American dream—no longer has enough foundation in fact to support a social consensus. In a rapidly changing and unpredictable world, a world of downward mobility, social upheaval, and chronic economic, political, and military crisis, authorities no longer serve very effectively as models and guardians. Their commandments no longer carry conviction. The nurturant, protective, benevolent side of social and parental authority no longer tempers its punitive side. Under these conditions, nothing will be gained by preaching against hedonism and self-indulgence. Instead of attempting to transmit and exemplify a clear ideal of moral conduct, those who hold positions of moral leadership would probably do better to teach survival skills, in the hope that resourcefulness, emotional toughness, and inner ego strength—as opposed to the security of an inherited morality—will enable the younger generation to weather the storms ahead.

The Liberal Ego: Nineteenth-Century Origins of the Therapeutic Ethic Liberal educators and social scientists have advocated ego-strengthening education, without calling it a program of personal survival, for some time. They have argued that a dynamic, pluralistic, and democratic society cannot live by the inherited moral wisdom of the past. According to the liberal theory of socialization, parents and other authorities recognize the futility of instilling in children practical skills and moral dogmas that will be outmoded by the time they become adults. Instead of merely transmitting the ethical and technical information accumulated in the past, they seek to train the inner resources that will enable the young to fend for themselves. According to liberal sociology, cultural alarmists mistake this educational realism for an abdication of parental and pedagogical authority, a breakdown of the family, a collapse of social order. As Talcott Parsons once put it, the modern family specializes in the "production of personality"—that is, the capacity for adaptation to unforeseen contingencies, for experimentation and innovation. John Dewey and his followers described the task facing the school system in much the same way. When they were accused of undermining respect for authority, they replied that democratic authority, like science, achieves its greatest success precisely in assuring its own supersession. It provides each new generation with the intellectual tools and emotional resources needed to challenge existing authority and to work out new ways of living better suited than the old ways to the changing conditions of a society constantly in motion.

The liberal tradition sides with the rational, reality-testing faculty, the ego, against both impulse and inherited morality. Even in the nineteenth century, when liberal education still drew on the cultural capital of the past, more heavily than it realized, liberal social theory envisioned a new type of autonomous personality emancipated from custom, prejudice, and patriarchal constraints. In its crudest form, liberalism identified itself with the utilitarian morality of enlightened self-interest, according to which the individual seeks to maximize pleasure and to avoid pain not, of course, by giving in to impulse but by putting off immediate gratification in the anticipation of future rewards. Today the morality of enlightened self-interest lives on in behavioral psychology, which conceives of moral education as moral conditioning accomplished largely through positive reinforcements. A behaviorist like B. F. Skinner stands squarely in the utilitarian tradition when he insists that punishment, an ineffective form of social control, has to give way to "nonaversive" controls. Skinner's belief that science can become the basis of a "better moral order," in which "there is no need for moral struggle," restates another tenet of utilitarianism, modified, as we shall see, by an overlay of twentieth-century progressivism.

The long-standing liberal critique of the superego found expression not only in utilitarianism and behaviorism but in nineteenth-century liberal religion, updated and secularized in the twentieth century by ego psychology, humanistic psychology, and other "reality-oriented" therapies. The nineteenth-century attack on Calvinism, denounced by liberal preachers as a religion of terror that bred either craven submission or revolt, illustrated very clearly the difference between two conceptions of social order, one founded on submission to omnipotent divine authority and the other on a system of rational "correction." Jacob Abbott, a Congregational clergyman, educator, and author still close enough to Calvinism to grasp its central doctrines, went to the heart of the issue when he distinguished between two conceptions of punishment, "vindictive retribution for sin" and "remedial" punishments administered with an eye to their "salutary" effects" on character. Retribution, Abbott explained, takes little or no account of "future acts"; it rests instead on a sense that justice demands punishment "as the natural and proper sequel and complement of the past act of transgression." Correction, on the other hand, employs punishment, along with rewards, in the interest of behavior modification, as it would be called today. A transitional figure, Abbott could still see value in retribution, which educates and satisfies our sense of justice. He found himself unable to decide whether God's punishment should be seen as vindictive or remedial, and the same uncertainty, he thought, extended to the machinery of penal justice administered by the state. But no one could have any doubts, he believed, about the undesirability of vindictive punishments in the school and family. "The punishment of a child by a parent, or of a pupil by a teacher, ought certainly, one would think, to exclude the element of vindictive retribution altogether, and to be employed solely with reference to the salutary influences that may be expected from it in time to come."

By the middle of the nineteenth century, most liberals had come to regard all forms of authority in the same light, even divine justice itself. They had come to believe that God punished sinners for their own good, not because punishment provides a fitting sequel to sin. Liberal preachers applied utilitarian conceptions of justice to theological problems and reinterpreted salvation and damnation as a rational apportionment of rewards and punishments designed to encourage good behavior and discourage bad. Just as penal reformers objected to corporal punishments and public torture on the grounds not only of their cruelty but of their ineffectiveness in preventing crime, so liberal theologians objected to the Calvinist doctrines of original sin and infant damnation on the grounds that they inadvertently encouraged moral irresponsibility and social disorder. Such was the burden of William Ellery Channing's celebrated "moral argument against Calvinism." "By shocking, as it does, the fundamental principles of morality, and by exhibiting a severe and partial Deity, [Calvinism] tends strongly to pervert the moral faculty, to form a gloomy, forbidding, and servile religion, and to lead men to substitute censoriousness, bitterness, and persecution, for a tender and impartial charity." The new ethic of personal accountability and "moral agency" insisted on punishments (human or divine) accorded strictly on the basis of individual merit and aimed at the moral enlightenment of the offender, along with the correction of the bad habits behind his offense.

   Psychoanalysis and the Liberal Tradition of Moral Optimism   Nineteenth-century liberal theology, with its insistence that health and happiness are a reward for clean living and high thinking, already contained the seeds of the remissive, therapeutic moralities that have flowered in such profusion in our own time. It is a commonplace that twentieth-century psychiatry serves as a substitute for religion, promising the traditional consolations of personal mastery, spiritual peace, and emotional security. Many of the founders of modern psychiatry, including the early popularizers of Freud—Ernest Rutherford Groves, Wilfred Lay, Edwin Bissell Holt—were brought up as liberal Christians and carried into their psychiatric work the ethical meliorism so characteristic of nineteenth-century Protestantism. Those who turned to psychoanalysis welcomed it as another form of mind-cure, another system of self-improvement and personal growth. From the beginning, the American version of psychoanalysis minimized the power of instinctual drives and stressed the possibility of subjecting them to rational control. In the "moral struggle" between infantile desires and the "spirit of social evolution," as Lay called it, the unconscious proved itself "willing to follow directions and gain the reward held out to it."

   According to Freud, psychoanalytic therapy could hope only to substitute "everyday unhappiness" for debilitating neurosis. By training intelligent self-awareness, it might reconcile men and women to the sacrifices exacted by civilized life, or at least make those sacrifices easier to bear. It might even help to encourage more enlightened public attitudes toward sex. But psychoanalysis held out no cure for injustice or unhappiness; nor could it satisfy the growing demand, in a world without religion, for meaning, faith, and emotional security. It was exactly belief and personal power, however, that Americans hoped to find in psychoanalysis. They turned to Freud's work in the hope that it would provide a new ethic grounded in study of human nature, an "ethic from below," in Holt's words, or in the expectation that it held the key to personal effectiveness and contentment. Popularizations of psychoanalysis, in the early years of its American acceptance, depicted it as a competitor of Christian Science. One journalist, Lucian Cary, compared a repressed memory to an abscess. "Lance an abscess and relief is instantaneous. Tell your painful memory and you will begin to forget it." "We have but to name these nervous diseases with their true name," wrote Max Eastman, ". . . and they dissolve like the charms in a fairy story."

The transformation of psychoanalysis into a cult of personal health and fulfillment, which occurred more rapidly and went further in America than anywhere else, had already been foreshadowed in Europe, in the early rebellions led by Alfred Adler and Carl Jung. Adler divested Freud's theories of their sexual content, reinterpreting libido as the "will-to-power." The "inferiority complex," not the Oedipus complex, underlay all human actions. The struggle to overcome feelings of inferiority, to attain the "masculine ideal" of "security and conquest," was the "fundamental fact of human development." Adler's stress on interpersonal relations and competition, his social democratic sympathy with the downtrodden, and his identification of the will-to-power with the striving for moral perfection appealed to many Americans. Large numbers of "Freudians" in the United States were actually closer to Adler and to Harry Stack Sullivan, who developed an indigenous psychology of interpersonal relationships that emphasized the need for power and security. This type of therapy, which assigned to willpower and self-mastery the healing role that Freud assigned to self-knowledge, blended more easily than stricter forms of psychoanalysis into a culture with its roots in nineteenth-century religious liberalism.

Even Jungian mysticism, in some of its manifestations at least, had a certain affinity with liberal traditions of moral striving and spiritual self-help. Jung saw the unconscious mind not as a tangled mass of desires—the Freudian view—but as a reservoir of collective experience, of saving myths. The task of therapy, as he saw it, was to bring to consciousness the buried imagery, the "archetypes," the eternal wisdom deeper than mere rationality, that slumbered in the soul. As Philip Rieff has shown, Jung addressed himself to a disease no less pervasive in modern society than the sense of personal inadequacy—the impoverishment of the spiritual imagination. He sought to restore the illusion of faith, if not its reality, by enabling the patient to construct a private religion made up of the decomposing remnants of former religions, all of them equally valid in Jung's eyes and therefore equally serviceable in the modern crisis of unbelief. Jung's spiritual eclecticism and Adler's self-improvement, radically different in so much of their tone and content, shared a central feature. Both replaced self-insight with ethical teaching, thereby transforming psychoanalysis into a "new religio-ethical system," as Freud put it. Jung's insistence on the individual's need to complete his "life-task"—to struggle against "psychic laziness" and to find his own destiny—resembled the Adlerian exhortation to master one's circumstances. For all his despair of science and rationality, Jung shared Adler's confidence that psychotherapy could serve as the basis of a new morality, based not on the old prohibitions but on a scientific understanding of human needs.

Even this sanitized reading of Freud proved unacceptable to most American psychiatrists, of course, and they proceeded to work out ever more affirmative and uplifting therapies that promised not only personal regeneration but, in many cases, social regeneration as well, a secular version of the Christianized social order envisioned by liberal Protestants. In the process, they jettisoned what remained of psychoanalysis. Carl Rogers, exposed as a young man to the idealism of the YMCA and to the bracing atmosphere of religious fellowship, found Freud's pessimism as revolting and incomprehensible as his spiritual forebears had once found Calvinism. "When a Freudian such as Karl Menninger tells me . . . that he perceives man as . . . 'innately destructive,' I can only shake my head in wonderment." Rogers's own approach to therapy, as a follower put it, was "as American as apple pie." It emphasized free will, in opposition to the determinism of both Freud and Skinner. It aimed to promote "total sensitivity to the client," "empathy," "unconditional positive regard," "congruence," and the importance of being "real." In the tradition of earlier doctrines of human perfectibility, it held that every organism has an innate "drive toward growth, health, and adjustment." Above all, it stressed the possibility of achieving rational control over the self and its environment.

The Quarrel between Behaviorism and Humanistic Psychiatry Modern psychiatric movements, which have carried on the tradition of liberal religion and self-improvement and shored it up with scientific pretensions, can be divided very generally into game therapies and growth therapies, both of which present themselves as "humanistic" solutions to the problems not just of unhappy individuals but of industrial society in general. In the first, one can recognize the ghost of Adler; in the second, the still more shadowy presence of Jung. Game therapies include the many schools of psychiatric thought that emphasize the importance of interpersonal relations, group dynamics, learning, communication, roles and role-playing, games and game theory. Eric Berne's transactional analysis, Albert Ellis's "rational therapy," William Glasser's "reality therapy," George Alexander Kelly's role-playing therapy, and Thomas Szasz's theory of "personal conduct," among others, belong to this category. Unlike psychoanalysis, which sees the human mind as the product of an unrelenting struggle between instinct and culture, these programs see mind as exclusively social. They concern themselves with the individual's relations to others rather than with inner conflicts. They subordinate the pursuit of self-knowledge to the pursuit of "meaningful goals." One of their principal objectives is to get the patient to set more "realistic" goals for himself and to renounce "perfectionist" illusions. Albert Ellis attempts to promote marital and sexual adjustment by attacking the unrealistic ideology of romantic love, the "myth" of the vaginal orgasm, and the "myth" of the simultaneous orgasm. George R. Bach and Peter Wyden condemn the "myth that sex and love must always go together," the "myth that simultaneous orgasm is a major requirement for good sexual adjustment," and other beliefs that allegedly encourage unrealistic expectations. Since the failure to live up to these expectations leads to self-denigration and feelings of inferiority, the most effective cure for inferiority, it appears, lies in persuading the patient to abandon illusory objectives.

Practitioners of the various humanistic or existential psychologies—Rogers, Abraham Maslow, Rollo May, Anthony J. Sutich, Ernest L. Rossi—have criticized game therapies on the grounds that games are repetitive and discourage growth, whereas psychotherapy should seek to transform the client's "inner reality," in Rossi's words, into "creative products." They have criticized psychoanalysis itself on similar grounds, accusing Freud of ignoring the capacity for emotional and intellectual development. Thus Charlotte Bühler insists that psychoanalysis aims only to bring about "homeostatic satisfaction" and ignores the human need for growth. She herself "conceives of man," she says ". . . as living with purpose. The purpose is to give meaning to life. . . . The individual . . . wants to create values." Here again, self-understanding gives way to self-improvement and moral education as the object of psychotherapy.*

Vigorously opposed not only to psychoanalysis but to behaviorism, game therapies and growth therapies advance their own version of behavior modification, as Rogers has admitted, in the hope of making the client self-directing. Since many behaviorists make the same claim, the controversy between "post-Freudian" psychotherapy and behaviorism collapses into differences of style and emphasis. In public debates with B. F. Skinner, Rogers has accused his adversary of using science "to enslave people in ways never dreamed of before, depersonalizing them, controlling them by means so carefully selected that they will perhaps never be aware of their loss of personhood." But he rejects Skinner's vision of a totally planned and administered society only to put in its place the survival artist's regimen of living

---

*Psychoanalysis not only discourages moral optimism but gives little support to the growing tendency to see human beings as victims of external circumstances: another reason for its increasing unpopularity. Psychoanalysis came into being when Freud began to understand that his patients could not have been sexually assaulted by their parents with the frequency they reported; that is, when he began to understand these reports as a recurring fantasy. Recent critics of psychoanalysis have attempted to revive the seduction theory in its original form. They insist that Freud's thought took a wrong turn when he gave it up. The seduction theory conforms to the prevailing definition of man as victim, the prevailing belief, as Janet Malcolm puts it, that "we are ruled by external reality rather than by our inner demons." It is this belief that unites many opponents of psychoanalysis, even those who seem at first, like the humanists and the behaviorists, to be deeply opposed.

"on a day-by-day basis," without reference to any goals beyond self-actualization. He warns of the political dangers of a psychiatric priesthood, but his own commitment to democracy rests on the unsupported belief that although the "behavior of the human organism may be determined by the influences to which it has been exposed," it may also reflect the "creative and integrative insight of the organism itself." Characteristically, he thinks the question can be decided only by further research. If "sound research" supports Skinner's view of human dependence, "then a social philosophy of expert control is clearly implied." If it indicates that men and women have at least a "latent capacity" for understanding and self-reliance, "then a psychological basis for democracy [will] have been demonstrated." After criticizing Skinner for advocating rule by a scientific elite, Rogers himself leaves it to science to decide whether democracy has a future. He too proposes, in effect, that the fate of democratic institutions be decided in the laboratory and the clinic—decided, moreover, by the very scientists whose work has already, by his own reckoning, laid an "effective technological basis for eventual control by the state." Instead of arguing that the capacity for understanding and self-mastery can flourish under democratic conditions alone, Rogers hopes that "objective study" will vindicate his faith in humanity. Such a humanism, which reduces to wishful thinking, poses no challenge to behaviorism.

The quarrel between behaviorism and liberal humanism, as exemplified by nineteenth-century liberal religion and by the twentieth-century psychotherapies that have tried to replace it, seems to support Arnold Rogow's contention that the only alternative to the superego is the superstate. From the beginning, liberals have argued that the capacity for rational self-direction makes it possible to dispense with external social controls and authoritative moral codes, or at least to reduce them to a minimum. Yet the destruction of the old creeds, the old commandments and constraints, seems to have released enormous capacities for aggression, which can be held in check, it appears, only by a return to some sort of collective superego or by a new system of scientific controls ostensibly administered in the interest of humanity as a whole—in the interest of its very survival, indeed—but vested in an enlightened managerial and technical elite. Since liberals refuse on principle to countenance a revival of moral "authoritarianism," as they see it, they find it increasingly difficult to resist the logic of a new social order "beyond freedom and dignity." The debate between Skinner and Rogers suggests that behaviorism cannot be refuted from a position based on an environmentalist, therapeutic ethic. Once you accept Skinner's premises—that "traditional" knowledge must give way to "scientific analysis"; that failure is the worst teacher; that the goal of social policy is to "avoid unhappiness"—it is not easy to resist his conception of utopia as a "world in which there is no need for moral struggle."

Skinner scandalizes liberals by carrying their own assumptions and prejudices to unpalatable conclusions. He makes explicit what liberal humanists prefer to ignore: that the therapeutic morality associated with twentieth-century liberalism destroys the idea of moral responsibility, in which it originates, and that it culminates, moreover, in the monopolization of knowledge and power by experts. Skinner is by no means a conservative, however. He shares the liberal faith that problems of modern social organization are administrative and psychological, not economic and political. He believes that social engineering holds the promise of a better world, once the techniques of social control are taken over by a disinterested managerial elite so that they can no longer be "used for personal aggrandizement in a competitive world." Like many socialists and progressives, he dismisses the danger of a scientific and technocratic tyranny with the offhand remark that "usurpation of power is a threat only in a competitive culture." His idea of the good society, as outlined in *Walden Two* and later in *Beyond Freedom and Dignity,* consists of clichés of twentieth-century liberalism. He wants to replace competition with cooperation, politics with administration, punishment with "treatment," rivalry with "general tolerance and affection," romantic love with "simple friendship," hero-worship with an egalitarian interchangeability of social parts, in which "there's no reason to feel that anyone is necessary to anyone else." Like the early progressive educators, he wants to teach not subjects but "scientific method." In *Walden Two,* he abolishes the study of history, on the grounds that it encourages hero-worship. He abolishes the family, which discriminates against women and perpetuates selfish individualism. He abolishes adolescence, replacing it with a "brief and painless" transition to adulthood. He gets rid of the "secrecy and shame" surrounding sex. He decrees the end of frustration, suffering, and failure. He dispenses with "simple democracy," relieving the masses of the "responsibility of planning" and freeing them for spiritual self-enrichment.

The difference between Skinner and his humanist critics is that he acknowledges the undemocratic implications of all this without a qualm. "You won't find very much 'simple democracy' here," he writes of his model community. The inhabitants of *Walden Two* vote as the "Planners" tell them to vote. It is not hard to see why liberals object to Skinner's ideas or why those ideas sometimes appeal, on the other hand, to a younger generation in revolt against the "hypocrisy" of its elders. As the charge of hypocrisy implies, many young people accept the prevailing values but demand a stricter observance of them. This kind of rebellion finds an ideal spokesman in Skinner, who draws on liberalism in order to convict liberals of sentimentality and evasion. His ideas appeal to many young readers in their insistence that utopian "change won't come about through power politics at all," but "at another level altogether." His frequent attacks on "consuming and polluting" echo important themes of the counterculture, as does his defense of "smallness" and his insistence on the social limits of growth. His egalitarianism reinforces the "anti-elitism" that has become almost the common denominator of contemporary politics. His pleas for the "complete equality of men and women," his attack on competitive sports and other forms of "personal triumph," and his dream of a "world without heroes" all participate in the current revulsion against invidious distinctions—a perversion of the democratic impulse that turns out to be perfectly compatible with acceptance of an oligarchy of experts, who claim no special powers or privileges beyond the impersonal authority of science.

Skinner's ideas may offend liberals, but they rest on a solid footing of liberal dogma: environmentalism, egalitarianism, social engineering. Behaviorism, moreover, confronts the weight of recent historical experience, which seems to indicate that liberals have exaggerated the power of rational intelligence to hold destructive impulses in check. Like psychoanalysis, to which it is otherwise unalterably opposed, behaviorism acknowledges the power of biological drives, ignored by "post-Freudian" psychotherapies or explained away as the product of "cultural conditioning." It denies that these drives can be overcome by means of moral education or by therapies designed to put people "in touch with their feelings." It prescribes stronger medicine: the skillful manipulation of social rewards by a scientific elite, supplemented, if necessary, by drugs, brain surgery, and genetic engineering.*

---

*Skinner himself, it should be noted, emphatically rejects drugs, brain surgery, and genetic engineering. Other behaviorists, however, do not share his scruples about such methods.

Hartmann's Ego Psychology: Psychoanalysis as Behavioral Engineering   Before concluding that liberal psychiatry has no answer at all to those who proclaim the death of freedom and dignity, we need to consider the tradition of ego psychology in psychoanalysis itself, which has tried to put the case for the ego on intellectual foundations more secure than those provided by therapies stressing interpersonal relations or personal growth. Ego psychology, like "neo-Freudian" and "post-Freudian" psychology, rejects the picture of man as a creature of instincts, restrained only by the fear of punishment or the hope of rewards; but it still tries to adhere to the moral realism provided by psychoanalytic concepts. It does not deny the existence of psychic conflict or suffering; nor does it confuse psychic health with personal salvation. It resists the temptation to set up psychotherapy as a panacea both for the individual and for the ills of society. It rejects the therapeutic morality according to which "there are not moral or immoral people," in Heinz Hartmann's paraphrase, but "only healthy and sick people." It refuses to endorse pure self-interest as the basis of a new morality of health and happiness. In his book *Psychoanalysis and Moral Values*, Hartmann attacks the misconception that psychoanalysis exposes moral imperatives and ideals as illusory or defines mental health as complete freedom from moral codes and guilt feelings. "The widely held expectation that a maximal consideration of self-interest would provide solutions most satisfactory from all points of view," Hartmann wryly notes, ". . . is not borne out by psychoanalytic experience."

While it resists the assimilation of morality to psychic health and personal well-being, ego psychology also rejects moral "absolutes" and extreme positions in general. It attempts to steer a middle course between moral dogmatism and moral debunking, between an ethics based on superego constraints and an ethics based on enlightened self-interest.

Its characteristic posture is the claim of scientific impartiality, which often serves as an excuse to avoid difficult questions. Its guiding ambition, to which everything else is secondary, is to remodel psychoanalysis as a "general developmental psychology," in Hartmann's words. It is this aspiration that distinguishes ego psychology, strictly speaking, from the work of those who seek merely to extend Freud's work by studying the defensive mechanisms adopted by the ego in the face of anxiety, the importance of "transitional objects" in the ego's attempt to master the external world, or the genesis and development of the ego ideal. Those most closely identified with this particular school of psychoanalytic thought—Hartmann, Ernest Kris, R. M. Lowenstein, David Rapaport, René Spitz, Roy Schafer—have taken the position that psychoanalysis needs to concern itself not only with psychopathology but with normal psychological development. The pursuit of this program leads not merely to intensified study of the ego but to a certain idealization of the ego. As Fred Weinstein and Gerald Platt note approvingly, psychoanalytic theory has "moved away from the notion of the helpless and beleaguered ego, caught on three sides by id, superego, and unrelenting reality, waging therefore a constant defensive struggle." Far more than Freud, ego psychologists emphasize the ego's capacity for masterful, creative action, even while they reproach others for exaggerating the power of human reason and ignoring the inevitability of psychic conflict.

In order to become a general psychology, Hartmann argues in his *Ego Psychology and the Problem of Adaptation*, psychoanalysis has to deal with aspects of "adaptive development" that are allegedly free of conflict—that is, with those "functions" of the ego that cannot be reduced to defensive mechanisms against the conflicting demands of the id and the superego. These include a remarkably broad range of activities: perception, thought, language, motor development, and even memory. To those who might argue that such matters lie outside the scope of psychoanalysis, Hartmann replies that "if we take seriously the claim of psychoanalysis to be a general theory of mental development, we must study this area of psychology too." But he never confronts the far more weighty objection that the assignment of all these important activities to the "conflict-free ego sphere," as Hartmann calls it, results precisely in their exemption from psychoanalytic scrutiny. The boldness of Freud's original challenge to academic psychology lay in his claim to have uncovered the unconscious dynamics underlying such ordinary mental phenomena as memory—memory above all—and thus to have made it impossible to regard them simply as mechanisms of "adaptation." His later work, interpreted by ego psychologists as a warrant for the abandonment of a narrow "id psychology," made it more difficult than ever to regard any "sphere" of the mind as free from unconscious conflicts, since it led to the conclusion that "not only what is lowest but also what is highest in the ego can be unconscious." Ego psychology, by explaining the higher activities of the mind as conflict-free, adaptive, and largely conscious techniques of personal and social evolution, has regressed to the position taken by pre-Freudian academic psychology.

Freud compared the ego to a "man on horseback, who has to hold in check the superior strength of the horse." For Hartmann and his followers, this image conveys an impression of man's power over nature, whereas Freud clearly intended it as a reminder of man's dependence on nature and of the precariousness of his mastery over natural forces— including his own capacity for destruction, which haunted everything Freud wrote after World War I. The beast within threatens to unseat the "rider," according to Freud; but for those who take ego psychology as their point of departure, reason steadily expands its control over the environment. A "better mastery of the environment" and a "better control of one's own person," as Hartmann puts it, reveal themselves both in the development of the individual and in human history as a whole. Freud's motto, "Where id was, there shall ego be"—although it "does not mean that there ever has been, or could be, a man who is purely rational"—expresses not only a therapeutic ideal but a "cultural-historical tendency," according to Hartmann. According to Weinstein and Platt, "We can identify historically a growing capacity among individuals for making conscious, ego-oriented choices." The "effects of the modernization process on personality," in their view, gradually free the ego both "from the compulsions of conscience and from impulsions of irrationality."

Ostensibly "value-free," ego psychology shares with other sciences and would-be sciences a commitment to the ideology of science itself. It assumes that scientific enlightenment means historical progress. It equates reason with technology—that is, with the problem-solving activities of the mind, the rational adjustment of means to ends—and then proceeds to remove technology, in effect, from psychoanalytic investigation by arguing that the problem-solving capacity leads an independent and "autonomous" existence, free from inner conflicts or ideological compulsions.* Psychoanalytic therapy itself, according to Hartmann,

---

*Hartmann takes his definition of rationality straight from Max Weber. An individual acts in a "purposively rational way," he says, when he "rationally balances the ends against the means, the means against the subsidiary consequences, and finally the various possible ends against each other," in Weber's words. This technical conception of reason ignores the long tradition of "practical reason" originating with Aristotle, according to which knowledge is to be used not to accomplish a given objective but to train the virtues specific to a given profession or calling or practice and, more generally, to encourage the development of character and the pursuit of moral perfection. Since psychoanalysis is a practice precisely in this sense, stressing moral insight as opposed to what are now called "practical" results, one might expect its practitioners to be among the last to accept a technical conception of rationality.

amounts to a "kind of technology," even though the "way from science to technology is on the whole much slower and more complex in the psychological and social than in the physical sciences." For this reason, control over the irrational elements in human nature often lags behind human control over the physical environment. "Historical development has brought now one and now the other of these to the fore as goals," Hartmann writes; at the present juncture, man's growing mastery of the external world needs to be balanced by a growing mastery of the inner world. The technology of the self, in other words, needs to catch up with industrial technology.

We see now why ego psychology answers the threat of behavioral engineering no more effectively than "humanistic" psychiatry. Once the problem is defined in this way— the rationalization of mental life as a counterpart to the rationalization of the natural environment and a corrective to the "irrationality implicit in mass psychology," as Hartmann puts it—the demand for a new form of behavior control far more rigorous than psychoanalysis becomes irresistible.

It is the underlying premises of this discussion—the premises of ego psychology and of the entire liberal celebration of the rational ego—that need to be called into question. What if technological progress is an illusion? What if it leads not to greater control over the physical environment but to an increasingly unpredictable environment, a return of the repressed capacity for destruction in nature herself? What if the impulse behind technological development (though not necessarily behind the spirit of scientific inquiry) is itself pathological? What if the drive to make ourselves entirely independent of nature, which never succeeds in reaching its goal, originates in the unconscious attempt to restore the illusion of infantile omnipotence?

In order to complete our consideration of the politics of the psyche, we turn now to the work of those who have not hesitated to raise these disturbing questions, normally banished from "scientific" discourse, and in doing so have challenged both liberal and conservative traditions of thought.

VII

The Ideological
Assault on the Ego

*The Exhaustion of Political Ideologies after World War
II* The terrible events of the 1930s and 1940s—the rise of
totalitarianism, the death camps, the strategic bombing of
Germany by the Allies, the use of the atomic bomb against
Japan—brought to the surface unsuspected or forgotten
depths of destructiveness, even in those fighting for democracy and freedom, and shook the foundations of liberal faith.
It was not simply that this revival of barbarism on a global
scale called into question naive conceptions of historical
progress and human perfectibility. The self-destructive
quality of the violence associated with it appeared to undermine even the premise that ordinary selfishness normally
restrains men from indulging their aggressive impulses in
complete disregard of the interests of others or the fear of
reprisals. The death-wish seemingly underlying the resur-
gence of mass murder, together with the failure of humanist

traditions to anticipate or illuminate it, led to a growing conviction that "contemporary social theory, both capitalist and socialist, has nothing to say," as Norman O. Brown put it in *Life against Death,* about the "real problem of our age."

Those who shared Brown's belief in the "superannuation of political categories" experimented, in the postwar period, with a variety of replacements. Some found in Christianity, specifically in "neo-orthodoxy," the basis for a new politics of "sin, cynicism, and despair," as Brown scornfully called it. Others proposed to replace politics with a new science of behavioral control, which envisioned the elimination of aggression by means of psychological conditioning and behavioral engineering. In effect, they held up a benign totalitarianism as the only answer to the savage totalitarianism of Stalin and Hitler. Such a solution continues to appeal to many people, in spite of its undemocratic implications, because it retains important elements of the liberal worldview, as we have seen: a belief in the predictability of human "behavior," a pleasure-pain psychology, insistence on the primacy of self-interest. Behaviorism provides a reassuringly familiar intellectual setting for a brave new world.

The demands of "emotional survival" prompted a third course of action, leading many "world-conscious people," as Dorothy Dinnerstein puts it, into attempts to renew the capacity for devotion on the modest scale of personal friendship and family life, "in the service of some spiritual equivalent of the ancients' household gods." The events of World War II reduced radicals of her generation, Dinnerstein writes, to a "state of moral shock," a condition of "historic despair so deep that few of us could recognize it clearly as despair." What made these events so shattering, she argues, was that they did not result simply from the actions of evil men but seemed to be rooted in large-scale social structures as such. "The impulse to build large-scale societal structures which would contain and eventually greatly reduce these nightmare forces was stalemated by massive evidence that large-scale societal structures *per se*—not just those in capitalist countries—were the habitat in which they managed most hideously to thrive."

Dinnerstein argues that the postwar generation, even in its flight from politics, communicated to the next generation its "infernal vision of society" and its "quasi-solutions to the problem of emotional survival." Thus it inadvertently planted the seeds of the cultural politics that flowered in the sixties and seventies. From this point of view, the radicalism of the sixties represented not so much a return to political commitments after a period of political retreat as a metamorphosis of personal life into politics. "Make love, not war." The most characteristic features of the new left derived from its attempt to "combine the 'personal' with the 'political,' " as Shulamith Firestone noted in 1970, and from its belief that the "old leafletting and pamphletting and Marxist analysis are no longer where it's at." The new left's suspicion of large-scale social organization; its rejection of democratic centralism; its distrust of leadership and party discipline; its faith in small groups; its repudiation of power and "power trips," work discipline, and goal-directed activity in general; its repudiation of "linear" thinking—these attitudes, the source of so much that was fruitful in the new left and of so much that was futile and self-defeating as well, originated in the central contention (as the San Francisco Redstockings put it in their 1970 manifesto) that "our politics begin with our feelings."

Such a politics can take many forms: radical feminism, environmentalism, pacifism, nihilism, a cult of revolutionary violence. "Cultural revolution" is an ambiguous slogan. In China, it was invoked on behalf of systematic attacks on intelligence and learning, a revolution against culture. In the West, a critique of "instrumental reason" has sometimes degenerated into a Dionysian celebration of irrationality.

The revolt against technological domination points toward new forms of community but also toward nihilism and "addled subjectivity," as Lewis Mumford has called it. But in spite of the anti-intellectualism, the infantile insurgency, and the taste for destruction so often associated with cultural politics, it addresses issues ignored by the dominant political tradition: the limits of reason; the unconscious origins of the desire for domination; the embodiment of this desire in industrial technology, ostensibly the highest product of the rational intelligence.

The Neo-Freudian Left   The best way to understand why the idea of a cultural revolution encourages such contradictory applications is to study its attempt to ground social theory in psychoanalysis, with the usual disclaimer that many exponents of this position take no interest in psychoanalysis at all. But those who did turn to Freud, in the years following World War II, did so for good reasons. His work—in particular *Civilization and Its Discontents*, which provided both Brown and Herbert Marcuse with a starting point for their investigations of culture—seemed to speak more directly than any other intellectual tradition to the question that haunted the postwar world: Why is it precisely the highest civilization that has developed and unleashed unprecedented powers of destruction?

In order to address this question, Brown and Marcuse had to discard an earlier tradition of psychoanalytic radicalism, developed in the 1930s by Wilhelm Reich, Erich Fromm, Karen Horney, Gregory Zilboorg, and other "neo-Freudians," who tried to press psychoanalysis into the service of social reform by emphasizing cultural instead of biological determinants of personality. The cultural school had set out to strip Freudian theory of its "biological determinism," its "disregard of cultural factors" and "social conditions," its undue emphasis on sexuality at the expense of "feelings of inferiority" and the "hunger of appreciation or affection," its neglect of "interpersonal relations," its "patriarchal" bias, its "hydraulic" theory of psychic energy—everything, in short, that allegedly stamped Freud's thought as a product of nineteenth-century mechanistic science and bourgeois culture. Reinterpreted in the light of Marxism, feminism, and cultural anthropology, psychoanalysis allegedly undermined the idea that sexual differences are divinely or biologically ordained and therefore unchangeable, destroyed the myth of the patriarchal family and monogamous marriage, and laid bare the psychological dynamics by means of which the patriarchal family and a repressive sexual morality served "to maintain the stability of class society," in Fromm's words. Feminism, Marxism, and psychoanalysis thus appeared to converge in an exposé of the authoritarian family and of the "patricentric" personality who experiences suffering as guilt instead of injustice, accepts his lot instead of trying to change the social conditions that make him unhappy, and "identifies with the aggressor" instead of attempting to unite the victims of aggression against the prevailing social system.

In their eagerness to bring psychoanalysis up to date and to reconcile it with progressive social philosophies, the "neo-Freudians" deleted whatever was distinctive and original in Freud's work and ended up with a psychological theory that merely confirmed what every literate, humane, right-thinking man or woman already knew. As Marcuse noted in his "Critique of Neo-Freudian Revisionism," they "flattened out" the "depth dimension of the conflict between the individual and his society" and turned psychoanalysis into a "moralistic philosophy of progress." According to Brown, they reversed the axiom that the child is father to the man, restated by Freud and supported with new evidence, and wrote instead as if toilet-training, parental injunctions against masturbation, and other child-rearing practices, repressive or enlightened, played the decisive role in psychological development. By dropping the "whole theory of infantile sexuality," they recovered optimism "cheaply." In place of psychoanalysis, they served up "lullabies of sweetness and light." Even Reich, who rightly argued that "to fulfill its own therapeutic promises, psychoanalysis has to envisage a social transformation," went astray, according to Brown, "in limiting the social transformation involved to the liberation of adult genital sexuality." As Marcuse tried to show, the transformation of the polymorphous perversity of the infant into genital sexuality already reflected the triumph of the performance principle, as he called it, over the pleasure principle. A social revolution that aimed to break the cycle of domination and rebellion could not stop with the creation of a more permissive sexual morality. A so-called sexual revolution that confined itself to genital pleasure could easily lend itself to new forms of domination. The task confronting the cultural revolution was not to set aside more opportunities for erotic indulgence, as a momentary release from the demands of alienated labor, but to eroticize work itself. The task was not to enlarge the domain of leisure but to abolish the very distinction between work and leisure, to make work into play, and to get rid of the aggressive, domineering attitude toward nature that informs the present organization of work.

Marcuse on "Surplus Repression" The postwar reformulation of psychoanalytic social theory had to begin, then, with an attempt to undo the damage done by the cultural school of Freudian revisionists. For Marcuse, Freud had to be approached much as Marx had approached David Ricardo, as a hardheaded ideological opponent whose work needed to be taken more seriously than that of well-meaning but tender-minded ideological allies—the utopian socialists for Marx, the neo-Freudian revisionists for Marcuse—and when properly understood, contradicted its own assumption that human happiness remains a mirage. "Freud's own theory," Marcuse insisted, "provides reasons for rejecting" Freud's pessimism. Marx had turned political economy against itself by arguing that the laws of the market, described by Adam Smith and Ricardo as natural, inevitable, and unchanging, derived from a particular series of historical developments and were therefore open to further modification. In the same way, Marcuse historicized Freud. Whereas Freud's theory of civilization derived the need for repression from the "natural" disproportion between human desires and the demands of reality, Marcuse tried to show that "natural" categories under close analysis proved to be historical and that repression originates not in the "struggle for existence but only in its oppressive organization." By distinguishing between repression and "surplus repression," Marcuse tried to give a psychological dimension to Marx's theory of alienated labor, according to which labor beyond what is necessary for human survival goes into the production of "surplus value." Surplus repression, as Marcuse called it, originates in the organized apparatus of class rule and domination, which forces men and women to labor beyond the satisfaction of their needs. As society becomes more complex, the relations of production become increasingly hierarchical and the psychological sanctions enforcing alienated labor correspondingly severe. Thus civilization inflicts on individuals a burden of renunciation, of psychological suffering and guilt, beyond what is strictly necessary to assure the reproduction of the race. The "unconscious sense of guilt and the unconscious need for punishment seem to be out of proportion with the actual 'sinful' impulses of the individual."

Just as Marx's critique of political economy demanded a historical analysis of alienated labor, Marcuse's position appears to demand a historical analysis of its psychological consequences, a history of surplus repression. Whereas Marx devoted much of his life to a study of changing modes of production, however, Marcuse fell back on Freud's dubious theory of the primal horde, which traced the origin of patriarchy to the abortive uprising against the primal father. The sons overthrow the father but internalize his authority and reimpose it on women and children. This "patriarchal counterrevolution," according to Marcuse, becomes the prototype of failed revolutions ever since. The alternating "rhythm of liberation and domination" arises out of the sons' unconscious identification with the hated father. Instead of ridding themselves of his rule, they reestablish it in the form of the "patriarchal monogamic family," which institutionalizes instinctual renunciation, channels "polymorphous perversity" into the single acceptable outlet of monogamous marriage, and enforces submission to social rules and the patriarchal compulsion to work. The uprising of the rebellious sons momentarily breaks the "chain of domination," according to Marcuse; "then the new freedom is again suppressed—this time by their own authority and action." Once established, this pattern repeats itself throughout history—as in the life and death of Jesus, which Marcuse reinterprets as a struggle against the patriarchal laws in the name of love, a struggle betrayed by Christ's disciples when they deified the son beside the father and codified his teachings in oppressive new laws.

The theory of the primal horde served Marcuse, as it has served other theorists of the Freudian left, as a substitute for historical analysis, an admittedly "speculative" and "symbolic" encapsulation of the entire course of patriarchal history. It is easy to see the idea's attraction for the left. It not only implicates the family in the origins of a repressive civilization but spells out the psychological linkages between them. It purports to show how the Oedipus complex, and with it the whole apparatus of patriarchal domination, transmits itself from one generation to the next. It traces the Oedipus complex back to the dawn of history and thus helps to define the need for a cultural revolution that transcends a mere change in power or institutions and breaks the cycle of rebellion and submission. But as Marcuse himself pointed out in his attack on the cultural school, psychoanalysis offers the "most concrete insights into the historical structure of civilization" precisely when it least concerns itself with developing a general theory of culture and sticks instead to clinical concepts—"concepts that the revisionists reject." This warning—unfortunately unheeded by most of those who attempt to remodel psychoanalysis as a social theory, including Marcuse—applies with particular force to Freud's speculations about group psychology, both in his essay of that name and in *Moses and Monotheism*, which rest on a model of mental conflict already discarded in the more strictly psychological writings of his last phase. Freud's increasing awareness of a more deeply buried layer of mental life underlying the Oedipus complex, his revision of his instinct theory, and his new psychology of women pointed to conclusions incompatible with many of the generalizations he continued to advance in his sociological writings. For one thing, this new line of analysis suggested that sexual pleasure is not the only object of repression. For another, it suggested that the agency of repression is not simply "reality." Accordingly the outcome of the Oedipus complex— the theory of which Freud now made explicit for the first time—cannot be seen simply as the submission of the pleasure principle to a reality principle imposed on the child by the father. It is not just that parental commands and prohibitions, toilet-training practices, and threats of castration play a less important role in the child's development than Freud had previously thought. The entire conceptual scheme that opposes pleasure and reality, equating the former with the unconscious and the latter with conscious adherence to parental morality, has to give way to a different model of the mind.

Marcuse himself challenged Freud's group psychology in an essay published in 1963, misleadingly entitled "The Obsolescence of the Freudian Concept of Man." Noting that Freud saw all social groups as revivals of the primal horde, with a "leader as a unifying agent" and the "transference of the ego ideal to the leader as father image," Marcuse went on to argue that modern societies have dispensed with patriarchal imagery and patriarchal authority. "The fascist leaders were no 'fathers,' and the postfascist and post-Stalinist top leaders do not display the traits of the heirs of the primal father—not by any stretch of the 'idealizing' imagination." The emergence of a "society without fathers," according to Marcuse, "invalidated" the "classical psychoanalytic model, in which the father and the father-dominated family were the agent of mental socialization." The "decline in the role of the father" reflected the "decline of the role of private and family enterprise" and "society's direct management of the nascent ego through the mass media, school and sport teams, gangs," and other agencies of collective socialization. These changes led to a "tremendous release of destructive energy," a "rampant" aggressiveness "freed from the instinctual bonds with the father as authority and conscience."

What these developments invalidate, of course, is not the "Freudian concept of man" but a social theory "extrapolated," in Marcuse's own words, from Freud's extrapolations of clinical data into prehistory. They invalidate the idea, already weakened by Freud's later work and by much of the work subsequently produced by Kleinians, object-relations theorists, and ego psychologists, that repression originates in the subjection of the pleasure principle to the patriarchal compulsion to labor. Yet Marcuse continues, even in his later writings, to condemn the "performance principle" as the primal source of human unhappiness and alienation. Forgetting even his own plea for the union of work and play, he insists that "no matter how justly and rationally the material production may be organized, it can never be a realm of freedom and gratification." Because work "serves ends outside itself," it remains "inevitably repressive" for Marcuse—a "neurosis." For this reason, he argues that the liberation of Eros demands the technological abolition of work. Disavowing any intention of advocating a "romantic regression behind technology," he insists on the liberating potential of industrial technology. "Is it still necessary to repeat," he asks in his *Essay on Liberation*, "that science and technology are the great vehicles of liberation, and that it is only their use and restriction in the repressive society which makes them into vehicles of domination?" Automation alone makes it possible for Orpheus and Narcissus to come out of hiding. The triumph of polymorphous perversity depends on its antithesis: instrumental rationality carried to the point of total regimentation. Presumably an exercise in dialectical thinking, this line of argument should give even Hegelians pause when they read (in *Eros and Civilization*) that the "transformation of sexuality into Eros . . . presupposes the rational reorganization of a large industrial apparatus, a highly specialized societal division of labor, the use of fantastically destructive energies, and the co-operation of vast masses." The achievement of "libidinal work relations," it appears, requires the organization of society into a vast industrial army.

Brown's Thanatology: The Pathology of Purposefulness
Brown, like Marcuse, condemns purposeful activity as a substitute for deeper gratifications, but he maintains this position more consistently, without any last-minute appeals to technological deliverance. He confronts the problem of "scarcity," moreover, in a spirit closer to Freud's. He traces

psychic conflict not to the demands of work but to separation anxiety, ultimately to the fear of death. For Marcuse, the "struggle for existence necessitates the repressive modification of the instincts chiefly because of the lack of sufficient means and resources for integral, painless and toilless gratification of instinctual needs." For Brown, the "lack of sufficient means and resources" derives not from the social organization of production but from the very urgency of instinctual demands. "Scarcity" is experienced first of all as a shortage of undivided mother-love. (From this point of view, the Oedipus complex merely reinforces a lesson the child learns much earlier.) "It is because the child loves the mother so much that it feels separation from the mother as death." The fear of separation contaminates the "narcissistic project of loving union with the world with the unreal project of becoming oneself one's whole world." It not only "activates a regressive death wish" but directs it outward in the form of aggression. Even the Oedipus complex, according to Brown, originates not so much in jealousy of the father as in the wish to overcome separation and dependence by "having a child by the mother [and thus] becoming father of oneself." Unable to bear either separation or dependence, the child conceives the fantasy of absolute self-sufficiency—the *causa sui* project, as Brown calls it, of becoming his own father—which the fear of castration (still another form of separation anxiety, because it threatens the instrument through which this project is to be carried out) forces him to repress.

Brown's reading of Freud is superior to Marcuse's in several respects. It disposes of the notion that sexual pleasure is the only object of repression. It disposes of the corollary that neurosis arises out of a conflict between pleasure and the patriarchal work ethic, between Eros and civilized morality. It exposes the dependence of these ideas on naive theories of historical progress abandoned by Freud in his later psychological writings. "Freud's early theory," Brown writes in *Life against Death,* "assumes that what is repressed is simply Eros (or play); it also assumes that repression comes from the outside—from the threatening father in the castration complex, from the toilet-training parents in the analogous anal trauma." The neo-Freudian schools of cultural anthropology and psychoanalytic revisionism, as Brown notes, carry these assumptions one step further. Since cultures differ in their attitude toward sexuality, since parental practices cover a wide range between permissiveness and repression, and since the structure of the family itself varies from one culture to another, it follows that culture, not biology, is the principal determinant of character, and furthermore that culture itself consists largely of the "variable actualities of infant-rearing practices," as Brown contemptuously puts it. Brown is a more trenchant critic of neo-Freudian revisionism than Marcuse. It is not only the "revisionist emphasis on the influence of 'social conditions' " that is misguided, as Marcuse contends. Revisionist theories of culture rest on the more fundamental misconception that repression originates in parental control over infantile sexuality. As Brown points out, "One of the relics of Freud's earlier theories, not consistently abandoned in his later formulations and still littering the textbook expositions of psychoanalysis, is the notion that the essence of the phallic stage of infantile sexuality is masturbation, and the essence of the castration complex is the repression of masturbation by the parental (usually paternal) threat to punish by castration." In his early years, Freud hoped that a relaxation of "civilized sexual morality" would reduce psychic conflict and suffering. Neo-Freudian revisionism clings to this humanitarian, reformist, "prophylactic" interpretation of the psychoanalytic mission, often tying it—as in the works of Fromm and Wilhelm Reich—to a socialist critique of "patricentric-acquisitive" institutions. The trouble with revisionism, then, is not that it "glorifies adjustment" and makes the individual conform to a repressive civilization, as Marcuse claims, but that its vision of sexual liberation remains embedded in simplistic theories of psychological conflict.

Having disposed of the neo-Freudian anthropology that occupies itself with superficial variations in child-rearing techniques, having rejected even Marcuse's distinction between repression and surplus repression, Brown finds it difficult to fend off the conclusion that "there are certain difficulties inherent in the very nature of culture," as Freud wrote in *Civilization and Its Discontents,* "which will not yield to any efforts at reform." Yet Brown cannot accept such a conclusion. Whereas Freud refused to "rise up as a prophet before my fellow men," bowing, he said, "to their reproach that I have no consolation to offer them," Brown insists that psychoanalysis must "transform itself into social criticism" and redefine itself as a "project to change human culture." The findings of psychoanalysis, with their "painful assault on human pride," would be insupportable, he thinks, if psychoanalysis could not "simultaneously offer a hope of better things." Only the hope of a "better way" makes it possible "to explore the bitter dregs of psychoanalytic theory."

It cannot be said of Brown, as Marcuse said of the neo-Freudians, that he recovers optimism cheaply. He builds his case for hope on Freud's hypothesis of a death instinct, the most "disheartening" of all his ideas, as Freud said, but also, unfortunately, the most speculative and dubious, the one least supported by clinical evidence. The postulate of a death instinct, Brown claims, points a "way out" of the human malaise—a "solution to the problem of aggression" and the "possibility of a consciousness not based on repression." Freud's insight that all instinctual activity seeks relief from tension—the Nirvana principle—means that at the biological level, according to Brown, life and death do not conflict.

The goal of life is death: that is, a state of absolute rest. "The lilies of the field . . . take no thought of the morrow." Man alone finds it impossible to accept the life "proper to his species," Brown argues. His "incapacity to accept death" condemns him to restless activity. He cannot conceive of the possibility of an existence that reconciles life and death. "Faustian characters as we are, we cannot imagine 'rest,' 'Nirvana,' 'eternity' except as death." Culture disrupts the "balanced equilibrium between tension and release of tension which governs the activity of animals." Culture deforms the death instinct, the instinctual search for peace, into a "fixation to the past, which alienates the neurotic from the present and commits him to the unconscious quest for the past in the future." Because man is afraid to die, unlike the animals, he directs the "innate self-destructive tendency of the death instinct" outward, according to Brown. Destructiveness in humans represents a cultural modification of the death instinct. It arises out of a neurotic and distinctively human "obsession with the past and the future," which leads man to deflect the urge to die into the urge to kill, to impose his will on others, to surround himself with heirs, and thus to achieve a spurious immortality.

The "way out" lies, then, in a new culture that recognizes the "possibility of activity which is also at rest." Such a culture would have to be based on play, the only satisfactory alternative to "our current mode of activity." In order to overcome the "emotional objection" that a life without striving, a life of "perfect felicity," would be equivalent to death, Brown suggests that we think of play as the ideal form of activity, the one that most nearly approximates Aristotle's definition of God: "perfection conceived as activity." Having condemned all compensatory gratifications as inherently pathological, Brown has to represent play, however, as pure desire, unrepressed and unsublimated. He ignores the most salient facts about the psychology of play: that it originates in the search for a mother-substitute, tries to recapture the lost Nirvana of infancy, and yet serves to reconcile us to its loss by enabling us to assert our growing mastery over our surroundings. Unwilling to concede any virtue in the impulse to master our surroundings, seeing it, on the contrary, as the source of everything destructive in culture, Brown has to claim a privileged status for the imagination. "Play is the erotic mode of activity," he says in a passage that resurrects an outmoded conceptual scheme that he elsewhere opposes: the "essential character of activity governed by the pleasure-principle rather than the reality-principle." Refusing to acknowledge the psychological compromise underlying play and art, Brown insists that art, "not being a compromise with the unconscious, . . . affords positive satisfaction, and cannot be simply classed . . . with dreams and neurosis as a substitute-gratification."

Brown's highly unpsychoanalytic view of play indicates that he has drawn the wrong conclusions from Freud's essay *Beyond the Pleasure Principle,* that most puzzling of all Freudian texts. Instead of basing his own theory on the hypothesis of a death instinct, he would have done better to follow Freud in his attempt to redefine the pleasure principle as something beyond the purely negative goal of a release from tension. Groping for an understanding of the sexual instinct that would not simply subsume it under the "Nirvana principle," a longing for inertia, Freud suggested that libidinal energy seeks union with objects other than itself, or, in another formulation, that the pleasure principle represents a "modification" of the so-called death instinct and cannot, therefore, be reduced to a drive toward homeostasis. These speculations seem to lead to the conclusion that it is precisely the impossibility of complete satisfaction that prevents Eros from taking the "backward path" to oblivion and impels it forward into the compensatory satisfaction provided by art, play, and romantic love—by culture in general.

Psychoanalysis does not bear out Brown's belief in the "morbidity of human sociability as such," though it refuses, on the other hand, to endorse the belief "that there is an instinct towards perfection at work in human beings," as Freud put it, "which has brought them to their present high level of intellectual achievement and ethical sublimation and which may be expected to watch over their development into supermen." It refuses to dissolve the tension between instinct and culture, which it regards as the source of the best as well as the worst in human life. It holds that sociability not only thwarts but at the same time fulfills instinctual needs; that culture not only ensures the survival of the human species but also provides the genuine pleasures associated with collective exploration and mastery of the natural world; that exploration, discovery, and invention themselves draw on playful impulses; and that culture represents for man precisely the life "appropriate to his species." All this disappears in Brown's reduction of culture to a massive conspiracy against human nature and happiness. If we follow Freud, we have to reject both the neo-Freudian view of man as exclusively the product of culture and the Brownian view of man as "nothing but body" and of culture as the "negation of the body." Accordingly we have to reject Brown's demand for a "resurrection of the body" as the only cure for the disease of human sociability.

Freudian Feminism The effort to base a theory of cultural revolution on psychoanalysis leads to such insurmountable difficulties that we need to remind ourselves of the reasons that made it seem important to make the effort in the first place. Neither liberalism nor Marxism provides an adequate explanation of the destructiveness that has erupted in the twentieth century. The violent history of our epoch makes it impossible to accept the liberal formula according to which aggression is a response to frustration or the Marxist version of this formula, which traces it to economic exploitation and class rule. The problem goes deeper than capitalism or economic inequality. The search for the underlying malignancy that deforms human enterprise and aspiration thus prompts renewed interest in civilization and its discontents.

The feminist movement has dealt another blow to liberal and Marxist ideologies. Historically the oppression of women precedes the oppression of workers and peasants; indeed it can plausibly be considered as the original source of oppression, from which all other forms of injustice derive. Moreover, it has a cultural and psychological dimension; it cannot be regarded as purely economic either in its causes or in its effects. The rise of the women's movement appears to strengthen the argument that social change has to go further than a change in institutions or the distribution of political and economic power, that it has to confront the psychology of power itself, and that it has to take the form, in other words, of a cultural revolution. For those who seek to ground the case for such a revolution in Freud's psychological realism, feminism promises a theoretical escape from the dead end reached by Brown. It holds out the hope that it is not enterprise itself that is malignant but masculine enterprise, masculine aggression and militarism, masculine technology, masculine rationality, the masculine compulsion to cheat death through the vicarious immortality of notable deeds, wars, conquest, bigger and bigger bombs.

Earlier feminists denounced Freud as an apologist for male supremacy. Either they refused to have anything to do with psychoanalysis at all, or, like Karen Horney, Clara Thompson, and other revisionists, they attempted to counter Freud's "biological determinism" by introducing a corrective emphasis on culture. Recent feminist criticism of Freud for the most part rejects such simplifications. It neither tries to base the argument for feminism on watered-down versions of Freudian theory from which all contradictions have been removed nor, on the other hand, contents itself with a reply to Freud and his followers that takes the form of a "simple ideological opposite," as Stephanie Engel puts it. Instead of dismissing or denaturing Freud, feminists therefore seek "to reappropriate what is powerful and coherent in psychoanalytic theory by writing women and the feminine experience back into the center of the vision."

The interpretive strategy that emerges in recent work by Engel, Nancy Chodorow, Dorothy Dinnerstein, and Jessica Benjamin depends on accepting Freudian theory, in its general outlines, as an accurate account of psychic development under the "patriarchal" conditions that have prevailed throughout history (which assign child-rearing exclusively to the care of women and subordinate the work of nurture to the masculine projects of conquest and domination), while holding out the possibility that a radically different system of work and nurture would produce a radically different personality structure. Psychoanalysis reveals its patriarchal bias, in this view, not in Freud's *obiter dicta* on female inferiority (expressions of personal opinion that should not be allowed to obscure what is useful in his theoretical work), but in its inability to imagine any path of psychological maturation that does not presuppose a radical rejection of the mother, fearful submission to the father, and the internalization of his authority in the form of a guilty conscience. Psychoanalysis is thus compromised by its uncritical acceptance of the "ideal of the guilty, self-controlled, and realistic bourgeois man."

The new psychoanalytic feminism seeks to carry on the critique of "instrumental rationality" initiated by Max Horkheimer, T. W. Adorno, Marcuse, and Brown and to feminize it, as it were, by showing that instrumental values vitiate "critical theory" itself, which equates psychological autonomy with bourgeois individualism and the "patriar-chal" family. This line of argument, which links feminism to the critique of enlightenment, becomes most explicit in Jessica Benjamin's article "A World without Fathers." Freud, Horkheimer, and their misguided followers assume, according to Benjamin, that "freedom consists of isolation" and that "denial of the need for the other" represents the only "route to independence." And indeed the "objectifying and instrumentalizing attitude which is so pronounced in western patriarchy . . . implies not merely the subjugation but the *repudiation* of the mother by the father." It is in this sense, Benjamin insists, that our society remains patriarchal, contrary to the claim advanced by Marcuse, Alexander Mit-scherlich, and others that a fatherless society has already emerged. "Insofar as instrumental rationality prevails, we are [still] far from fatherless."

According to this line of argument, patriarchal values will continue to prevail as long as society assigns children exclu-sively to the care of women and subordinates the work of nurture to the masculine projects of conquest and domi-nation. Freudian feminists advocate more than an expanded role for men in child-care. In company with many other kinds of feminists, they call for the collectivization of child-rearing, on the grounds not only that the nuclear family oppresses women but that it produces an acquisitive, aggres-sive, authoritarian type of personality. "Studies of more col-lective childrearing situations," writes Nancy Chodorow, "(the kibbutzim, China, Cuba) suggest that children develop more sense of solidarity and commitment to the group, less individualism and competitiveness, are less liable to form intense, exclusive adult relations, than children reared in Western nuclear families." The nuclear family provides the psychological underpinning, in other words, of Brown's "nightmare of infinitely expanding technological progress." Because technological progress seems to have reached a dangerous dead end, it has become imperative to identify an alternative to the "patricentric" personality in the form of a narcissistic, Dionysian, or androgynous personality type. Now that Promethean man apparently stands on the brink of self-destruction, Narcissus looks like a more likely survivor. What some critics condemn as cultural and psychological regression looks to many feminists like a long overdue "feminization of American society," as Engel calls it. If the "basic feminine sense of self is connected to the world," as Nancy Chodorow argues, while the "basic masculine sense of self is separate," modern society obviously has no future as long as men hold the upper hand. Hence the Freudian feminists' "challenge to traditional psychoanalytic definitions of autonomy and morality," in Engel's words, and their attempt "to articulate conceptions of autonomy that are premised not simply on separation but also on the experiences of mutuality, relatedness, and the recognition of an other as a full subject."

The Case for Narcissism: "Masculine" Enterprise against "Feminine" Mutuality The conservative analysis of modern culture, as we have seen, attributes the increase in destructive violence to a decline of the superego, while liberal critics attribute it to a failure of the rational ego. Advocates of a cultural revolution point to the destructiveness of reason itself and side, in effect, with the ego ideal in its striving to recapture a sense of oneness with the world. Stephanie Engel makes this identification with the ego ideal explicit when she criticizes the "ideal of the radically autonomous and individuated man" allegedly upheld by Freud and cites Chasseguet-Smirgel's work on the ego ideal to support the possibility of psychological development and cultural creation "that is 'engendered' rather than fabricated." In a carefully balanced passage, she pleads for a union of the ego ideal and the superego.

The super-ego, heir to the oedipus complex, insists on reality and the separation of the child from the mother, whereas the ego-ideal, heir to the state of primary narcissism, restores the promise of the imagination, of desire, and the fantasy of re-fusion. The exclusive reign of the ego-ideal, the infantile fantasy of narcissistic triumph, forms the basis of illusion, of blind adherence to ideology, and of the perpetual desire . . . character-istic of narcissists. Yet the desire to reconcile ego and ego-ideal, the drive to return to the undifferentiated infantile state of primary narcissism, helps to provide the content and drive for imagination as well as for the emotions that are the heart of our creative life. Thus an alternative [to the Freudian model of emotional development, with its alleged overemphasis on the superego] is the insistence that neither agency of morality should overpower the other—this challenge to the moral hegemony of the super-ego would not destroy its power but would instead usher in a dual reign.

The case for narcissism has never been stated more persua-sively. The case collapses, however, as soon as the qualities associated respectively with the ego ideal and the superego are assigned a gender so that feminine "mutuality" and "relatedness" can be played off against the "radically autono-mous" masculine sense of self. That kind of argument dis-solves the contradiction held in tension by the psy-choanalytic theory of narcissism: namely, that all of us, men and women alike, experience the pain of separation and simultaneously long for a restoration of the original sense of union. Narcissism originates in the infant's symbiotic fusion with the mother, but the desire to return to this blissful state cannot be identified with "feminine mutuality" without ob-scuring both its universality and the illusions of "radical autonomy" to which it also gives rise, in women as well as in men. The desire for complete self-sufficiency is just as much a legacy of primary narcissism as the desire for mutu-ality and relatedness. Because narcissism knows no distinction between the self and others, it expresses itself in later life both in the desire for ecstatic union with others, as in romantic love, and in the desire for absolute independence from others, by means of which we seek to revive the original illusion of omnipotence and to deny our dependence on external sources of nourishment and gratification. The technological project of achieving independence from nature embodies the solipsistic side of narcissism, just as the desire for a mystical union with nature embodies its symbiotic and self-obliterating side. Since both spring from the same source—the need to deny the fact of dependence—it can only cause confusion to call the dream of technological omnipotence a masculine obsession, while extolling the hope of a more loving relation with nature as a characteristically feminine preoccupation. Both originate in the undifferentiated equilibrium of the prenatal state, and both, moreover, reject psychological maturation in favor of regression, the "feminine" longing for symbiosis no less so than the solipsistic "masculine" drive for absolute mastery.

The only way out of the impasse of narcissism is the creation of cultural objects, "transitional objects," that simultaneously restore a sense of connection with mothers and with Mother Nature and assert our mastery over nature, without denying our dependence on mothers or nature. It is precisely this compensatory activity, however, that is condemned by the party of the ego ideal—the party of Narcissus—on the grounds that substitute-gratifications are inherently pathological. Even Dorothy Dinnerstein, who reproaches Brown for confusing the "malignant aspect" of enterprise with enterprise in general, shares his prejudice against compensatory gratification. Purposeful activity, she argues, "gives us pleasure as straightforward as the pleasure of lovemaking"; it takes on a "malignant aspect" only when it serves as a substitute for the "early magic of the body." In fact, however, all purposeful activity, including play—

which Brown tries to privilege in the same way that Dinnerstein privileges enterprise uncontaminated by the "masculine" drive for mastery—carries this "implausible burden," as she calls it.* Lovemaking, artistic creation, and play do not provide "straightforward" satisfaction at all. Indeed they become most deeply satisfying when they remind us of the tension that precedes release, the separation that precedes reconciliation, the loss underlying restoration, the unavoidable otherness of the other. Purposeful activity becomes pathological not when it serves to compensate us for earlier losses but when it serves to deny those losses. It becomes pathological when it tries to keep alive the illusion of omnipotence: for example, by assuring us that we can make ourselves absolute masters over nature and thus want for nothing.

With their fear of "masculine" rationality and their exaggerated admiration for the narcissistic ego ideal, which embodies an allegedly feminine counterweight to the rational ego, the advocates of a cultural revolution hold up narcissism as the cure for a disease that springs from the same

---

*Notwithstanding their contempt for ego psychology, Brown, Marcuse, and their followers fall back on the very same strategy, at a crucial point in their argument, that Hartmann adopts in his theory of a conflict-free sphere of the ego: the strategy, that is, of exempting certain favored activities from psychoanalytic scrutiny. For Hartmann, it is purposeful activity and problem-solving that are privileged in this fashion; for the Freudian left, art and play, or in Dinnerstein's case, "straightforward" purposefulness that serves no hidden compensatory ends, carries no "implausible burden." Whereas Freud insisted on the underlying kinship between art and neurosis, Brown, Marcuse, and Dinnerstein try to salvage art and playful creativity from the psychoanalytic critique of human pretensions, just as Hartmann tries to salvage perception, language, and memory.

Art resembles the most deeply regressive psychosis in its attempt to restore a sense of oneness with the primal mother. What distinguishes art from psychosis or neurosis is that it also acknowledges the reality of separation. Art rejects the easy way of illusions. Like religion, it represents a hard-won restoration of the sense of wholeness, one that simultaneously reminds us of the sense of division and loss. Peter Fuller, drawing on the work of Hanna Segal, notes that a "working through of the conflict [between union and separation] must penetrate the work, even if the final outcome is cheerful or serene. . . . In the most aesthetically satisfying works, the formal resolution is never quite complete."

source. They recommend a narcissistic symbiosis with nature as the cure for technological solipsism, itself narcissistic
in its origin. This kind of thinking, shorn of its psychoanalytic subtleties and reduced to a handful of shopworn
slogans and platitudes, now permeates not only the women's
movement but the environmental movement and the peace
movement as well, whose adherents blindly follow feminists
in conceiving of "feminine" virtues as the remedy for environmental devastation, imperialism, and war. A recent book
on "men's liberation" by Jack Nichols outlines an argument
that has become commonplace. "If the survival of our species is our concern, it is certain that masculinist values have
outlived their usefulness in a nuclear age and are downright
dangerous." In another book on the "changing faces of
American manhood," one of an outpouring of such books,
Mark Gerzon makes the same point: "The 'masculine' traits
that formerly assured survival will now, if not balanced by
the 'feminine,' assure destruction. The manliness that
women once revered because it protected them is now increasingly condemned because it endangers them." Philip
Slater, Theodore Roszak, William Irwin Thompson, and
any number of feminist fellow-travelers have echoed this
now familiar line of psychocultural analysis. The culture of
industrialism is a phallic culture, according to Thompson,
which "climaxes in the technological rape of Vietnam."
"The adolescent who was sold his Honda by an ad in *Play-
boy* that showed it parting the thighs of a bikini-clad girl is
the same man who is now socking it to female Asia in his
bullet-spurting gunship." The predictable quality of such
arguments shows how deeply psychopolitical clichés,
thanks to feminism, psychiatry, and the culture of psychic
self-help, have penetrated into popular thinking.

Criticism of "patriarchal" values directs itself not merely
against the obvious targets—aggressiveness, militarism,
combativeness, the cult of toughness—but against the com-

pulsion to work, the "myth of objective consciousness" (as Roszak calls it), and the search for vicarious immortality through achievements, all of which are seen, from this point of view, as elements of a pathology specific to males. According to Slater, men suffer, as women do not, from the compulsion "to monumentalize themselves all over the environment." This is why women, in his view, "are in a better position to liberate our society emotionally." Men are programmed for competitive achievement, alienated from their bodies and from the emotions associated with bodily pleasure, as opposed to goal-directed orgasmic release. They envy the creative power of women, which alone brings new life into the world, and try to appropriate it for themselves by inventing machines and launching far-flung enterprises that simulate life and make women dispensable. "This effort to displace the female," Thompson writes, "seems to be the archetypal foundation for civilization, for mankind has been at it ever since. Whether he is challenging Mother Nature in flying away from her in rockets, or in changing her on earth through genetic engineering, man has not given up on the attempt to take away the mysteries of life from the Great Mother and the conservative female religion." According to Mary Daly, "male demonic destructiveness" originates in the dream of dispensing with women altogether, of creating life without the collaboration of women. Masculine projects —war in particular—provide a "cover for personal emptiness" and inadequacy. As Roszak explains it, war and military technology arise out of a "castration-haunted psychology." The political establishment professes to concern itself with "higher politics and heady ideology," but "its space rocket and ballistic missile rivalry all too clearly" embody a "world-wide contest of insecure penises out to prove their size and potency." Valerie Solanas offers the same reductive interpretation of war in her *S.C.U.M. Manifesto.* "The male, because of his obsession to compensate for not being female combined with his inability to relate and to feel compassion, . . . is responsible for WAR. The male's normal method of compensation for not being female, namely, getting his Big Gun off, is grossly inadequate, as he can get it off only a very limited number of times; so he gets it off on a really massive scale, and proves to the entire world that he's a 'Man.' "

Women stand for the "sympathetic resonance of subject and object," according to Thompson, and therefore serve as the source and inspiration of a "holistic epistemology." Again and again, critics of militarism, corporate enterprise, and industrial technology insist that "masculine" individualism, which puts us at odds with our neighbors and with nature, has to give way to a new sense of solidarity. "A new consciousness is rising," June Singer announces in *Androgyny*, a "feminine consciousness" that rejects individualism, separation, "logical thinking," and "linear reasoning." The old ego-centered psychology is yielding to a "holistic" psychology that sees the self as part of an ecological continuum, a "vast over-all plan." The new sensibility, according to Marilyn Ferguson, rests on a recognition of the limits of rational thought" and a rejection of "causality," "scientific proof," "logic," and a linear view of the world." Ralph Metzner argues that "analysis probes, goes into, takes apart." "It is a masculine, dynamic function." Synthesis, on the other hand, "contains, combines, encloses: it is a feminine magnetic function." The emergence of a new "ecology of mind," according to Lewis J. Perelman, requires an abandonment of our "obsolete selves," a "reduction of the scope of the conscious self," and a repudiation of the "conceptual separation of man from nature." The "appropriate emergent values will tend to be communal rather than individualistic," Robert Hunter writes in *The Storming of the Mind*. Ecological awareness, drugs, television, rock music, and Eastern religions have helped to "diffuse the boundaries between the inside of the mind and the outside, thus bringing a quality of 'one-ness' into the world." In a recent study of evangelical and charismatic movements, Jeremy Rifkin and Ted Howard agree that "the notion of self-reliance and the centrality of the individual (which is so intimate a part of the Protestant ethic and the liberal ethos) will continue to lose its driving force as society makes its final transformation into a service economy and as increased economic scarcity places a greater pressure on the public sector to serve as a forum for the resolution and advancement of collective economic needs." According to Henry Malcolm, the cultural value of narcissism lies in the "nondifferentiation of the self from the world."

The appeal of these ideas lies in their seeming ability to address some of the most obviously important issues of the times: the arms race and the danger of nuclear war, the technological destruction of the environment, the limits of economic growth. As Barbara Gelpi contends, it has become "urgently important for the men in our patriarchal society to recognize the feminine within themselves before the untrammelled combination of masculine science and masculine aggressiveness destroys us all." The "metaphysical reconstruction" advocated by E. F. Schumacher and other environmentalists appears to hinge on the cultivation of a new sense of oneness with nature, an understanding, as Kai Curry-Lindahl puts it in his *Conservation for Survival,* that "man is as dependent on nature as an unborn child on its mother." In an essay entitled "Prometheus Rebound," Jean Houston traces the environmental crisis to the "dualistic agony of man separate from nature." "It is enormously significant," she writes, "that the current crisis in consciousness . . . occurs concomitantly with the ecological destruction of the planet by technological means." The need to "reverse the ecological plunder" gives urgency and direction to a mounting dissatisfaction with consumerism and competitive individualism. Humanity's very survival depends on the discovery of "new forms of consciousness and fulfillment apart from the traditional ones of consumption, control, aggrandizement, and manipulation. The time has come to take off the psychological shelf all the dormant potentials that were not immediately necessary to man in his role as Promethean Man-over-Nature." The "ecological conscience," according to Robert Disch, renounces the "illusion of separateness from and superiority over" nature. It recognizes the need for a "universal symbiosis with land," as Aldo Leopold put it many years ago. Gregory Bateson, another forerunner and prophet of the "ecological psyche," as it has been called, argued on many occasions that Western conceptions of selfhood had to be replaced by an understanding of the way "personal identity merges into all the processes of relationship in some vast ecology or aesthetics of cosmic interaction." The "concept of 'self,' " Bateson maintained, can "no longer function as a nodal argument in the punctuation of experience," since we now understand, thanks to cybernetics, that the ecological system as a whole is more important than the individual organisms that comprise it. Indeed the "unit of survival—either in ethics or in evolution—is not the organism or the species" but the entire environment on which the organism depends. "The 'self' is a false reification of an improperly delimited part of this much larger field of interlocking processes." Linear, purposive thinking ignores the interconnections characteristic of complex, "cybernetically integrated" systems. It exaggerates the importance of conscious control, as when Freud turns the proper relations between thought and feeling "upside down" and tries to replace the id with the ego. Psychoanalysis, in Bateson's view, is the "product of an almost totally distorted epistemology and a totally distorted view of what sort of thing a man, or any other organism is." In common with other varieties of scientific materialism, it overlooks the "vast and integrated network of mind." It amounts to a "monstrous denial of the integration of that whole."

Purposefulness, Nature, and Selfhood: The Case for a Guilty Conscience   The critique of the rational or "masculine" ego, which has now found a political home in a number of important movements for social and cultural change, not only addresses issues of growing concern but identifies weaknesses in the dominant political traditions, especially in the liberal tradition, that can no longer be ignored. My objections to the "new consciousness" must not be misunderstood as a defense of liberal humanism or as an attack on feminism, environmentalism, or the peace movement. I believe in the goals of these movements and join in their demand for a realignment of political forces, an abandonment of the old political ideologies, and a reorientation of values. I share their conviction that a "cultural revolution" is an essential precondition of political change, though not a substitute for it. It is precisely because the party of Narcissus, as I have called it, has gone so much further than others in calling attention to the dangers of "instrumental reason" and industrial technology that its ideas need to be subjected to careful scrutiny. A new politics of conservation has to rest on a solid philosophical foundation, not on a critique of instrumental reason that extends to every form of purposeful activity. It has to rest on a respect for nature, not on a mystical adoration of nature. It has to rest on a firm conception of selfhood, not on the belief that the "separate self is an illusion." A brief review of these three issues—purposefulness, nature, and selfhood—will bring this essay to a conclusion.

The antidote to instrumental reason is practical reason, not mysticism, spirituality, or the power of "personhood." In the Aristotelian tradition of political theory, *phronesis* or practical reason describes the development of character, the moral perfection of life, and the virtues specific to various forms of practical activity. Technique, on the other hand, concerns itself exclusively with the means appropriate to a given end. The highest form of practice, for Aristotle and his followers, is politics, which seeks to promote the good life by conferring equal rights on all citizens and by establishing rules and conventions designed not so much to solve the problems of social living as to encourage citizens to test themselves against demanding standards of moral excellence (for example, in contests of oratorical skill and physical prowess) and thus to develop their gifts to the highest pitch. The Aristotelian conception of practice has more in common with play than with activities defined as practical in the modern sense. Practices in the Aristotelian sense have nothing to do, as such, with the production of useful objects or with satisfying material needs. This goes even for the practice of politics. Only in the sixteenth century did Machiavelli and Thomas More define material survival, the physical maintenance of life, as the chief business of the state. From that position it was a short step to the modern conception of politics as political economy, which assumes, as Jürgen Habermas points out, that "individuals are exclusively motivated to maximize their private wants, desires, and interests."

The classical conception carries with it a certain contempt for the production of material comforts and useful objects (which it assigns to the lowly realm of the household) and an unacceptably restrictive definition of citizenship (one that includes only those who have freed themselves from material necessity); but it nevertheless enables us to identify one of the distinctive features of the industrial worldview: its instrumentalization and debasement of practical activity. Instrumentalism regards the relation of ends and means as purely external, whereas the older tradition, now almost forgotten, holds that the choice of the means appropriate to a given end has to be considered as it contributes to internal goods as well. In other words, the choice of means has to be governed by their conformity to standards of excellence designed to extend human capacities for self-understanding and self-mastery. Industrial societies conceive of the extension of human powers only as the replacement of human labor by machinery. As work and politics lose their educative content and degenerate into pure technique, the very distinction between technique and practice becomes incomprehensible. Industrial societies have almost completely lost sight of the possibility that work and politics can serve as character-forming disciplines. These activities are now understood strictly as means of satisfying material needs. Moral ideas, meanwhile, lose their connection with practical life and with the virtues specific to particular practices and become confused instead with the exercise of purely personal choices and the expression of personal prejudices and tastes, which can be neither justified nor explained and which should therefore not be regarded as binding on anyone else.

It is the deterioration of public life, together with the privatization and trivialization of moral ideas, that prevents a collaborative assault on the environmental and military difficulties confronting modern nations. But the party of Narcissus does not understand the source of these difficulties: the confusion of practice with technique. It shares this confusion and thus repudiates all forms of purposeful action in favor of playful, artistic pursuits, which it misunderstands, moreover, as activities without structure or purpose. When it insists on the pathology of purposefulness, it merely reverses industrial ideology. Where the prevailing ideology swallows up practice into a cult of technique, the "counterculture" indiscriminately rejects both and advocates a renunciation of will and purpose as the only escape from Promethean technology. Disparaging human inventiveness, which it associates only with destructive industrial technologies, it defines the overriding imperative of the present age as a return to nature. It ignores the more important need to restore the intermediate world of practical activity, which binds man to nature in the capacity of a loving caretaker and cultivator, not in a symbiotic union that simply denies the reality of man's separation from nature.

An environmental ethic ought to affirm the possibility of living in peace with nature while acknowledging that separation. Nature sets limits to human freedom, but it does not define freedom; nor does it, by itself, offer us a home. Our home is the earth, which includes a marvelously salubrious natural environment but also includes the durable world of human objects and associations. The crowning indictment of industrial civilization is not merely that it has ravaged nature but that it has undermined confidence in the continuity and permanence of the man-made world by surrounding us with disposable goods and with fantastic images of commodities. Confusion about the distinction between practice and technique is closely bound up with confusion about man's relation to nature. Human beings are part of an intricately interconnected evolutionary chain, but self-consciousness—the capacity to see the self from a point of view outside the self—distinguishes humanity from other forms of life and leads both to a sense of power over nature and to a sense of alienation from nature. Dependent on nature yet capable of transcending it, humanity wavers between transcendent pride and a humiliating sense of weakness and dependency. It seeks to dissolve this tension either by making itself altogether self-sufficient or by dreaming of a symbiotic reunion with the primordial source of life. The first path leads to the attempt to impose human will on nature through technology and to achieve an absolute independence from nature; the second, to a complete surrender of the will.

If men were moved solely by impulse and self-interest,

they would be content, like other animals, simply to survive. Nature knows no will-to-power, only a will-to-live. With man, needs become desires; even the acquisitive enterprise has a spiritual dimension, which makes men want more than they need. This is why it is useless to urge men to renounce material pleasures in favor of a more spiritual existence. It is precisely the spiritual side of human experience that makes men want more than is good for them. It is equally useless to urge men to be governed, in the interest of their survival as a species, strictly by their biological needs. Even those who understand the "wide gulf between the purely natural impulse of survival and the distinctively human and spiritual impulse of pride and power," as Reinhold Niebuhr once observed, too often tend to seek a quick and easy return to the harmony of a purely natural existence. "The perversity of romantic naturalism," Niebuhr wrote—which reappears in many phases of the contemporary environmental movement—"consists in its primitivistic effort to regain the innocency of nature" and "to reconstitute the harmony of nature on a new level of historical decision." Such a program misunderstands human freedom, which makes it impossible to recreate natural harmony in history. The innocence of nature is harmony without freedom.

At this point in history, it is essential to question the boundless confidence in human powers that acknowledges no limits, which finds its ultimate expression in the technology of nuclear warfare. But this cannot be done by disavowing all forms of purposive intelligence or by dissolving the subject-object distinction that allegedly underlies it—the "strange dualistic epistemology characteristic of Occidental civilization," as Bateson calls it. Selfhood—an obsolete idea, according to Bateson and other proponents of the "new consciousness"—is precisely the inescapable awareness of man's contradictory place in the natural order of things. Advocates of a cultural revolution echo the dominant culture not only in their confusion of practice with technique but in their equation of selfhood with the rational ego. Like their opponents, they see rationality as the essence of selfhood. Accordingly, they argue for a "resurrection of the body," for "feminine" intuition and feeling against the instrumental reason of the male, for the alleged aimlessness of play, and for the "poetic imagination," as Bateson puts it, as a corrective to "false reifications of the 'self.' " The distinguishing characteristic of selfhood, however, is not rationality but the critical awareness of man's divided nature. Selfhood expresses itself in the form of a guilty conscience, the painful awareness of the gulf between human aspirations and human limitations. "Bad conscience is inseparable from freedom," Jacques Ellul reminds us. "There is no freedom without an accompanying critical attitude to the self," and this "excess of freedom and the critical turning back upon the self that freedom begets," he adds, "are at the source of dialectical thinking and the dialectical interpretation of history."

Both the champions and the critics of the rational ego turn their back on what remains valuable in the Western, Judaeo-Christian tradition of individualism (as opposed to the tradition of acquisitive individualism, which parodies and subverts it): the definition of selfhood as tension, division, conflict. As Niebuhr pointed out, attempts to ease an uneasy conscience take the form of a denial of man's divided nature. "Either the rational man or the natural man is conceived as essentially good." If the party of the ego glorifies the rational man, the party of Narcissus seeks to dissolve tension in its own way, by dreaming of a symbiotic reunion with nature. It glorifies the natural man, often after redefining nature itself, however, as an aspect of some universal mind.

As for the party of the superego, it equates conscience not with an awareness of the dialectical relationships between freedom and the capacity for destruction but with adherence to a received body of authoritative moral law. It hankers for the restoration of punitive sanctions against disobedience, above all for the restoration of fear. It forgets that conscience (as distinguished from the superego) originates not so much in the "fear of God" as in the urge to make amends. Conscience arises not so much from the dread of reprisals by those we have injured or wish to injure as in the capacity for mourning and remorse. In individuals, its development signifies the child's growing awareness that the parents he wishes to punish and destroy are the same parents on whom he relies for love and nourishment. It represents the simultaneous acceptance of dependence—on fathers, on mothers, on nature—and of our inevitable separation from the primordial source of life.

In the history of civilization, the emergence of conscience can be linked among other things to changing attitudes toward the dead. The idea that the dead call for revenge, that their avenging spirits haunt the living, and that the living know no peace until they placate these ancestral ghosts gives way to an attitude of genuine mourning. At the same time, vindictive gods give way to gods who show mercy as well and uphold the morality of loving your enemy. Such a morality has never achieved anything like general popularity, but it lives on, even in our own enlightened age, as a reminder both of our fallen state and of our surprising capacity for gratitude, remorse, and forgiveness, by means of which we now and then transcend it.

Acknowledgments and Bibliographical Notes

Instead of burdening the text of this book with a cumbersome apparatus of reference notes, I have decided to acknowledge my sources and obligations in the following essay, which not only provides publishing information about works already referred to but elaborates further on some of them, discusses a number of other relevant works, and, in general, tries to convey some sense of this book's intellectual and theoretical background.

First I wish to acknowledge a number of more immediate obligations. My research assistants, Everett Akam, Jonathan Elwitt, Shelley Gurstein, and David Steigerwald, helped to gather material for this book. The manuscript benefited from a close reading by my wife Nell. Jean DeGroat typed the final copy. The American Council of Learned Societies and the Ford Foundation provided financial support at a crucial stage in its composition. I am grateful to all of them.

I INTRODUCTION: CONSUMPTION, NARCISSISM, AND MASS CULTURE

The State of American Culture Both the right-wing critique of "secular humanism," pacifism, and permissiveness and the liberal critique of consumerism, alluded to at the beginning of this chapter, are too familiar to require documentation: such arguments are the common coin of recent political and cultural debate. On the other hand, those who deny the existence of a "national malaise" or "crisis of confidence" have formulated their position very explicitly in books that try to assess the state of American culture and to refute its detractors. As already noted, those who take this position do not always agree among themselves. They agree only in their opposition to the characterization of contemporary culture as a "culture of narcissism." Some are themselves very critical of consumerism —even, in Philip Slater's case, of "narcissism," which he defines as the masculine illusion of independence and self-sufficiency. See his *Pursuit of Loneliness* (Boston: Beacon Press, 1970) and *Earthwalk* (Garden City, New York: Anchor Press, 1974); Theodore Roszak, *Person/Planet* (Garden City, New York: Doubleday, 1978); and Paul L. Wachtel, *The Poverty of Affluence: A Psychological Portrait of the American Way of Life* (New York: Free Press, 1983). Other works in this vein, not addressed, however, to the controversy about "narcissism," include Gregory Bateson, *Steps toward an Ecology of Mind* (San Francisco: Chandler, 1972); Morris Berman, *The Reenchantment of the World* (Ithaca, New York: Cornell University Press, 1981), which draws heavily on Bateson's work; and the many books and articles written in opposition not merely to consumer capitalism but to Western rationalism, Western technology, and the Western sense of selfhood, listed below in the bibliographical notes to chapter VII. In their sensitivity to ecological issues and their understanding that an ecologically sensible way of life requires profound economic changes as well as cultural changes, all these analyses differ from ones that belittle talk of a political and economic crisis and advocate a "cultural revolution," in effect, as a substitute for political and economic changes.

In *New Rules: Searching for Self-Fulfillment in a World Turned Upside Down* (New York: Random House, 1981), Daniel Yankelovich explicitly recommends investigation of the "genuine cultural revolution" allegedly in progress as an antidote to gloom. "I want to show that while a prognosis of our future based solely on our political/economic prospects may leave us pessimistic, even desperate, one based on our cultural prospects —our shared values—may, rather unexpectedly, point the way toward a brighter future." Other books that try to point the same effortless way toward a brighter future include Peter Clecak, *America's Quest for the Ideal Self: Dissent and Fulfillment in the 60s and 70s* (New York: Oxford University Press, 1983); Marilyn Ferguson, *The Aquarian Conspiracy* (Los Angeles: J. P. Tarcher, 1980); Alvin Toffler, *The Third Wave* (New York: William Morrow, 1980); Betty Friedan, *The Second Stage* (New York:

Summit Books, 1981); Duane Elgin, *Voluntary Simplicity: An Ecological Lifestyle That Promotes Personal and Social Renewal* (New York: Bantam Books, 1981); and, among the older works in this mold, Charles Reich, *The Greening of America* (New York: Random House, 1970), and Henry Malcolm, *Generation of Narcissus* (Boston: Beacon Press, 1971).

Mass Culture Patrick Brantlinger provides a rather confusing introduction to the controversy about mass culture in his *Bread and Circuses: Theories of Mass Culture as Social Decay* (Ithaca, New York: Cornell University Press, 1983)—confusing, because he devotes most of the book to an attack on the "doomsday syndrome" only to concede, at the last minute, that our "social landscape . . . in great measure merits the doomsaying" advanced by critics of mass culture. Those critics include Max Horkheimer, "Art and Mass Culture," *Studies in Philosophy and Social Science* 9 (1941): 290–304; Dwight Macdonald, "A Theory of Popular Culture," *Politics* 1 (February 1944): 20–23; Max Horkheimer and Theodor W. Adorno, "The Culture Industry: Enlightenment as Mass Deception," in their *Dialectic of Enlightenment*, originally published in 1944 (New York: Herder and Herder, 1972), pp. 120–67; Irving Howe, "Notes on Mass Culture," *Politics* 5 (Spring 1948): 120–23; Leo Lowenthal, "Historical Perspectives of Popular Culture," *American Journal of Sociology* 55 (1950): 323–32; Dwight Macdonald, "A Theory of Mass Culture," *Diogenes* 3 (Summer 1953): 1–17; and Dwight Macdonald, "Masscult and Midcult," *Partisan Review* 27 (1960): 203–33, reprinted in his *Against the American Grain* (New York: Random House, 1962), pp. 3–75. Some of these essays are collected, together with many others on both sides of the debate, in Bernard Rosenberg and David Manning White, eds., *Mass Culture: The Popular Arts in America* (Glencoe, Illinois: Free Press, 1957).

All these attacks on mass culture come from the left. Mass culture has also been attacked from the right; but the conservative critique is less interesting than the radical one, partly because it is ideologically predictable, partly because it starts from the dubious premise that the masses have actually overthrown established elites and gained political power for themselves. The best example of this kind of argument is Jose Ortega y Gasset, *The Revolt of the Masses* (New York: W. W. Norton, 1932).

The standard arguments in opposition to the critique of mass culture appear in Edward Shils, "Daydreams and Nightmares: Reflections on the Criticism of Mass Culture," *Sewanee Review* 65 (1957): 587–608, and in Herbert Gans, *Popular Culture and High Culture: An Analysis and Evaluation of Taste* (New York: Basic Books, 1974). For the argument that

264 | Acknowledgments and Notes

"modernization" exposes people to an ever-increasing abundance of personal choices, see Fred Weinstein and Gerald M. Platt, *The Wish to Be Free: Society, Psyche, and Value Change* (Berkeley: University of California Press, 1969).

The coerciveness of the mass culture debate and the difficulty of reformulating it are suggested by Gans's reply to an article of mine ("Mass Culture Reconsidered," *democracy* 1 [October 1981]: 7–22), in which I argued against the "belief that if democratic institutions were to prosper, the masses would have to be roused from their age-old intellectual torpor and equipped with the tools of critical thought." Taking as a point of departure Randolph Bourne's contention that true cosmopolitanism has to be rooted in particularism, I maintained that the experience of uprootedness, so characteristic of modern mass societies, leads not to cultural pluralism but to aggressive nationalism, centralization, and the consolidation of state and corporate power. Gans nevertheless managed to find in this argument only the old claim that the "capitalistic mass media," in his paraphrase, "continue to keep the masses in their 'age-old intellectual torpor' and . . . that America could not be a political democracy until and unless Americans were cultured." In other words, he attributed to me the very beliefs I had tried to refute. (This exchange appeared in *democracy* 2 [April 1982]: 81–92. Needless to say, Gans never acknowledged his misreading of my position.)

Pluralism The theory of pluralism, which underlies the defense of mass culture advanced by Gans and Clecak, has an intellectual ancestry so complicated that I can do no more than to list some of the major works. We need a historical study of this concept, just as we still need a historical guide to the controversy about mass culture. The basic postwar texts include Louis Hartz, *The Liberal Tradition in America* (New York: Harcourt, Brace, 1955); Daniel Boorstin, *The Genius of American Politics* (Chicago: University of Chicago Press, 1953); Richard Hofstadter, *The Age of Reform* (New York: Alfred A. Knopf, 1955), and *Anti-Intellectualism in American Life* (New York: Alfred A. Knopf, 1963); Robert A. Dahl, *Who Governs? Democracy and Power in an American City* (New Haven: Yale University Press, 1963); Bernard Berelson, Paul F. Lazarsfeld, and William N. McPhee, *Voting* (Chicago: University of Chicago Press, 1954); and David Truman, *The Governmental Process* (New York: Alfred A. Knopf, 1951). Criticism of pluralist theory has concerned itself almost exclusively with its political dimension, even though it has wider application, as yet unstudied and uncriticized, as a theory of culture. See Theodore Lowi, "The Public Philosophy: Interest-Group Liberalism,"

American Political Science Review 61 (1967): 5–24; Michael Parenti, "Power and Pluralism: A View from the Bottom," *Journal of Politics* 32 (1970): 501–30; Peter Bachrach and Morton S. Baratz, "Two Faces of Power," *American Political Science Review* 56 (1962): 947–52; and Peter Bachrach, *The Theory of Democratic Elitism: A Critique* (Washington, D.C.: University Press of America, 1980).

Consumption, Work, and Social Discipline   Daniel Bell's *Cultural Contradictions of Capitalism* (New York: Basic Books, 1976) has already been discussed; see also his *Coming of Post-Industrial Society* (New York: Basic Books, 1973). My own analysis of the connection between consumerism and the degradation of work begins with Harry Braverman's *Labor and Monopoly Capital: The Degradation of Work in the Twentieth Century* (New York: Monthly Review Press, 1974), which examines the introduction of scientific management and the division of labor between the planning and execution of tasks. Once industrial labor had been reduced to a routine, two things followed. First, workers had to be encouraged to find satisfactions in consumption that could no longer be found in work. Second, new forms of labor discipline had to be devised in order to deal with the problems of "motivation" and "morale" that began to arise when workers lost control of the design and rhythm of work. The new "human services" or "helping professions"—such is my contention—played a central part in both developments. Along with the advertising and public relations industries, they articulated the values—self-expression, creativity, personal mobility—on which a culture of consumption had to rest. They also upheld a new conception of authority and a new therapeutic style of social discipline, which they introduced into the factory as the solution to the "human factor of production," as they called it. Later they extended the new techniques of social management —which depended above all, as I have argued, on the systematic observation and measurement of allegedly symptomatic data—into politics, education, and almost every other phase of social life.

This argument draws, rather eclectically, on a variety of intellectual traditions. It draws on the historical analysis of the "tutelary complex" worked out by Michel Foucault, *Discipline and Punish*, Alan Sheridan, trans. (New York: Pantheon, 1977), and especially by Jacques Donzelot, *The Policing of Families*, Robert Hurley, trans. (New York: Pantheon, 1979), a book that reinforces many of the points advanced in my *Haven in a Heartless World: The Family Besieged* (New York: Basic Books, 1977). My interpretation of consumerism and the new therapeutic system of social discipline also draws, though much more selectively, on recent historical scholarship dealing with the rise of professionalism and its relation to reform movements: Robert Wiebe, *The Search for Order* (New York: Hill and Wang, 1967); Burton Bledstein, *The Culture of Professionalism* (New York: W. W. Norton, 1976); and Magali Sarfati Larson, *The Rise of Professionalism* (Berkeley: University of California Press, 1977), among others. It draws on Ivan Illich's studies of professionalism and technology, especially *Medical Nemesis* (New York: Pantheon, 1976), and on other critiques of professionalism, notably Eliot Freidson, *Professional Dominance: The Social Structure of Medical Care* (New York: Atherton, 1970), and Nicholas N. Kittrie, *The Right to Be Different: Deviance and Enforced Therapy* (Baltimore: Johns Hopkins University Press, 1970). It also draws, of course, on primary sources, especially those concerning the rise of "human relations" in management and the extension of these techniques into other areas: Elton Mayo, *The Human Problems of an Industrial Civilization* (New York: Macmillan, 1933); Fritz J. Roethlisberger and William J. Dickson, *Management and the Worker* (Cambridge: Harvard University Press, 1939); Thomas North Whitehead, *The Industrial Worker* (New York: Oxford University Press, 1938); and the files of such journals as *Applied Anthropology, Human Relations,* and *Psychiatry,* which throw a great deal of light on the merger of social science, the management of industrial relations, and the applied science of social pathology. Some of this ground has already been covered in my *Haven in a Heartless World,* in *The Culture of Narcissism* (New York: W. W. Norton, 1979), and in "Democracy and the 'Crisis of Confidence,' " *democracy* 1 (January 1981): 25–40, in which the reader will also find further indications of my sources and obligations.

On politics as an object of consumption, see David Riesman, *The Lonely Crowd* (New Haven: Yale University Press, 1950), still one of the most suggestive analyses, and Walter Dean Burnham, "Party Systems and the Political Process," in William Nisbet Chambers and Walter Dean Burnham, eds., *The American Party Systems,* 2nd ed. (New York: Oxford University Press, 1975). On consumption in general, see Stewart Ewen, *Captains of Consciousness: Advertising and the Social Roots of Consumer Culture* (New York: McGraw-Hill, 1976); Stewart Ewen and Elizabeth Ewen, *Channels of Desire: Mass Images and the Shaping of American Consciousness* (New York: McGraw-Hill, 1982); and the essays in Richard Wightman Fox and T. J. Jackson Lears, eds., *The Culture of Consumption* (New York: Pantheon, 1983).

My analysis of the "fantastic world of commodities" and its obliteration of the distinction between the self and not-self owes more to art and literature (see below, chap. IV) than to social theory or social criticism;

but see, on the general subject of spectacle, Edgar Morin, *L'ésprit du temps* (Paris: Bernard Grasset, 1962); Guy Debord, *La Société du Spectacle* (Paris: Buchet-Chastel, 1967); and Jean Baudrillard, *For a Critique of the Political Economy of the Sign*, Charles Levin, trans. (St. Louis: Telos Press, 1981). On "Sloanism," see Emma Rothschild, *Paradise Lost: The Decline of the Auto-Industrial Age* (New York: Random House, 1973). See also Hannah Arendt, *The Human Condition* (Chicago: University of Chicago Press, 1958), on the importance of the durable world of man-made objects, especially chapter XII, "The Thing-Character of the World."

Identity   Erving Goffman, *The Presentation of Self in Everyday Life* (Garden City, New York: Doubleday, 1959), and *Stigma: Notes on the Management of Spoiled Identity* (Englewood Cliffs, New Jersey: Prentice-Hall, 1963); Erik H. Erikson, *Identity: Youth and Crisis* (New York: W. W. Norton, 1968); and Peter L. Berger, *Invitation to Sociology: A Humanistic Approach* (Garden City, New York: Doubleday, 1963), bear most directly on my discussion. Philip Gleason provides a good introduction to the recent history of this concept in "Identifying Identity: A Semantic History," *Journal of American History* 69 (1983): 910–31.

II THE SURVIVAL MENTALITY

The subjects explored in this chapter can be divided—with some difficulty, since they overlap with each other—into three compartments: the growing interest in extreme situations and total institutions and in the need to prepare for the worst; the attempt to apply lessons drawn from the experience of extreme adversity to everyday life; and the controversy about the political implications of a morality that subordinates everything else to the demands of survival. Before discussing sources that bear on each of these categories, I must acknowledge a more general debt to a pair of books on American literature since World War II, both of which treat survivalism as a unifying theme in recent American writing: Warner Berthoff, *A Literature without Qualities* (Berkeley: University of California Press, 1979), and Josephine Hendin, *Vulnerable People* (New York: Oxford University Press, 1978). The Berthoff study is particularly astute; I have drawn on it again in chapter IV (below). See also the wide-ranging article by Robert B. Reich, "Ideologies of Survival," *New Republic* 188 (September 20 and 27, 1982): 32–37, and two articles by Louise Kaegi, which offer a necessary corrective to Reich's contention that social Darwinism is an exclusively right-wing ideology: "The Debate over Sex

Education," *Update* 5 (Spring 1981): 14–59, and "A Conspiracy against the Inner Life," *Update* 6 (Fall 1982): 32–57. Kaegi replied more directly to Reich in an unpublished letter to the *New Republic*, September 29, 1982.

Extreme Situations, Total Institutions, and the Hard Times Ahead
Relevant writings on extreme situations include not only those dealing with or inspired by the Nazi death camps and concentration camps (see below, chap. III), by the prison camps and forced-labor camps in Stalinist Russia (see especially Alexander I. Solzhenitsyn, *The Gulag Archipelago*, vol. II, Thomas P. Whitney, trans. [New York: Harper and Row, 1975]), by Hiroshima and Nagasaki (see, for example, Robert Jay Lifton, *Death in Life: Survivors of Hiroshima* [New York: Touchstone Books, 1976]), and by twentieth-century genocide in general, but all those books and articles (not to mention films and television programs) dealing with shipwrecks, airplane crashes, floods, hurricanes, earthquakes, mining accidents, military combat, and other disasters: in other words, with life-and-death emergencies, predictable or unexpected, that compel individuals to summon up all their psychic and physical resources against overwhelming odds. From a sampling of writings on these subjects, I conclude that most of them advance a double message, one troubling, one allegedly hopeful. Modern man, the product of a soft, flabby, comfortable, and permissive environment, has lost the toughness necessary for survival; but by regaining his poise and self-discipline under adverse conditions, even if it means deliberately exposing himself to adversity, he can once again make himself what he so obviously is not in his normal everyday life: "master of his fate," as Dougal Robertson puts it in an account of his thirty-eight-day ordeal as a castaway, *Survive the Savage Sea* (New York: Praeger, 1973). "The enormous difference between actively fighting for survival and passively awaiting rescue or death effects a complete change in the castaway's outlook," according to Robertson. When he and his family understood that they would survive only by their own efforts, he says—having been passed by a ship that failed to see them—they experienced a new sense of strength. "That was the word from now on, 'survival' not 'rescue' or 'help' or dependence of any kind, just survival. . . . I felt the bitter aggression of the predator fill my mind. . . . From that instant on, I became a savage."

The same hankering for danger, for the challenge of adversity denied to men and women in an affluent society, runs through much of the commentary on the darkening future. My understanding of hard-core "survivalists"—and of many other subjects considered in this essay—rests on personal impressions and on various newspaper accounts too scattered and ephemeral to document; but I have also relied on several detailed reports in national news magazines ("Surviving the End of the World," *New West* 5 [February 25, 1980]: 17–29; "Doomsday Boom," *Newsweek* 96 [August 11, 1980]: 56 ff.; "Planning for the Apocalypse Now," *Time* 116 [August 18, 1980]: 69–71) and on an examination of Kurt Saxon's monthly magazine, *The Survivor* 1–2 (1976–1977).

On the promise of space travel, see Stewart Brand, ed., *Space Colonies* (New York: Penguin Books, 1977), a collection of articles and letters from *CoEvolution Quarterly*; Gerard O'Neill, *The High Frontier: Human Colonies in Space* (New York: William Morrow, 1977); and Ben Bova, *The High Road* (New York: Pocket Books, 1981). The preoccupation with survival among environmentalists, together with the tendency to define environmentalism as a "survival movement," sometimes leads them to endorse space travel and other technological fantasies that environmentalists might be expected to oppose. The sense that time is running out, moreover, encourages strategies of political action that work against a conservationist ethic and a democratic politics of conservation. Instead of trying to base the conservation movement on a broad popular following, too many conservationists, moved by a sense of almost unbearable urgency, advocate central administrative planning, reforms instituted by an enlightened elite, or rearguard "survival colonies" open only to those qualified to serve as custodians of Western civilization in the dark days ahead. In *The Last Days of Mankind: Ecological Survival or Extinction* (New York: Simon and Schuster, 1971), Samuel Mines notes approvingly that "conservationists have learned that protest and publicity, valuable as they are—indispensable in the long run—take effect too slowly to prevent much needless damage being done." Unwilling to wait for a change in public attitudes, they call for reforms instituted at the highest level of government and for a greater concentration of political power. Mines quotes Mike McCloskey, a Sierra Club member and U.S. senator in the early seventies, as saying that the "true enemy of conservation" is the system of government based on local and county units. Robert Heilbroner concludes his *Inquiry into the Human Prospect* (New York: W. W. Norton, 1974) with the argument that controls against overpopulation and environmental pollution can be imposed only by a central government equipped with unprecedented powers. This kind of thinking often culminates in a plea for world government. In his recent essay on the nuclear arms race, *The Fate of the Earth* (New York: Alfred A. Knopf, 1982)—an otherwise invaluable piece of work—Jonathan Schell concludes that the system of national sovereignty, the "deepest source" of the world's difficulties, needs to be replaced by a new international state. According to

Richard Falk, *This Endangered Planet* (New York: Random House, 1971), the "defense of life on earth," which has to rest on a "vision of the earth's wholeness," requires "nothing less than a new system of world order." As immediate steps toward this goal, he advocates an international Declaration of Ecological Emergency, the establishment of "survival universities or colleges of world ecology," and the formation of a world political party. Although he recognizes that a unified "city of man" might become a "new center of demoniac power with the potentiality for tyrannizing and exploiting mankind," Falk brushes these reservations aside and emphasizes the possibility of a new "era of world harmony." With a few lingering misgivings, he commends the suggestion of Warren Wagar that ecologists prepare for Armageddon by setting up survival colonies in isolated, thinly populated parts of the world. This "ark of civilization," as Wagar calls it in his book *The City of Man* (Boston: Houghton Mifflin, 1963), would serve as the nucleus of a world government when the inevitable catastrophe finally persuades mankind of its necessity. Consumed with the feverish expectation of world-historical collapse but lacking any real sense of history or of the social conditions conducive to political change, Wagar believes that "there is no more opportune moment for radical change than in the aftermath of a world catastrophe." "At war's end," he writes, a survival colony of the ecologically enlightened "would emerge as a conspiratorial task force dedicated to persuading the other survivors throughout the world to form an indissoluble world union as man's last hope of preventing complete extinction or reversion to savagery."

The effort to dramatize environmental issues by dwelling on the problem of survival leads all too easily, then, to a mood of apocalyptic urgency, to proposals for a world government enjoying quasi-dictatorial powers, and to fantasies of a global revolution engineered by self-selected colonies of survivors. It is reassuring to find environmentalists like Paul R. Ehrlich and Richard L. Harriman, *How to Be a Survivor: A Plan to Save Spaceship Earth* (New York: Ballantine Books, 1971), advocating—notwithstanding the melodramatic title of their book—more modest political strategies: "public education," "consumer boycotts," "grassroots power." But even Ehrlich, a few years after writing this book, succumbed to the panacea of space travel—hardly an example of a grassroots approach to environmental problems.

On Doris Lessing and the spiritual discipline of survival, see *The Four-Gated City* (New York: Alfred A. Knopf, 1969); *Briefing for a Descent into Hell* (New York: Alfred A. Knopf, 1971); *The Memoirs of a Survivor* (New York: Alfred A. Knopf, 1975); her recent series of novels, *Canopus in Argos: Archives*, especially *Shikasta* (New York: Alfred A. Knopf, 1979);

and the following interviews: with Florence Howe, *Contemporary Literature* 14 (1966): 418–36; with Minda Bikman, *New York Times Book Review*, March 30, 1980, 1 ff.; and with Lesley Hazelton, *New York Times Magazine*, July 25, 1982, 21 ff. See also Nancy Hardin, "Doris Lessing and the Sufi Way," in Annis Pratt and L. S. Dembo, eds., *Doris Lessing: Critical Studies* (Madison: University of Wisconsin Press, 1973), pp. 148–64; Marion Vlastos, "Doris Lessing and R. D. Laing: Psychopolitics and Prophecy," *Publications of the Modern Language Association* 91 (1976): 245–58; and my own essay, "Doris Lessing and the Technology of Survival," *democracy* 3 (Spring 1983): 28–36.

I must not conclude this section without mentioning the ur-manual on survival, Herman Kahn's *On Thermonuclear War* (Princeton: Princeton University Press, 1960), or the article that raises the ur-question about the concentration camps, Hilde O. Bluhm, "How Did They Survive? Mechanisms of Defense in Nazi Concentration Camps," *American Journal for Psychotherapy* 2 (1948): 3–32.

Everyday Survival   On victimization and "victimology," see William F. Ryan, *Blaming the Victim*, rev. ed. (New York: Vintage Books, 1976); Margaret Atwood, *Survival: A Thematic Guide to Canadian Literature* (Toronto: Anansi, 1972), which shows how difficult it is to talk about survival without also talking about the "basic victim positions"; William H. Parsonage, ed., *Perspectives on Victimology* (Beverly Hills, California: Sage Publications, 1979); Stefan A. Pasternack, ed., *Violence and Victims* (New York: Spectrum, 1974); Robert Reiff, *The Invisible Victim: The Criminal Justice System's Forgotten Responsibility* (New York: Basic Books, 1979); Joe Hudson and Burt Galaway, eds., *Victims, Offenders, and Alternative Sanctions* (Lexington, Massachusetts: Lexington Books, 1980); Terence P. Thornberry and Edward Sagarin, *Images of Crime: Offenders and Victims* (New York: Praeger, 1974); Elaine Hilberman, *The Rape Victim* (New York: Basic Books, 1976); Jane Roberts Chapman and Margaret Gates, eds., *The Victimization of Women* (Beverly Hills, California: Sage Publications, 1978); LeRoy J. A. Parker, *What the Negro Can Do about Crime* (New Rochelle, New York: Arlington House, 1974); Leroy G. Schultz, ed., *The Sexual Victimology of Youth* (Springfield, Illinois: Thomas, 1980); and Paul H. Hahn, *Crimes against the Elderly: A Study in Victimology* (Santa Cruz, California: Davis, 1976). The unidentified author quoted on the pervasiveness of victimization is Zvonimir P. Separovic, "Victimology: A New Approach in the Social Sciences," in Israel Drapkin and Emilio Vianoa, eds., *Theoretical Issues in Victimology* (vol. I of *Victimology: A New Focus* [Lexington, Massachusetts: Lexington

Books, 1974]). On "gynocide," see Mary Daly, *Gyn/Ecology: The Metaethics of Radical Feminism* (Boston: Beacon Press, 1978). On the moral elevation of the victim, see Jacques Ellul, *The Betrayal of the West*, Matthew J. O'Connell, trans. (New York: Seabury, 1978), chapter II; Richard Sennett, *Authority* (New York: Alfred A. Knopf, 1980), pp. 142–54; and Warner Berthoff, *A Literature without Qualities*, chapter III.

There is no need to document the journalistic evidence I have used to show the way in which the rhetoric of survival now pervades discussion of everyday life. I shall list only a few titles dealing with large organizations and "total institutions," beginning with Erving Goffman's *Asylums: Essays on the Social Situation of Mental Patients and Other Inmates* (Garden City, New York: Doubleday, 1961) and his *Presentation of Self in Everyday Life* (Garden City, New York: Doubleday, 1959), which have done so much to shape this discourse. On total institutions, see also Stanley Cohen and Laurie Taylor, *Psychological Survival: The Experience of Long-Term Imprisonment* (New York: Vintage Books, 1974); Hans Toch, *Living in Prison: The Ecology of Survival* (New York: Free Press, 1977); and Goffman's "Characteristics of Total Institutions," in Maurice R. Stein, Arthur J. Vidich, and David Manning White, eds., *Identity and Anxiety: Survival of the Person in Mass Society* (Glencoe, Illinois: Free Press, 1960). Guides to survival in large organizations include Chester Burger, *Survival in the Executive Jungle* (New York: Macmillan, 1964) and *Executives under Fire* (New York: Macmillan, 1966); Michael Korda, *Success!* (New York: Random House, 1977); Melville Dalton, "Conformity," in Robert Manley and Seon Manley, eds., *The Age of the Manager: A Treasury of Our Times* (New York: Macmillan, 1962); Andrew J. DuBrin, *Survival in the Sexist Jungle* (Chatsworth, California: Books for Better Living, 1974); Betty Lehan Harragan, *Games Mother Never Taught You: Corporate Gamesmanship for Women* (New York: Warner Books, 1977); and Barrie S. Greiff and Preston K. Munter, *Tradeoffs: Executive, Family, and Organizational Life* (New York: New American Library, 1980). See also Dale Tarnowieski, *The Changing Success Ethic* (New York: American Management Association, 1973).

Vincent Canby reviewed Wertmüller's *Seven Beauties* in the *New York Times*, January 22, 1976, and January 25, 1976.

Stanley Elkins applied research on the Nazi concentration camps to the study of American Negro slavery in his *Slavery: A Problem in American Institutional and Intellectual Life* (Chicago: University of Chicago Press, 1959).

Grove Press (New York) published the screenplay for *My Dinner with André*, by Wallace Shawn and André Gregory, in 1981.

The Cold-War Critique of Survival Sidney Hook's attack on Russell and Kennan, "The Morality of Survival in a Nuclear Face-Off," appeared in the *Los Angeles Times*, May 11, 1983. Attacks on the peace movement from the left include Cornelius Castoriadis, "Facing the War," *Telos*, no. 46 (Winter 1981): 43–61; another article by Castoriadis, " 'Facing the War' and the Socio-Economic Roots of Re-Armament: A Rejoinder," *Telos*, no. 52 (Summer 1982): 192–98; and Ferenc Feher and Agnes Heller, "The Antinomies of Peace," *Telos*, no. 53 (Autumn 1982): 5–16. See also Seyla Benhabib, "The West German Peace Movement and Its Critics," *Telos*, no. 51 (Spring 1982): 148–58, which concludes with a reminder that "reason in the service of self-preservation triumphs in the world only by destroying the human subjects in whose benefit it was first set into motion"; Andrew Arato and Jean Cohen, "The Peace Movement and Western European Sovereignty," *Telos*, no. 51 (Spring 1982): 158–71, which accuses advocates of nuclear disarmament of appealing to the "lowest common denominator around which they can mobilize large masses, namely life and fear"; and Orville Lee III, "Metacritique of Non-Criticism: A Reply to Breines *et al.*, " *Telos*, no. 52 (Summer 1982): 108–13, which argues that "survival in itself only prepares the subject for further brutalization." Russell Jacoby's observation about narcissism and self-sacrifice appears in his "Narcissism and the Crisis of Capitalism," *Telos*, no. 44 (Summer 1980): 58–65.

Reinhold Niebuhr's condemnation of the Munich agreement, originally published in *Radical Religion* (1938), is quoted in Donald B. Meyer, *The Protestant Search for Political Realism, 1919–1941* (Berkeley: University of California Press, 1960), pp. 359–60. Mumford's analysis of the moral paralysis of liberalism appeared in "The Corruption of Liberalism," *New Republic* 102 (April 29, 1940): 568–73.

III THE DISCOURSE ON MASS DEATH

The "Holocaust" In tracing the history and implications of the idea of the "Holocaust," I have relied heavily on Jacob Neusner's *Stranger at Home: 'The Holocaust,' Zionism, and American Judaism* (Chicago: University of Chicago Press, 1981). My account makes no claim to cover the vast literature on this subject. The following studies can serve as an introduction: Raul Hilberg, *The Destruction of the European Jews* (Chicago: Quadrangle, 1961); Nora Levin, *The Holocaust: The Destruction of European Jewry, 1933–1945* (New York: Thomas Y. Crowell, 1968); Lucy

S. Dawidowicz, *The War against the Jews, 1933–1945* (New York: Holt, Rinehart, and Winston, 1975); Richard L. Rubenstein, *The Cunning of History: Mass Death and the American Future* (New York: Harper and Row, 1975); and the same author's *The Age of Triage: Fear and Hope in an Over-Crowded World* (Boston: Beacon Press, 1983). See also Lucy S. Dawidowicz, *The Holocaust and the Historians* (Cambridge: Harvard University Press, 1981); Yehuda Bauer, *The Holocaust in Historical Perspective* (Seattle: University of Washington Press, 1978); Gerd Korman, "The Holocaust in American Historical Writing," *Societas* 2 (1972): 251–76; Emil Fackenheim, "The Nazi Holocaust as a Persisting Trauma for the Non-Jewish Mind," *Journal of the History of Ideas* 36 (1975): 369–76; and Lawrence L. Langer, *The Holocaust and the Literary Imagination* (New Haven: Yale University Press, 1975).

Begin's remark, "I know what is a holocaust," was reported by *Newsweek* 100 (September 27, 1982): 83. David L. Kirp reports some good examples of the debasement and trivialization of the concept of genocide in the *Los Angeles Times*, June 13, 1983. After quoting a migrant worker who accuses county officials of committing "genocide" against the poor, Kirp goes on: "Arthur Robbins isn't the only one with a penchant for such rhetoric. A cohort of elderly women, migrants to Miami, recently were spotted carrying picket signs denouncing their landlord as a Nazi; it turned out that he had been remiss in the heat-and-hot-water department. A Fort Lauderdale doctor, opposed to legislation on medical fees, wrote to the local newspaper, 'We will not go quietly, as the Jews went to the gas chambers, but will fight back.' Most notoriously, Arab militants have repeatedly described Israel's activities in the West Bank, and latterly in Lebanon, as designed to impose a 'final solution' on the Palestinian people."

In *The Fate of the Earth*, Jonathan Schell argues that the genocide committed against the Jews in World War II may serve as a model and portent for the nuclear annihilation of humanity as a whole.

Totalitarianism   Among the first writers to use the concept of totalitarianism were Hermann Rauschning, *The Revolution of Nihilism* (New York: Longmans, Green, 1939); Franz Borkenau, *The Totalitarian Enemy* (London: Faber and Faber, 1940); Arthur Koestler, *Darkness at Noon* (New York: Macmillan, 1941); and James Burnham, *The Managerial Revolution* (New York: John Day, 1941). The idea finds its classical expression in George Orwell's anti-utopian novels, *Animal Farm* (New York: Harcourt, Brace, 1946) and *Nineteen Eighty-Four* (New York: Harcourt, Brace, 1949), and in Hannah Arendt's *Origins of Totalitarianism*

(New York: Harcourt, Brace, 1951). On the background of Orwell's novels, see William Steinhoff, *George Orwell and the Origins of 1984* (Ann Arbor: University of Michigan Press, 1975), and Bernard Crick, *George Orwell: A Life* (London: Secker and Warburg, 1981). On Arendt, see Elisabeth Young-Bruehl, *Hannah Arendt: For Love of the World* (New Haven: Yale University Press, 1982); Stephen J. Whitfield, *Into the Dark: Hannah Arendt and Totalitarianism* (Philadelphia: Temple University Press, 1980); Margaret Canovan, *The Political Thought of Hannah Arendt* (New York: Harcourt Brace Jovanovich, 1974); and Melvyn A. Hill, ed., *Hannah Arendt: The Recovery of the Public World* (New York: St. Martin's Press, 1979). Dwight Macdonald's observations about the irrationality of totalitarianism, originally published in *Politics* 2 (March 1945): 82–93, can be found in his *Memoirs of a Revolutionist: Essays in Political Criticism* (New York: Meridian Books, 1958).

The growing tendency to equate totalitarianism with "direct democracy" and utopian social planning can be followed in J. L. Talmon, *The Origins of Totalitarian Democracy* (London: Secker and Warburg, 1952); Karl Popper, *The Open Society and Its Enemies* (London: Routledge and Kegan Paul, 1945); and Norman Cohn, *The Pursuit of the Millennium* (London: Secker and Warburg, 1957). For the concept of totalitarianism in political and social science, see Carl J. Friedrich and Zbigniew K. Brzezinski, *Totalitarian Dictatorship and Autocracy*, 2nd ed. (Cambridge: Harvard University Press, 1965); Carl J. Friedrich, Michael Curtis, and Benjamin R. Barber, *Totalitarianism in Perspective: Three Views* (New York: Praeger, 1969); Robert Burrowes, "Totalitarianism: The Revised Standard Version," *World Politics* 21 (1969): 272–94; Les K. Adler and Thomas G. Paterson, "Red Fascism: The Merger of Nazi Germany and Soviet Russia in the American Image of Totalitarianism," *American Historical Review* 75 (1970): 1046–64. Some of the more prominent examples of the left's equation of capitalism, racism, and almost any use of political power with "totalitarianism," drawn almost at random from the rhetorical exaggerations of the sixties, include, besides Herbert Marcuse's *One-Dimensional Man* (Boston: Beacon Press, 1964), Norman Mailer's frequent allusions to the totalitarian character of American society, as in *Armies of the Night* (New York: New American Library, 1968), where he refers to the "diseases of America, its upcoming totalitarianism, its oppressiveness, its smog" ; James Baldwin's standard reference to the United States as the "Fourth Reich"; and H. Rap Brown's reference to Lyndon Johnson as "Hitler's Illegitimate Child," reported by James Ridgeway, "Freak-Out in Chicago: The National Conference of New Politics," *New Republic* 157 (September 16, 1967): 11.

The Death Camps and Concentration Camps Here again, my account makes no pretense of exhaustive coverage. I have consulted the most obvious first-hand reports: David Rousset, *The Other Kingdom*, Ramon Guthrie, trans. (New York: Reynal and Hitchcock, 1947); Eugen Kogon, *The Theory and Practice of Hell*, Heinz Norden, trans. (New York: Farrar, Straus, 1953); Elie A. Cohen, *Human Behavior in the Concentration Camp*, M. H. Braaksma, trans. (New York: W. W. Norton, 1953); Elie Wiesel, *Night*, Stella Rodway, trans. (New York: Hill and Wang, 1960); and Alexander Donat, *The Holocaust Kingdom* (New York: Holt, Rinehart, and Winston, 1965); but I have singled out for special attention a handful of works—themselves written by survivors, in several cases—that seem crucial to the debate about whether the concentration camps offer lessons applicable to ordinary life. Bruno Bettelheim's works on extreme situations and survival include "Individual and Mass Behavior in Extreme Situations," *Journal of Abnormal and Social Psychology* 38 (1943): 417–52, reprinted in his *Surviving and Other Essays* (New York: Alfred A. Knopf, 1979); *The Informed Heart: Autonomy in a Mass Age* (Glencoe, Illinois: Free Press, 1960); and "The Holocaust—One Generation Later," in *Surviving*. This last essay quotes Elie Wiesel's protest (1975) against the "cheapening" of the Holocaust and his explanation of survivor guilt. Viktor Frankl's *From Death Camp to Existentialism*, Ilse Lasch, trans., was published by Beacon Press (Boston) in 1959. The relevant writings by Terrence Des Pres are *The Survivor: An Anatomy of Life in the Death Camps* (New York: Oxford University Press, 1976); his review of *Seven Beauties*, "Bleak Comedies: Lina Wertmüller's Artful Method," *Harper's* 252 (June 1976): 26–28; and his philippic against Bettelheim, "The Bettelheim Problem," *Social Research* 46 (1979): 619–47, which also contains his revised opinion of *Seven Beauties*. Other reviews of this film, on the whole quite laudatory, include the two by Vincent Canby, already cited, and those by Pauline Kael, *New Yorker* 52 (February 16, 1976): 104–9; Russell Baker, *New York Times*, February 17, 1976; Jerzy Kozinski, *New York Times*, March 7, 1976; Gary Arnold, *Washington Post*, March 18, 1976; Jay Cocks, *Time* 107 (January 26, 1976): 76; Jack Kroll, *Newsweek* 87 (January 26, 1976): 78–79; Robert Hatch, *Nation* 222 (February 7, 1976): 155–156; William S. Pechter, *Commentary* 61 (May 1976): 72–76; Judith Crist, *Saturday Review* 3 (February 21, 1976): 49–50; John Simon, *New York* 9 (February 2, 1976): 24; and Marcia Cavell Aufhauser, *New Leader* 59 (February 16, 1976): 23–24.

"Comparative survivor research" tries to link studies of the concentration camps with studies of everyday life. See, for an introduction, Joel E. Dimsdale, ed., *Survivors, Victims, and Perpetrators: Essays on the Nazi*

Holocaust (Washington, D.C.: Hemisphere, 1980), which contains, among other essays, Robert Jay Lifton's reflections on survivor guilt, "The Concept of the Survivor"; Dimsdale's "Coping Behavior of Nazi Concentration Camp Survivors"; and the important essay by Patricia Benner, Ethel Roskies, and Richard S. Lazarus, "Stress and Coping under Extreme Conditions." Other examples of this kind of work include Henry Krystal, ed., *Massive Psychic Trauma* (New York: International Universities Press, 1968); Elmer Luchterhand, "Early and Late Effects of Imprisonment in Nazi Concentration Camps: Conflicting Interpretations in Survivor Research," *Social Psychology* 5 (1970): 102–10; Alan Monat and Richard S. Lazarus, eds., *Stress and Coping* (New York: Columbia University Press, 1977); and Paul Chodoff, "The German Concentration Camp as a Psychological Stress," *Archives of General Psychiatry* 22 (1970): 78–87. For a small sample of other works on stress and coping, see Marion R. Just et al., *Coping in a Troubled Society: An Environmental Approach to Mental Health* (Lexington, Massachusetts: Lexington Books, 1974); Irving L. Janis, *Psychological Stress* (New York: Wiley, 1958); Richard S. Lazarus, *Psychological Stress and the Coping Process* (New York: McGraw-Hill, 1966); Aaron Antonovsky, *Health, Stress, and Coping* (San Francisco: Jossey-Bass, 1979); William J. Mueller and Bill L. Kell, *Coping with Conflict* (New York: Appleton-Century-Crofts, 1972); Gustave Simmons, *Coping with Crisis* (New York: Macmillan, 1972); Norma Haan, *Coping and Defending: Processes of Self-Environmental Organization* (New York: Academic Press, 1972); William N. Morris et al., "Collective Coping with Stress: Group Reactions to Fear, Anxiety, and Ambiguity," *Journal of Personality and Social Psychology* 33 (1976): 674–79; Alan Monat, "Temporal Uncertainty, Anticipation Time, and Cognitive Coping under Threat," *Journal of Human Stress* 2 (1976): 32–43; J. K. Hashimi, "Environmental Modification: Teaching Social Coping Skills," *Social Work* 26 (1981): 323–26; Roma M. Harris, "Conceptual Complexity and Preferred Coping Strategies in Anticipation of Temporally Predictable and Unpredictable Threat," *Journal of Personality and Social Psychology* 41 (1981): 380–90; Suzanne C. Kobasa, "Stressful Life Events, Personality, and Health: An Inquiry into Hardiness," *Journal of Personality and Social Psychology* 37 (1979): 1–11; Mark S. Pittner and B. Kent Houston, "Response to Stress, Cognitive Coping Strategies, and the Type A Behavior Pattern," *Journal of Personality and Social Psychology* 39 (1980): 147–57; Lizette Peterson and Carol Shigetomi, "The Use of Coping Techniques to Minimize Anxiety in Hospitalized Children," *Behavior Therapy* 12 (1981): 1–14; Thomas M. Beers, Jr., and Paul Karoly, "Coping Strategies, Expectancy, and Coping Style in the Control of Pain," *Journal of Consult-*

ing and Clinical Psychology 47 (1979): 179–80; Michael Girodo and Julius Roehl, "Cognitive Preparation and Coping Self-Talk: Anxiety Management during the Stress of Flying," *Journal of Consulting and Clinical Psychology* 46 (1978): 978–89; and Alan Monat, James R. Averill, and Richard S. Lazarus, "Anticipating Stress and Coping Reactions under Various Conditions of Uncertainty," *Journal of Personality and Social Psychology* 24 (1972): 237–53.

IV THE MINIMALIST AESTHETIC

In addition to Berthoff's *A Literature without Qualities*, already cited, I have drawn on John W. Aldridge's astringent analysis of recent fiction, *The American Novel and the Way We Live Now* (New York: Oxford University Press, 1983), and on Tony Tanner, *City of Words: American Fiction, 1950–1970* (London: Jonathan Cape, 1971), which is often astute in its interpretations of particular authors but strikes me as too generous in its general assessment of the state of American writing. See also Wylie Sypher, *Loss of the Self in Modern Literature and Art* (New York: Vintage Books, 1962), the source, among other things, of several statements by Jean Dubuffet.

Philip Roth's essay "Writing American Fiction" appeared in *Commentary* 31 (March 1961): 223–33. Merce Cunningham's observations about the deemphasis of climactic effects are quoted by Barbara Rose in her minimalist manifesto "ABC Art" (1965), reprinted in Gregory Battcock, ed., *Minimal Art: A Critical Anthology* (New York: Dutton, 1968). Battcock's collection provides a good introduction to the subject. I have quoted from his introduction, from the Rose essay, and from John Perreault's essay "Minimal Abstracts." See also Yvonne Rainer's contribution, "A Quasi Survey of Some 'Minimalist' Tendencies in . . . Dance," which shares Cunningham's opposition to "phrasing," "development and climax," "variation," "rhythm, shape, dynamics," and the "virtuosic movement feat." Reminiscent also of Reinhardt's principles for a new academy, Rainer's list of self-denying ordinances shows how easily the minimalist program, first formulated in opposition to "narcissistic," "self-indulgent" painting and sculpture, can be extended not merely to dance but to music and literature as well. "Much of the Western dancing we are familiar with," Rainer says, "can be characterized by a particular distribution of energy: maximal output or 'attack' at the beginning of a phrase, followed by abatement and recovery at the end, with energy often arrested somewhere in the middle." The *grand jeté*, she argues, typifies this interest in the "suspended movement of climax." "Like a romantic, overblown plot, this particular kind of display—with its emphasis on nuance and skilled accomplishment, its accessibility to comparison and interpretation, its involvement with connoisseurship, narcissism, and self-congratulatoriness—has finally in this decade [the sixties] exhausted itself."

Another useful collection, Nikos Stangos, ed., *Concepts of Modern Art* (New York: Harper and Row, 1974), includes Jasia Reichardt's notes on op art (1966) and Roberta Smith's analysis of conceptualism (1980)—the source of Robert Barry's warning against the manipulation of reality. See also Nicolas Calas and Elena Calas, *Icons and Images of the Sixties* (New York: Dutton, 1971); Calvin Tomkins, *The Bride and the Bachelors: The Heretical Courtship in Modern Art* (New York: Viking, 1965), which contains essays on Marcel Duchamp, John Cage, and Robert Rauschenberg; Harold Rosenberg, *The De-definition of Art: Action Art to Pop to Earthworks* (New York: Horizon Press, 1972); Christopher Finch, *Pop Art: Object and Image* (New York: Dutton, 1968); Robert Pincus-Witten, *Postminimalism* (New York: Out of London Press, 1977); and Douglas Davis, "Post-Everything," *Art in America* 68 (February 1980): 11–14. For the somewhat misguided objection that minimalism creates a hallucinatory effect—precisely its intention—see H. H. Rookmaaker, *Modern Art and the Death of a Culture* (London: Inter-Varsity Press, 1970). Lucy R. Lippard's *Six Years: The Dematerialization of the Art Object* (New York: Praeger, 1973), a kind of scrapbook, contains a great deal of useful material, including Robert Smithson's statements (1969) on the "expressive fallacy" and on the "yawning gap" that constitutes our future; Adrian Piper's declaration of withdrawal (1970); and the announcement about the importance of "clearing the air of objects" (1970) by Ian Burn and Mel Ramsden. Sol LeWitt's strictures against subjectivity can be found in his "Paragraphs on Conceptual Art," *Artforum* 5 (Summer 1967): 79–83. For Ad Reinhardt, see Lucy R. Lippard's biography, *Ad Reinhardt* (New York: Harry N. Abrams, 1981), which contains Reinhardt's opinions on the irresponsibility of color, his praise of icons, his "Twelve Rules for a New Academy" (1957), and the defense of subject matter (1943) by Rothko and Gottlieb.

On the New York painters, see E. A. Carmean, *American Art at Mid-Century* (Washington, D.C.: National Gallery of Art, 1978), the source of Gorky's remark about inner infinity, of Eliza Rathbone's illuminating comparison between Reinhardt and Rothko, and of Nicolas Calas's description of Reinhardt's black paintings as "veils covering the obvious." See also Clement Greenberg, "American-Type Painting," in his *Art and Culture: Critical Essays* (Boston: Beacon Press, 1961).

Peter Fuller, *Beyond the Crisis in Art* (London: Writers and Readers Publishing Cooperative, 1980), contains several admirable essays and interviews, from which I have taken statements by Carl Andre, Frank Stella, and Fuller himself. Carter Ratcliff's beautifully argued essay, "Robert Morris: Prisoner of Modernism," appeared in *Art in America* 67 (October 1979): 96–109.

My analysis of recent fiction, like my analysis of the visual arts, slights realism on the grounds that realism in the arts, whatever its intrinsic merits, now goes against the grain of our culture. Even my treatment of experimental authors is admittedly selective, though not arbitrary, I hope: it deals with those who exemplify the literary equivalent of the minimalist program and sensibility, and whose work, moreover, like so much of minimal and pop art, derives its inspiration, at least in part, from the saturation of everyday life with images and mass-produced art objects. Quotations from Henry Miller come from his *Tropic of Cancer*, originally published in 1934 (New York: Grove Press, 1961). My discussion of William Burroughs rests on *Naked Lunch* (New York: Grove Press, 1959); *Nova Express* (New York: Grove Press, 1964); *Cities of the Red Night* (New York: Holt, Rinehart, and Winston, 1981); and the conversations and interviews recorded in Victor Bockris, *With William Burroughs: A Report from the Bunker* (New York: Seaver Books, 1981). J. G. Ballard's *Love and Napalm: Export U.S.A.* (New York: Grove Press, 1972) includes a preface by Burroughs. For the program of the "new novel," see Nathalie Sarraute, *The Age of Suspicion: Essays on the Novel*, Maria Jolas, trans. (New York: Braziller, 1963)—the title essay originally appeared in 1950— and Alain Robbe-Grillet, *For a New Novel: Essays on Fiction*, Richard Howard, trans. (New York: Grove Press, 1965), which consists of essays most of which were written in the fifties. Thomas Pynchon has published three novels: *V.* (Philadelphia: J. B. Lippincott, 1963); *The Crying of Lot 49* (Philadelphia: J. B. Lippincott, 1966); and *Gravity's Rainbow* (New York: Viking, 1973), all available in Bantam reprints.

Walter Benjamin's essay, "The Work of Art in the Age of Mechanical Reproduction," originally published in Germany in 1936, appears in his *Illuminations*, Hannah Arendt, ed., Harry Zohn, trans. (New York: Schocken Books, 1969), pp. 217–51.

V   THE INNER HISTORY OF SELFHOOD

John Cage   The quotations from Cage and Christian Wolff come from Cage's *Silence* (Middletown, Connecticut: Wesleyan University Press, 1961); see also his *Empty Words: Writings, '73–'78* (Middletown, Connecticut: Wesleyan University Press, 1979). Cage's praise of artistic anonymity; his insistence that nothing happens offstage, as it were ("At a given moment, we are when we are. The nowmoment"); his contention that "anything goes" in art; and of course his long association with Merce Cunningham link him to the minimalist sensibility; while his frequent allusions to Norman O. Brown and Buckminster Fuller, his opposition to all forms of ownership and possession, his advocacy of a global culture, and his belief that local attachments impede the development of such a culture link his ideas to the ecological counterculture discussed in chapter VII. Both sides of his thought, the aesthetic and the social-cultural, are evident in this condemnation of memory and climax, from a "Lecture on Nothing" first given in 1949 or 1950: "Our poetry now is the reali-zation that we possess nothing. . . . We need not destroy the past: it is gone. . . . [Musical] continuity today, when it is necessary, is a demonstration of disinterestedness. That is, it is a proof that our delight lies in not pos-sessing anything. Each moment presents what happens. How differ-ent this form sense is from that which is bound up with memory: themes and secondary themes; their struggle; their development; the climax; the recapitulation (which is the belief that one may own one's own home). But actually, unlike the snail, we carry our homes within us, which enables us to fly or to stay,—to enjoy each."

The Psychoanalytic Theory of Separation: Works by Freud   In his seminal but confusing paper, "On Narcissism: An Introduction" (1914), in James Strachey, trans. and ed., *The Standard Edition of the Complete Psychological Works of Sigmund Freud* (New York: W. W. Norton, 1976) 14: 73–102, in the course of which he refers to the ego ideal as a "substitute for the lost narcissism of . . . childhood," Freud presents two different conceptions of narcissism itself. The first identifies it with a withdrawal of libidinal interest from the outside world and with the libidinal invest-ment of the ego. The second seems to presuppose a state of "primary narcissism" antecedent to object-relations or even to any awareness of separate objects; thus Freud speaks of the infant's "blissful state of mind"; of his "unassailable libido-position"; of his "narcissistic perfection." It may have been his growing preoccupation with narcissism in this second sense that pointed Freud toward the ill-conceived hypothesis of a death instinct (*Beyond the Pleasure Principle* [1920], *Standard Edition* 18: 7–64), better described as a longing for absolute equilibrium: the Nirvana princi-ple, as he aptly called it. But the hypothesis of a death instinct also grew out of Freud's growing awareness of aggression, so that the death instinct too has a second meaning, as when Freud calls the superego a "pure culture of the death instinct" (*The Ego and the Id* [1923], *Standard Edition* 19: 13–66), meaning that it redirects aggressive instincts against the ego itself. The ambiguity surrounding these concepts should not prevent us from appreciating the profound intuition underlying them: that a part of the mind seeks not the gratification of instinctual desire but a primordial, "oceanic" contentment beyond desire (*Civilization and Its Discontents* [1930], *Standard Edition* 21: 64–145) and turns away from this "backward path" (*Beyond the Pleasure Principle*) only because the disappointments and frustrations inflicted by experience eventually make it impossible to sustain the infantile illusion of oneness and omnipotence, the illusion that the infant is the "possessor of all perfections" ("On Narcissism")—which illusion remains, nevertheless, the source of all subsequent ideas of perfection.

This line of thought, together with the discovery of the "Minoan-Mycenean" stage of mental development underlying the Oedipal stage and centering on the relations between the infant and its mother ("Female Sexuality" [1931], *Standard Edition* 21: 225–43), led Freud to give more and more attention to separation anxiety as the prototype of all other forms of anxiety, including the fear of castration (*The Ego and the Id; Inhibitions, Symptoms, and Anxiety* [1926], *Standard Edition* 20: 87–174). Even the superego, it appears—the "heir of the Oedipus complex"—has an earlier origin: a conclusion prompted not only by the general course of Freud's later work but by specific statements linking it to aggressive instincts redirected against the ego, characterizing it as the representative of the id rather than of external reality, and stressing its "extraordinary harshness and severity" (*The Ego and the Id; New Introductory Lectures on Psychoanalysis* [1933], *Standard Edition* 22: 5–182). The further suggestion that the Oedipal superego modifies the cruelty of the archaic superego by adding a more impersonal principle of authority appears, rather misleadingly, in the context of a discussion of gender differences ("Some Psychical Consequences of the Anatomical Distinction between the Sexes" [1925], *Standard Edition* 19: 248–58). Freud's essays on the psychology of women reinforce the view that the "Oedipus complex is a secondary formation" ("Some Psychical Consequences"); but the assertion that this is true only for women remains still another source of confusion about the implications of the structural theory of mind. So does the claim that penis envy exists only in women, which seems to be undercut by the important observation, in *Beyond the Pleasure Principle*, that the child's sexual desires are "incompatible" with the "inadequate stage of development which the child has reached." This observation suggests that penis envy, like envy in general, derives from the child's discovery of his inferiority, helplessness, and dependence, so painfully at odds with his precocious sexual desires. It also helps to explain why men suffer so intensely from the fear of dependence and passivity, as Freud noted in his last paper ("Analysis Terminable and Interminable" [1937], *Standard Edition* 23: 216–53).

Separation Anxiety and Narcissism: Later Psychoanalytic Theory The discovery of the pre-Oedipal mother, of the importance of separation anxiety, and of this broader dimension of envy opened the way for the advances in psychoanalytic theory achieved by Melanie Klein, by the object-relations school, and finally by recent students of narcissism. I shall refer only to work that bears directly on the problem of separation or on other subjects touched on in the course of my own discussion. Melanie Klein's "Envy and Gratitude" (1957), in her *Envy and Gratitude and Other Works, 1946–1963* (New York: Delacorte Press, 1975), pp. 176–235, deals with the connections between envy, greed, and anxiety. Her "Reflections on 'The Oresteia' " (1963), in the same volume, pp. 275–99, continue this discussion and also take up the concept of *hubris.* An earlier essay, "Love, Guilt and Reparation" (1937), in *Love, Guilt and Reparation and Other Works, 1921–1945* (New York: Delacorte Press, 1975), pp. 306–43, examines the impulse to make amends and the distinction between the conquest of nature and the loving exploration of nature. See also Hannah Segal, *Melanie Klein* (New York: Viking, 1979). Ernest Jones examines the fantasy of the phallic mother in "The Phallic Phase," *International Journal of Psychoanalysis* 14 (1933): 1–33. On early object relations, see Margaret S. Mahler, *On Human Symbiosis and the Vicissitudes of Individuation* (New York: International Universities Press, 1968); her essay, "On Sadness and Grief in Infancy and Childhood: Loss and Restoration of the Symbiotic Love Object," *Psychoanalytic Study of the Child* 16 (1961): 332–51; Michael Balint, *Primary Love and Psychoanalytic Technique* (London: Hogarth Press, 1952); Anna Freud, *The Ego and the Mechanisms of Defense* (New York: International Universities Press, 1946); Edith Jacobson, *The Self and the Object World* (New York: International Universities Press, 1964); and Joyce McDougall, "Primal Scene and Sexual Perversion," *International Journal of Psychoanalysis* 53 (1972): 371–91. On transitional objects, see Donald W. Winnicott, *The Child, the Family, and the Outside World* (Baltimore: Penguin Books, 1964), and his *Playing and Reality* (Harmondsworth, England: Penguin Books, 1974). On play, see also Johan Huizinga, *Homo Ludens: A Study of the Play Element in Culture* (Boston: Beacon Press, 1955).

My understanding of narcissism derives principally from Otto Kernberg, *Borderline Conditions and Pathological Narcissism* (New York: Jason Aronson, 1975); from Jean Laplanche, *Life and Death in Psychoanalysis*, Jeffrey Mehlman, trans. (Baltimore: Johns Hopkins University Press, 1976), which helps to clarify the difference between Freud's two concepts of narcissism and also explains the transformation of biological needs into human desires; from Béla Grunberger, *Narcissism: Psychoanalytic Essays*, Joyce S. Diamanti, trans. (New York: International Universities Press, 1979); and from the more specialized studies of the ego ideal cited below. See also Sydney E. Pulver, "Narcissism: The Term and the Concept," *Journal of the American Psychoanalytic Association* 18 (1970): 319–41. Grunberger's book is the source of Cioran's statement about the humiliating sense of weakness and insecurity and of a number of other statements already acknowledged; but the extent of my debt to Grunberger's work and to that of his wife Janine Chasseguet-Smirgel goes beyond what is already evident. Their work raises the study of narcissism to a new level. It traces the "profoundly regressive" character of narcissism to the longing for a lost paradise but disentangles the concept of a Nirvana principle from the concept of a death instinct. It shows, on the other hand, that narcissism does not serve the instinct of self-preservation and that it cannot be defined, therefore, as a libidinal investment of the ego. It forces us to see that it is precisely tumultuous instinctual desires that first disturb narcissistic equilibrium and that "maintaining the illusion of omnipotence in which he was born," as Grunberger puts it in a pregnant observation, "seems more important to [man] than instinctual gratification proper." Narcissism bears a dialectical and contradictory relation to the ego, according to Grunberger. On the one hand, its indifference to the requirements of ordinary bodily survival makes it contemptuous of the ego's compromises both with reality and with instinctual demands; on the other hand, it bequeaths to the ego an exacting ideal of perfection that encourages exploration and mastery of the world, the basis for a solid self-esteem, instead of an attempt to take refuge in illusions. This "continual dialectic between the instinctual ego and the narcissistic self" explains, among other things, why the "narcissistic person," in Grunberger's words, "is one who loves himself well, but also one who loves himself poorly or not at all."

The Ego Ideal   My discussion of this subject rests on the following studies: Annie Reich, "Narcissistic Object Choice in Women," *Journal of the American Psychoanalytic Association* 1 (1953): 22–44; Samuel Novey, "The Role of the Superego and Ego-Ideal in Character Formation," *International Journal of Psychoanalysis* 36 (1955): 254–59; René Spitz,

"On the Genesis of Superego Components," *Psychoanalytic Study of the Child* 13 (1958): 375–404; Paul Kramer, "Note on One of the Preoedipal Roots of the Superego," *Journal of the American Psychoanalytic Association* 6 (1958): 38–46; Michael Balint, "Primary Narcissism and Primary Love," *Psychoanalytic Quarterly* 29 (1960): 6–43; Joseph Sandler, "On the Concept of the Superego," *Psychoanalytic Study of the Child* 15 (1960): 128–62; Roy Schafer, "The Loving and Beloved Superego in Freud's Structural Theory," *Psychoanalytic Study of the Child* 15 (1960): 163–88; Heinz Hartmann and Rudolph M. Loewenstein, "Notes on the Superego," *Psychoanalytic Study of the Child* 17 (1962): 42–81; Jeanne Lampl-de Groot, "Ego Ideal and Superego," *Psychoanalytic Study of the Child* 17 (1962): 94–106; Herbert Rosenfeld, "The Superego and the Ego-Ideal," *International Journal of Psychoanalysis* 43 (1962): 258–71; "Superego and Ego Ideal: A Symposium," *International Journal of Psychoanalysis* 43 (1962): 258–71; Erik H. Erikson, *Childhood and Society*, 2nd ed. (New York: W. W. Norton, 1963), pp. 261–63 ("Identity vs. Role Confusion"); John M. Murray, "The Transformation of Narcissism into the Ego Ideal," *Bulletin of the Philadelphia Association for Psychoanalysis* 13 (1963): 143–145; Joseph Sandler, Alex Holder, and Dale Meers, "The Ego Ideal and the Ideal Self," *Psychoanalytic Study of the Child* 18 (1963): 139–58; Grete L. Bibring, "Some Considerations on the Ego Ideal," *Journal of the American Psychoanalytic Association* 12 (1964): 517–21; Helene Deutsch, "Clinical Considerations on the Ego Ideal," *Journal of the American Psychoanalytic Association* 12 (1964): 512–16; Ives Hendrick, "Narcissism and the Prepuberty Ego Ideal," *Journal of the American Psychoanalytic Association* 12 (1964): 522–28; John M. Murray, "Narcissism and the Ego Ideal," *Journal of the American Psychoanalytic Association* 12 (1964): 477–511; Stephen Hammerman, "Conceptions of Superego Development," *Journal of the American Psychoanalytic Association* 13 (1965): 320–55; Martin Stein, "Current Status of Superego Theory," *Journal of the American Psychoanalytic Association* 13 (1965): 172–80; Peter Blos, "The Function of the Ego Ideal in Adolescence," *Psychoanalytic Study of the Child* 27 (1972): 93–97; George E. Gross and Isaiah A. Rubin, "Sublimation," *Psychoanalytic Study of the Child* 27 (1972): 334–59; and Esther Menaker, "The Ego-Ideal: An Aspect of Narcissism," in Marie Coleman Nelson, ed., *The Narcissistic Condition* (New York: Human Sciences Press, 1977), pp. 248–64. The contributions of Janine Chasseguet-Smirgel include "Perversion, Idealization and Sublimation," *International Journal of Psychoanalysis* 55 (1974): 349–57; "Some Thoughts on the Ego Ideal: A Contribution to the Study of the 'Illness of Ideality'," *Psychoanalytic Quarterly* 45 (1976): 345–73; and "Freud and Female Sexuality," *International Journal of Psychoanalysis* 57 (1976): 275–

86. These essays, in different form, serve as the basis of her full-length study, *L'Idéal du Moi: Essai psychoanalytique sur la "maladie d'idéálité"* (Paris: Tchou, 1975). An English translation of this work will be published by Free Association Books (London) and by W. W. Norton in 1985.

Childhood in a Narcissistic Culture   Bruno Bettelheim's observations about the threat of desertion and about the pedagogical revolt against fairy tales come from *The Uses of Enchantment: The Meaning and Importance of Fairy Tales* (New York: Alfred A. Knopf, 1976). Recent studies of childhood include Marie Winn, *Children without Childhood* (New York: Pantheon, 1983); Vance Packard, *Our Endangered Children: Growing Up in a Changing World* (Boston: Little, Brown, 1983); and Valerie Polakow Suransky, *The Erosion of Childhood* (Chicago: University of Chicago Press, 1982). The psychoanalytic material in this section comes from the studies by Joyce McDougall, Annie Reich, and Janine Chasseguet-Smirgel ("Some Thoughts on the Ego Ideal"), already cited. I have dealt in more detail with the transformation of the family in advanced industrial society in my *Haven in a Heartless World: The Family Besieged* and *The Culture of Narcissism*.

On the high incidence of incest, see Joel Greenberg, "Incest: Out of Hiding," *Science News* 117 (April 5, 1980): 218–20; on the movement to weaken the incest taboo, see Benjamin DeMott, "The Pro-Incest Lobby," *Psychology Today* 13 (March 1980): 11–16.

VI   THE POLITICS OF THE PSYCHE

The Party of the Superego   I must caution the reader once again that the three positions I have tried to characterize in the last two chapters of this study are ideal types. In this somewhat stylized form, they will not be found in any of the works of any one author; nor will they appear under the labels I have assigned to them. In describing the "party of the superego," I have had principally in mind works by Lionel Trilling, *Beyond Culture* (New York: Viking, 1965), and *Sincerity and Authenticity* (Cambridge: Harvard University Press, 1972); by Daniel Bell, *The Cultural Contradictions of Capitalism* (New York: Basic Books, 1976); and by Philip Rieff, *The Triumph of the Therapeutic* (New York: Harper and Row, 1966), and *Fellow-Teachers* (New York: Harper and Row, 1973). It occurs to me that my own book, *The Culture of Narcissism*, could easily be read, or misread, as a defense of this position. Although it links narcissism in contemporary culture not so much to a decline of the superego as to an archaic superego, that book is not sufficiently critical of superego controls. The same thing is true of the paper by Henry Lowenfeld and Yela Lowenfeld, "Our Permissive Society and the Superego," *Psychoanalytic Quarterly* 39 (1970): 590–607, and of Arnold Rogow's chapter, "The Decline of the Superego," in *The Dying of the Light* (New York: Putnam's, 1975).

The Party of the Ego   Parsons's comment on the "production of personality" comes from his essay, "The Link between Character and Society" (1961), in *Social Structure and Personality* (New York: Free Press, 1964). John Dewey's idea of the relation between "scientific method" and liberal education is succinctly stated in an early essay, "Science as Subject-Matter and as Method," *Science*, n.s. 31 (January 28, 1910): 121–27. For similar arguments, see Thorstein Veblen, "The Place of Science in Modern Civilization," *American Journal of Sociology* 11 (1906): 585–609, and Karl Mannheim, "The Democratization of Culture" (1933), in Kurt H. Wolff, ed., *From Karl Mannheim* (New York: Oxford University Press, 1971), pp. 271–346. The work of Lawrence Kohlberg provides a more recent example of the liberal philosophy of education: see his "Development of Moral Character and Moral Ideology," in Martin L. Hoffman and Louis W. Hoffman, eds., *Review of Child Development Research* (New York: Russell Sage, 1964) 1:383–431; "The Adolescent as a Philosopher: The Discovery of the Self in a Postconventional World," in Jerome Kagan and Robert Coles, eds., *Twelve to Sixteen: Early Adolescence* (New York: W. W. Norton, 1973); and "Moral Development and the Education of Adolescents," in R. F. Purnell, ed., *Adolescents and the American High School* (New York: Holt, Rinehart, and Winston, 1970). Kohlberg and his followers, notably Carol Gilligan, take the position that clear thinking about moral issues is more important than ever in a society where conventional reinforcements of moral conduct have fallen into disarray. In such a society, they argue, the family and the school must take on the job of turning out not just healthy, well-adjusted personalities but morally enlightened personalities as well. They assume that "moral maturity"—an intellectual grasp of moral issues, a successful passage through the various "stages of moral development"—leads to good conduct. This assumption, of course, is the weak link in the liberal chain of argument. As conservatives have always pointed out, knowing good from bad does not necessarily mean doing good. This is exactly why moral knowledge, in their view, has to be reinforced by the emotional sanctions of shame and guilt. For liberals, on the other hand, shame and guilt are deeply irrational and culturally retrograde: outworn relics of our unenlightened past.

My analysis of the nineteenth-century origins of the modern liberal ethic rests on Jacob Abbott, *Gentle Measures in the Management of the Young* (New York: Harper, 1872), and on a number of other treatises on child-rearing, discipline, and punishment: Theodore Dwight, Jr., *The Father's Book*, 2nd ed. (Springfield, Massachusetts: Merriam, 1834); Artemus B. Muzzey, *The Fireside: An Aid to Parents* (Boston: Crosby and Nichols, 1856); William A. Alcott, *The Young Wife* (Boston: George W. Light, 1837); and Lydia Maria Child, *The Mother's Book* (New York: C. S. Francis, 1844), among others. See also Anne L. Kuhn, *The Mother's Role in Childhood Education: New England Concepts* (New Haven: Yale University Press, 1947), and Peter Gregg Slater, *Children in the New England Mind* (Hamden, Connecticut: Archon Books, 1977). Nineteenth-century authorities on punishment sometimes confused the issue of vindictive punishments, as Abbott called them, with that of corporal punishment. (So do many historians today.) Those who did not grasp the distinction between retribution and remedial justice welcomed Abbott, because he did not object to corporal punishment as such, as an ally in their campaign against the new "indulgence." In the 1840s, Horace Mann's opposition to corporal punishment in the classroom ran into resistance from a group of Boston schoolmasters, who cited this along with other issues in their attempt to oust Mann from his position as Massachusetts Commissioner of Education. Mann condemned corporal punishment on the usual grounds that it appealed not to the spirit of cooperation and repentance but to fear, "a most debasing, dementalizing passion." The schoolmasters argued that Mann's policy was undermining classroom discipline. In support of their position, they cited works by Abbott, whom they regarded—as do many historians—as a traditionalist in matters of discipline. A closer study of Abbott's position would have dispelled this impression at once. He refused to be diverted by the specific issue of corporal punishment. He took the common view that it should be used only as a last resort. But the important point, in his mind, was that corporal punishments, like other punishments, should be administered in the interest of correction.

William Ellery Channing's "Moral Argument against Calvinism" (1820) can be found in his *Works* (Boston: George C. Channing, 1849) 1:217–41. See also, on the decline of Calvinism, Daniel Walker Howe, "The Decline of Calvinism," *Comparative Studies in Society and History* 14 (1972): 306–27; Ann Douglas, *The Feminization of American Culture* (New York: Alfred A. Knopf, 1977); and Joseph Haroutunian, *Piety versus Moralism: The Passing of the New England Theology* (New York: Henry Holt, 1932), still the best study on this subject.

On the Americanization of psychoanalysis, see Nathan G. Hale, Jr., *Freud and the Americans: The Beginnings of Psychoanalysis in the United States, 1876–1917* (New York: Oxford University Press, 1971), which contains the quotations from Lay, Holt, Cary, and Eastman. On Adler, see Heinz L. Ausbacher and Rowena R. Ausbacher, eds., *The Individual Psychology of Alfred Adler: A Systematic Presentation in Selections from His Writings* (New York: Basic Books, 1956); on Jung, his *Memories, Dreams, Reflections*, Richard Winston and Clara Winston, trans. (New York: Pantheon, 1963); on Sullivan, his *Interpersonal Theory of Psychiatry* (New York: W. W. Norton, 1953). Freud's reference to Jung's "new religio-ethical system" appears in his "On the History of the Psycho-analytic Movement" (1914), *Standard Edition* 14: 7–66.

Exponents of nonpsychoanalytic approaches to psychotherapy include Eric Berne, *Transactional Analysis in Psychotherapy* (New York: Grove Press, 1961), and *Games People Play* (New York: Grove Press, 1964); William Glasser, *Reality Therapy* (New York: Harper and Row, 1965), and *Schools without Failure* (New York: Harper and Row, 1969); Albert Ellis, *Reason and Emotion in Psychotherapy* (New York: Lyle Stuart, 1962), and *The American Sexual Tragedy* (New York: Lyle Stuart, 1959); Thomas S. Szasz, *The Myth of Mental Illness* (New York: Harper and Row, 1961); Charlotte Bühler, *Values in Psychotherapy* (Glencoe, Illinois: Free Press, 1962); Abraham Maslow, *Toward a Psychology of Being* (Princeton, New Jersey: Van Nostrand, 1962); Rollo May, *Existential Psychology* (New York: Random House, 1961), and *Love and Will* (New York: W. W. Norton, 1969); George Alexander Kelly, *The Psychology of Personal Constructs* (New York: W. W. Norton, 1955); A. J. Sutich and M. A. Vich, *Readings in Humanistic Psychology* (New York: Free Press, 1969); George R. Bach and Peter Wyden, *The Intimate Enemy: How to Fight Fair in Love and Marriage* (New York: William Morrow, 1969); George R. Bach and Herb Goldberg, *Creative Aggression* (Garden City, New York: Doubleday, 1974); A. J. Sutich, "The Growth-Experience and the Growth-Centered Attitude," *Journal of Psychology* 28 (1949): 293–301; and Ernest Lawrence Rossi, "Game and Growth: Two Dimensions of Our Psychotherapeutic Zeitgeist," in Sutich and Vich, *Readings in Humanistic Psychology*.

Carl Rogers's version of humanistic psychology is outlined in his book *On Becoming a Person* (Boston: Houghton Mifflin, 1961), and in the worshipful biography by Howard Kirschenbaum, *On Becoming Carl Rogers* (New York: Delacorte Press, 1979), which reports his debate with B. F. Skinner at the annual meeting of the American Psychological Association in 1956. For Skinner, see his *Science and Human Behavior* (New York:

Macmillan, 1953); *Walden Two* (New York: Macmillan, 1948); *Beyond Freedom and Dignity* (New York: Alfred A. Knopf, 1971); and his autobiography, *The Shaping of a Behaviorist* (New York: Alfred A. Knopf, 1979).

The best introduction to ego psychology that I have managed to find is Gertrude Blanck and Rubin Blanck, *Ego Psychology: Theory and Practice* (New York: Columbia University Press, 1974); see also Marshall Edelson, *Ego Psychology, Group Dynamics, and the Therapeutic Community* (New York: Grune and Stratton, 1964). My discussion of Heinz Hartmann rests mainly on two works, *Ego Psychology and the Problems of Adaptation* (New York: International Universities Press, 1958), and *Psychoanalysis and Moral Values* (New York: International Universities Press, 1960); see also his *Essays on Ego Psychology: Selected Problems in Psychoanalytic Theory* (New York: International Universities Press, 1964). Fred Weinstein and Gerald W. Platt attempt to integrate ego psychology and social science in *Psychoanalytic Sociology* (Baltimore: Johns Hopkins University Press, 1973). In *Ego and Instinct: The Psychoanalytic View of Human Nature—Revised* (New York: Random House, 1970), Daniel Yankelovich and William Barrett likewise attempt to "break down the barriers [between psychoanalysis] and other disciplines," in the hope of revitalizing liberalism and countering the trend toward behavioral engineering. "In the years that lie ahead," they write, "we will need new guideposts to replace those 'liberal' ideologies that are tied to an unreasonable faith in environmentalism, in rationalization, in technology, and in one-sided social planning. The utopia of B. F. Skinner's Walden Two—a logical extension of this faith—is a modern nightmare growing straight out of some of the old philosophy. It is the *reductio ad absurdum* of the old liberalism which so many students now reject."

VII   The Ideological Assault on the Ego

The Postwar Exhaustion of Ideologies and the Rise of Cultural Politics   Dorothy Dinnerstein's reminiscences of the postwar atmosphere appear in *The Mermaid and the Minotaur: Sexual Arrangements and the Human Malaise* (New York: Harper and Row, 1976). Norman O. Brown opens *Life against Death: The Psychoanalytic Meaning of History* (Middletown, Connecticut: Wesleyan University Press, 1959) with a discussion of the "superannuation of political categories." His contention that "contemporary social theory, both capitalist and socialist, has nothing to say about the real problem of the age" has served, also, in a somewhat different form, as the point of departure for many feminists. Thus a manifesto issued by the Stanton-Anthony Brigade (1969) took the position that capitalism is not the cause of women's oppression and that socialism will not bring it to an end. In other words, power itself, not just the unequal distribution of power, is the "real problem of the age." (For this manifesto and that of the San Francisco Redstockings, see Roberta Salper, "The Development of the American Women's Liberation Movement, 1967–1971," in Roberta Salper, ed., *Female Liberation: History and Current Politics* [New York: Alfred A. Knopf, 1972], pp. 169–84.) It was a belief in the pathology of power, domination, purposefulness, and "instrumental reason" that distinguished the new left from the old and gave the movement whatever theoretical coherence and unity it achieved.

Not that a cultural conception of politics ever dominated the new left. The works of Marx and Lenin soon supplemented and even replaced the works from which the new left had taken so much of its original inspiration: Brown's *Life against Death*; Herbert Marcuse's *Eros and Civilization* (Boston: Beacon Press, 1955); Erich Fromm's *The Sane Society* (New York: Holt, Rinehart, and Winston, 1955); Paul Goodman's *Growing Up Absurd* (New York: Random House, 1960). The amorphousness of the "counterculture" created a demand for organizational and intellectual rigor eagerly exploited by more conventional socialist sects and ideologies. Many socialists dismissed the counterculture and its offshoot, radical feminism, as expressions of "bourgeois subjectivity" lacking in "revolutionary potential"—middle-class in their composition, concerned only with private issues, and hopelessly reformist, in the words of Bernadine Dohrn, in their fascination with "personal liberation" and their "evasion of practice" (quoted in Kathy McAfee and Myrna Wood, "Bread and Roses" [1969], in Salper, ed., *Female Liberation*). When women first raised the issue of "male chauvinism" in SDS, they were reminded that "women are not oppressed as a class" and advised to organize around working-class issues: equal pay for working-class women employed in universities, equal rights in universities where working-class women were educated (Salper, "The Development of the American Women's Liberation Movement"). Marlene Dixon complained in 1972 that the "mysticism of sisterhood" ignored "class struggle, nationalization of medicine, abolition of welfare, and the ultimate destruction of American imperialism" and concerned itself instead with "reformist," "subjective" issues interesting only to women rich enough to "worry about their spirits instead of their bellies" (Marlene Dixon, "Why Women's Liberation?" in Salper, ed., *Female Liberation*, pp. 184–200). In the same vein, Karen Frankel argued that feminist demands for "control of your own body" capitulated, "in a totally idealist and subjective manner," to "middle-class subjectivity" (quoted in Celestine Ware, *Woman Power: The Movement for Women's Liberation* [New York: Tower Publications, 1970]).

Cultural radicalism could not be silenced by such rhetoric, however, because it provided an explanation, of sorts—tentative, confused, and contradictory as it may have been—of the cultural, psychological, and environmental devastation inherent in large-scale industrial organization and high-level technology. Proponents of a "cultural revolution" addressed issues ignored by the old left: the limits of reason; the unconscious origins of the desire for domination; the embodiment of this desire in industrial technology. In its feminist form, furthermore, cultural radicalism addressed women's concrete sense of injury and grievance, instead of exhorting them to join a hypothetical revolution led by the proletariat. A book like Shulamith Firestone's *Dialectic of Sex: The Case for Feminist Revolution* (New York: William Morrow, 1970) shows how closely the concerns of radical feminists overlapped, in the late sixties and early seventies, with those of Marcuse, Brown, R. D. Laing, and other theorists of cultural revolution. It also shows how easily those concerns could be reduced to slogans and clichés. Like many other theorists associated with the new left, Firestone tried "to correlate the best of Engels and Marx . . . with the best of Freud." The need for such a synthesis, she argued, grew out of the old left's failure to study the "psychology of power," to trace the "structure of the economic class system to its origins in the sexual class system, the model for all other exploitative systems," or to draw the appropriate conclusion that only a sexual revolution, one that incorporates and transcends the socialist revolution, can put an end not just to "male privilege" but to all other forms of exploitation, even to the "sex distinction itself." The sexual revolution, according to Firestone, will abolish repression and reconcile advanced technology with the taste for beauty. In the feminist utopia, "control and delay of 'id' satisfactions by the 'ego' will be unnecessary; the id can live free."

Lewis Mumford's condemnation of this politics of "addled subjectivity" appears in *The Pentagon of Power* (New York: Harcourt Brace Jovanovich, 1970), chapter XIII; see also Russell Jacoby, "The Politics of Subjectivity," in *Social Amnesia: A Critique of Conformist Psychology from Adler to Laing* (Boston: Beacon Press, 1975), pp. 101–18.

The Neo-Freudian Left The leading expositions of the "cultural school" of psychoanalytic revisionism are Wilhelm Reich, *Character-Analysis*, 3rd ed., Theodore P. Wolfe, trans. (New York: Farrar, Straus, 1949), and *The Sexual Revolution*, Theodore P. Wolfe, trans. (New York: Farrar, Straus, and Cudahy, 1962); Erich Fromm, *The Crisis of*

Psychoanalysis (New York: Holt, Rinehart, and Winston, 1970), which includes his important essay "The Method and Function of an Analytic Social Psychology" (1932), one of the earliest attempts to reconcile Marx and Freud and the starting-point for many subsequent attempts; Karen Horney, *The Neurotic Personality of Our Time* (New York: W. W. Norton, 1937), and *Feminine Psychology* (New York: W. W. Norton, 1967), a collection that includes some of the earliest attempts to combine psychoanalysis with feminism, notably her "Flight from Womanhood" (1926); Clara Thompson, *Psychoanalysis: Evolution and Development* (New York: Hermitage House, 1950), and "The Role of Women in This Culture" (1941), in Patrick Mullahy, ed., *A Study of Interperpersonal Relations: New Contributions to Psychiatry* (New York: Grove Press, 1957); and Gregory Zilboorg, "Masculine and Feminine: Some Biological and Cultural Aspects" (1944), in Jean Baker Miller, ed., *Psychoanalysis and Women* (New York: Brunner-Mazel, 1973), an anthology that contains a number of other essays by neo-Freudian revisionists.

Herbert Marcuse's "Critique of Neo-Freudian Revisionism," in *Eros and Civilization* (Boston: Beacon Press, 1955), is itself badly flawed, for reasons already explained; see also his exchange with Fromm, *Dissent* 2 (Autumn 1955): 342–49 and 3 (Winter 1956): 79–83. Marcuse has more in common than he thinks with Fromm and especially with Wilhelm Reich, whose simple-minded theory of sexual liberation he largely exempts from his strictures against other neo-Freudians. In spite of his attempt to confront the profound pessimism of Freud's later work, Marcuse's interpretation of psychoanalytic theory, like that of the neo-Freudians, rests almost entirely on Freud's early work, in which mental suffering originates in the pleasure principle's submission to an oppressive, externally imposed reality. In spite of his condemnation of the neo-Freudians' "moralistic philosophy of progress," Marcuse shares their faith—part of the intellectual legacy of the nineteenth-century socialist movement and of the Enlightenment in general—that the progress of reason and technology, once these are freed from capitalist constraints, will eventually make life pleasant and painless. *Eros and Civilization* concludes with the pious hope that even death, like work and "other necessities," can "be made rational—painless."

Marcuse, Brown, and the Freudian Feminists   My discussion of Marcuse rests for the most part on *Eros and Civilization*, already cited; on *An Essay on Liberation* (Boston: Beacon Press, 1969); and on *Five Lectures: Psychoanalysis, Politics, and Utopia* (Boston: Beacon Press, 1970), which includes "The Obsolescence of the Freudian Concept of Man" (1963). My discussion of Brown rests entirely on *Life against Death;* I have not attempted to follow the increasingly mystical, cryptic, and aphoristic works of his later phase, *Love's Body* (New York: Random House, 1966) and *Closing Time* (New York: Random House, 1973). The central point of Brown's later work, as I understand it—that the "distinction between inner self and outside world, between subject and object" must be "overcome," as he writes in *Love's Body*—is already implicit in *Life against Death.* See also the exchange between Marcuse and Brown in *Commentary* 43 (February 1967): 71–75 and 43 (March 1967): 83–84, in the course of which Brown declares: "The next generation needs to be told that the real fight is not the political fight, but to put an end to politics." Since our subject here is the concept of cultural politics, there is not much point in dealing with works that reject politics as such, even a politics that seeks an end to power and domination.

My consideration of recent Freudian feminism is similarly selective. It pays no attention, for example, to the work of Juliet Mitchell, since she too rejects cultural politics, for reasons the opposite of Brown's. Whereas Brown can see no value in politics at all, Mitchell clings to a Leninist conception of politics, notwithstanding her interest in Freud and Lacan and her hope that psychoanalysis can become a "science" (*Psychoanalysis and Feminism* [New York: Pantheon, 1974]). She takes no interest in the possibility that feminism can substitute a whole new political agenda for the old agenda of power and conquest. She admits that the recent feminist revival testifies to the "inadequacy of classical socialist theory," but she thinks that this inadequacy can somehow be corrected by a "scientific socialist analysis of our oppression," as she puts it in *Woman's Estate* (New York: Pantheon, 1971). She criticizes feminists who try to "make a 'theory' of the concrete *experience* of oppression." Quoting Lenin on the impossibility of a "middle course" between "bourgeois and socialist ideology," she insists that feminists who refuse to become socialists support capitalism by default. Oppressed groups, she explains, have a right to "their oppressed consciousness," but this consciousness becomes revolutionary only when assimilated to the socialist movement: in other words, only when oppressed women, workers, and racial minorities consent to be led by accredited socialist intellectuals. Mitchell accepts as an article of faith Lenin's dictum that "to belittle the socialist ideology *in any way, to turn aside from it in the slightest degree,* means to strengthen bourgeois ideology."

Women's "confinement" in the family, according to Mitchell, makes them small-minded, jealous, dependent, passive, and politically conservative. These qualities derive not from men's desire to lord it over women or from conventional denigration of the female sex but from "the *woman's objective conditions within the family.*" Women, like peasants, inhabit a "small and backward world" and, "as a potential revolutionary force, present comparable problems." Their backwardness reveals itself, most distressingly, in a distrust of leaders and of the principle of leadership. Mitchell thinks that the "refusal to allow leaders to arise" in the women's movement is "dangerous because, not yet having any theoretical scientific base from which to understand the oppression of women, it leaves us vulnerable to the return of our own repressed, oppressed characteristics. . . . In not wishing to act like 'men,' there is no need for us to act like 'women.' The rise of the oppressed should not be a glorification of oppressed characteristics." Women need to forsake "feminine virtues," according to Mitchell, and to "learn self-defense and aggression." In other words, they need to become as ruthless, cruel, and domineering as men.

As a classic specimen of "revolutionary" thought—which in our time has become increasingly indistinguishable from bureaucratic thought—Mitchell's argument has its own fascination, but it has nothing in common with the kind of feminism under consideration here, which originates in a distrust not merely of "revolutionary" leadership but of the whole Marxist tradition, with which "democratic centralism" has been so closely associated. No doubt there was a great deal of foolishness in the new left's opposition to leadership in any form. Now that many attitudes formerly associated with the "counterculture" have spread to American society as a whole, the pretense of absolute equality in small groups and the transformation of leaders into "resource persons" and "facilitators" has become not merely foolish but nauseating and sentimental as well, because this pseudodemocratic symbolism serves to give an appearance of participatory democracy to hierarchically organized institutions. But there is nothing sentimental about the idea of participatory democracy itself. That idea was the new left's most important contribution to political life; and the attempt to revive "scientific" socialism, as a corrective to the anarchy and irrationalism of the new left, is an ominous development, a regression to dogmas the "superannuation" of which was widely acknowledged a generation ago.

The most closely argued of the feminist works considered here is Dinnerstein's *Mermaid and the Minotaur*, already cited. The others are Nancy Chodorow, *The Reproduction of Mothering: Psychoanalysis and the Sociology of Gender* (Berkeley: University of California Press, 1978); Stephanie Engel, "Femininity as Tragedy: Re-examining the 'New Narcissism,'" *Socialist Review*, no. 53 (September–October 1980): 77–104; and Jessica Benjamin, "Authority and the Family Revisited: Or, a World

296 | Acknowledgments and Notes

without Fathers," *New German Critique*, no. 13 (Autumn 1978): 35–57. See also Richard Wollheim, "Psychoanalysis and Feminism," *New Left Review*, no. 93 (September–October 1975): 61–69, together with rejoinders by Nancy Chodorow and Eli Zaretsky, *New Left Review*, no. 96 (March–April 1976): 115–18 and the Lacan Study Group, *New Left Review*, no. 97 (May–June 1976): 106–9; Jessica Benjamin, "The End of Internalization: Adorno's Social Psychology," *Telos*, no. 32 (Summer 1977): 42–64; Nancy Chodorow, "Feminism and Difference: Gender, Relation, and Difference in Psychoanalytic Perspective," *Socialist Review*, no. 46 (July–August 1979): 51–69; Eli Zaretsky, "Male Supremacy and the Unconscious," *Socialist Revolution*, nos. 21–22 (January 1975): 7–55; Karen Rotkin and Michael Rotkin, "Freud: Rejected, Redeemed, and Rejected," *Socialist Revolution*, no. 24 (June 1975): 105–31; "Women's Exile: Interview with Luce Irigaray," *Ideology and Consciousness* 1 (1977): 57–76; Monique Plaza, " 'Phallomorphic Power' and the Psychology of 'Woman,' " *Ideology and Consciousness* 4 (1978): 4–36; and, on the Freudian left in general, David Fernbach, "Sexual Oppression and Political Practice," *New Left Review*, no. 64 (November–December 1970): 87–96; Igor Caruso, "Psychoanalysis and Society," *New Left Review*, no. 32 (July–August 1965): 24–31; Richard Lichtman, "Marx and Freud," *Socialist Revolution*, no. 30 (October–December 1976): 3–55, no. 33 (May–June 1977): 59–84, and no. 36 (November–December 1977): 37–78; Jerry Cohen, "Critical Theory: The Philosophy of Marcuse," *New Left Review*, no. 57 (September–October 1969): 35–51; Morton Schoolman, *The Imaginary Witness: The Critical Theory of Herbert Marcuse* (New York: Free Press, 1980); Paul A. Robinson: *The Freudian Left: Wilhelm Reich, Géza Róheim, Herbert Marcuse* (New York: Harper and Row, 1969); and André Stéphane, *L'Univers Contestationnaire* (Paris: Payot, 1969), a psychoanalytic study of the May movement that also considers the influence of psychoanalytic theory on the movement and discusses such writers as Marcuse. The Freudian left in France, with its return to the early Freud, its celebration of the pleasure principle, and its critique of "sexual oppression," has also been analyzed in Sherry Turkle, *Psychoanalytic Politics: Freud's French Revolution* (New York: Basic Books, 1978); in the various articles on "French Freud," *Yale French Studies*, no. 48 (1972); in David James Fisher, "Lacan's Ambiguous Impact on Contemporary French Psychoanalysis," *Contemporary French Civilization* 6 (Fall-Winter 1981–1982): 89–114; and in Maud Mannoni, "Psychoanalysis and the May Revolution," in Charles Posner, ed., *Reflections on the Revolution in France: 1968* (Harmondsworth, England: Penguin Books, 1970). Representative texts include Jacques Lacan, *The Language of the Self*, Anthony Wilden, trans. (New York: Delta Books, 1975); Gilles

Deleuze and Félix Guattari, *Anti-Oedipus: Capitalism and Schizophrenia*, Robert Hurley et al., trans. (New York: Viking, 1977); Louis Althusser, "Freud and Lacan," *New Left Review*, no. 55 (May–June 1969): 51–65; Luce Irigaray, *Spéculum: De l'autre femme* (Paris: Editions de Minuit, 1974); and Armando Verdiglione, ed., *Psychanalyse et Politique* (Paris: Editions de Seuil, 1974), which includes essays by Julia Kristeva and Philippe Sollers, among others. One of the principal dogmas advanced by this movement, already referred to in another connection, holds that Freud should never have given up his original theory that children are regularly seduced by their parents. When he decided that seduction takes place only in the child's fantasies, Freud allegedly shifted the blame for psychic suffering from the parents to the child. In reality, "Guilt is an idea projected by the father before it is an inner feeling experienced by the son," according to Deleuze and Guattari. "The first error of psychoanalysis is in acting as if things began with the child. This leads psychoanalysis to develop an absurd theory of fantasy, in terms of which the father, the mother, and their real actions and passions must first be misunderstood as 'fantasies' of the child." Contemptuous of neo-Freudian revisionism and of ego psychology, said to water down Freud in the interest of "adjustment" and "conformity," the psychoanalytic left in France goes much farther in divesting Freud's thought of critical content. The emphasis on "real actions" represents a return to pre-Freudian psychology.

For other attempts to revive the seduction theory—newly appealing, as already noted, because it conforms so closely to the current equation of selfhood with victimization—see Janet Malcolm's two-part essay (*New Yorker* 59 [December 5, 1983]: 59–152 and 59 [December 12, 1983]: 60–119) on Jeffrey Masson and Peter Swales, two adventurers who have both tried, quite independently of each other, to build careers on the exposure of Freud's intellectual cowardice and dishonesty in suppressing the shocking facts of parental seduction.

For the Frankfurt school, the critique of instrumental reason, and the theory of "society without the father," see Max Horkheimer and Theodor W. Adorno, *Dialectic of Enlightenment*; Max Horkheimer, *The Eclipse of Reason* (New York: Oxford University Press, 1947); Max Horkheimer, "Authority and the Family Today," in Ruth Nanda Anshen, ed., *The Family: Its Function and Destiny* (New York: Harper and Row, 1949), pp. 359–74; and Alexander Mitscherlich, *Society without the Father*, Eric Mosbacher, trans. (New York: Schocken Books, 1970).

Freud proposed his theory of the primal horde in *Moses and Monotheism* (1939), *Standard Edition* 23: 7–137, the Freudian text preferred by almost all commentators on the left, often followed by *Group Psychology and the*

Analysis of the Ego (1921), *Standard Edition* 18: 65–143. Another work that lends itself to a "prophylactic" interpretation of psychoanalysis, as Anna Freud called it in *The Ego and the Mechanisms of Defense* (that is, to an interpretation that stresses the social roots of neurosis and hopes to pull them out by means of enlightened social policies), is his early essay, "Civilized Sexual Morality and Modern Nervous Illness" (1908), *Standard Edition* 9: 181–204. There he deplores the restrictions on sexual activity imposed by middle-class culture and asks "whether our 'civilized' sexual morality is worth the sacrifice which it imposes upon us." The various writings having their origin in the theory of narcissistic "Nirvana" are more "disheartening," as Freud said *(Beyond the Pleasure Principle)* of his theory of the death instinct. In *Civilization and Its Discontents*, he announced his refusal to "rise up as a prophet before my fellow men" with a message of hope and consolation. In *Beyond the Pleasure Principle*, he rejected the hypothesis of an "instinct toward perfection."

The Party of Narcissus   Recent books on "men's liberation" include Jack Nichols, *Men's Liberation: A New Definition of Masculinity* (New York: Penguin Books, 1975); Mark Gerzon, *A Choice of Heroes: The Changing Faces of American Manhood* (Boston: Houghton Mifflin, 1982); Herb Goldberg, *The New Man: From Self-Destruction to Self-Care* (New York: William Morrow, 1979); Marc Feigen Fasteau, *The Male Machine* (New York: McGraw-Hill, 1974); Warren Farrell, *The Liberated Man* (New York: Random House, 1974); Joseph E. Pleck, *The Myth of Masculinity* (Cambridge, M.I.T. Press, 1981); Karl Bednarik, *The Male in Crisis*, Helen Sebba, trans. (New York: Alfred A. Knopf, 1970); Joe L. Dubbert, *A Man's Place: Masculinity in Transition* (Englewood Cliffs, New Jersey: Prentice-Hall, 1979); Peter Filene, *Him/Her/Self* (New York: Harcourt Brace Jovanovich, 1975); Hal Lyon, *Tenderness Is Strength: From Machismo to Manhood* (New York: Harper and Row, 1978); and Betty Roszak and Theodore Roszak, eds., *Masculine/Feminine* (New York: Harper and Row, 1969). See also Barbara Ehrenreich, *The Hearts of Men: American Dreams and the Flight from Commitment* (Garden City, New York: Doubleday, 1983).

On androgyny, see Carolyn G. Heilbrun, *Toward a Recognition of Androgyny* (New York: Alfred A. Knopf, 1973); June Singer, *Androgyny: Toward a New Theory of Sexuality* (Garden City, New York: Doubleday, 1976); Alexandra G. Kaplan and Joan P. Bean, eds., *Beyond Sex-Role Stereotypes: Readings toward a Psychology of Androgyny* (Boston: Little, Brown, 1976); Sandra Lipsitz Bem et al., "Sex Typing and Androgyny: Further Explorations of the Expressive Domain," *Journal of Personality and Social Psychology* 34 (1976): 1016–23; Barbara Charlesworth Gelpi, "The Politics of Androgyny," *Women's Studies* 2 (1974): 151–60; Cynthia Secor, "Androgyny: An Early Appraisal," *Women's Studies* 2 (1974): 162–69.

On the links between feminism, "men's liberation," and ecology, see Mary Daly, *Gyn/Ecology*, already cited; Susan Griffin, *Woman and Nature* (New York: Harper and Row, 1978); Rosemary Redford Reuther, *New Woman, New Earth* (New York: Seabury, 1975); and Delores La Chappelle, *Earth Wisdom* (Los Angeles: Tudor, 1978).

On the search for an "environmental ethic," see, among an enormous number of works, Aldo Leopold, *A Sand County Almanac* (New York: Oxford University Press, 1949); Ernest Partridge, ed., *Responsibilities to Future Generations: Environmental Ethics* (Buffalo: Prometheus Books, 1981); K. S. Shrader-Frechette, *Environmental Ethics* (Pacific Grove, California: Boxwood Press, 1981); Science Action Coalition, *Environmental Ethics: Choices for Concerned Citizens* (Garden City, New York: Doubleday, 1979); Barry Commoner, *Science and Survival* (New York: Viking, 1967); Donella H. Meadows et al., *The Limits to Growth* (New York: New American Library, 1972); E. F. Schumacher, *Small Is Beautiful* (New York: Harper and Row, 1973), and *A Guide for the Perplexed* (New York: Harper and Row, 1977); René Dubos, *The Wooing of Earth: New Perspectives on Man's Use of Nature* (New York: Scribner's, 1980); Kenneth Boulding, "The Interplay of Technology and Values: The Emerging Superculture," in Kurt Baier and Nicholas Rescher, eds., *Values and the Future: The Impact of Technological Change on American Values* (New York: Free Press, 1969); Kai Curry-Lindahl, *Conservation for Survival: An Ecological Strategy* (New York: William Morrow, 1972); Raymond Dasmann, *The Conservation Alternative* (New York: Wiley, 1975); Harold W. Helfrich, *Agenda for Survival: The Environmental Crisis* (New Haven: Yale University Press, 1970); Kimon Valaskasis, et al., *The Conserver Society* (New York: Harper and Row, 1979); Robert Disch, ed., *The Ecological Conscience: Values for Survival* (Englewood Cliffs, New Jersey: Prentice-Hall, 1970); Anne Chisholm, *Philosophers of the Earth: Conversations with Ecologists* (New York: Dutton, 1972); Jean Houston, "Prometheus Rebound: An Inquiry into Technological Growth and Psychological Change," in Dennis L. Meadows, ed., *Alternatives to Growth: A Search for Sustainable Futures* (New York: Ballinger, 1977); Lewis J. Perelman, *The Global Mind: Beyond the Limits of Growth* (New York: Mason-Charter, 1976); Garrett Hardin, *Exploring New Ethics for Survival* (New York: Viking, 1972); Robert Hunter, *The Storming of the Mind* (Garden City, New York: Doubleday, 1971); Ralph Metzner, *Maps of Consciousness: I Ching, Tantra, Tarot, Alchemy, Astrology, Actualism* (New York: Collier

Books, 1971); William Irwin Thompson, *At the Edge of History: Specula-tions on the Transformation of Culture* (New York: Harper and Row, 1979), and *The Time Falling Bodies Take to Light: Mythology, Sexuality, and the Origins of Culture* (New York: St. Martin's Press, 1981); Adam Daniel Finnerty, *No More Plastic Jesus* (New York: Orbis Books, 1977); Henlee Barnett, *The Church and the Environmental Crisis* (Grand Rapids, Michigan: Eerdmans, 1972); Steven M. Tipton, *Getting Saved from the Sixties: Moral Meaning in Conversion and Cultural Change* (Los Angeles: UCLA Press, 1982); Jeremy Rifkin, *The Emerging Order: God in the Age of Scarcity* (New York: Putnam's, 1979), and *Entropy: A New World View* (New York: Viking, 1980); Theodore Roszak, *The Making of a Counter Culture* (Garden City, New York: Doubleday, 1969), and *Where the Wasteland Ends: Politics and Transcendence in Postindustrial Society* (Garden City, New York: Doubleday, 1972); Philip Slater, *The Pursuit of Loneliness* (Boston: Beacon Press, 1970), and *Earthwalk* (Garden City, New York: Anchor Press, 1974); Henry Malcolm, *Generation of Narcissus* (Boston: Little, Brown, 1971); Gregory Bateson, *Steps toward an Ecology of Mind* (San Francisco: Chandler, 1972); Murray Bookchin, *The Ecology of Free-dom* (Palo Alto, California: Cheshire Books, 1982); André Gorz, *Ecology as Politics*, Jonathan Cloud and Patsy Vigderman, trans. (Boston: South End Press, 1980); Rudolph Bahro, *Socialism and Survival*, David Fernbach, trans. (London: Heretic Books, 1982); and the following reports on the Green Party of West Germany: Steve Wasserman, "The Greens' Whole-Earth Politics: A Talk with Rudolf Bahro," *Nation* 237 (October 8, 1983): 296–99; William Sweet, "Can Green Grow?" *Progressive* 47 (May 1983): 26–33; and James M. Markham, "Germany's Volatile Greens," *New York Times Magazine*, February 13, 1983, 37 ff.

Purposefulness, Nature, Selfhood My discussion of practical rea-son rests on Jürgen Habermas, *Theory and Practice*, John Viertel, trans. (Boston: Beacon Press, 1973); Hannah Arendt, *The Human Condition* (Chicago: University of Chicago Press, 1958); Richard J. Bernstein, *The Restructuring of Social and Political Theory* (Philadelphia: University of Pennsylvania Press, 1978); and Alasdair MacIntyre, *After Virtue: A Study in Moral Theory* (Notre Dame, Indiana: University of Notre Dame Press, 1981). For nature and selfhood, see Jacques Ellul, *The Betrayal of the West*, Matthew J. O'Connell, trans. (New York: Seabury, 1978), on the impor-tance of bad conscience as a condition of freedom; and Reinhold Niebuhr, *The Nature and Destiny of Man* (New York: Scribner's, 1964). In the preface to the 1964 edition of this work (originally published in 1941), Niebuhr briefly describes the divided self as viewed by the Christian tradition and notes that "modern 'ego-psychology,' particularly as elaborated by my friend Erik Erikson, has developed this paradoxical position of the self scientifically." Although Niebuhr misread the implications of ego psychology, his suggestion that psychoanalysis recaptures some of the deepest insights of the Judaeo-Christian tradition rests on a very solid intuition.

Index